TABLE OF CONTENTS

12. Monty Penkower (Machon Lander Graduate School of Jewish Studies), The Dreyfus Affair and Its Echoes
13. Rochelle L. Millen (Wittenberg University), A Meditation on Memory and Mortality

Introduction

Jonathan C. Friedman
West Chester University

Of all the books I've prepared in my nearly two decades of working in academia, this is perhaps the most difficult. My father, Saul S. Friedman, to whom this volume is dedicated, was an extraordinary man. In his forty year career as a professor in the history department at Youngstown State University from 1969 to 2009, he was beloved as a teacher, imposing as a scholar with twelve books and numerous articles, and stalwart as an advocate for the Jewish community. He was my inspiration and guide on my own journey of self-discovery. He was always more than just "dad." On March 31, 2013, just twenty-three days after his 76th birthday (and five days after my 47th), he died from Parkinson's Disease.

Born in Uniontown, Pennsylvania in 1937, dad experienced poverty as a child, but private hardship coupled with a precocious awareness of the impact of World War II, compelled him at a young age to make a difference in his life. He was already a strong writer by the age of twelve, and as a teenager, he wrote articles on sports for some of the local Cleveland newspapers. By twenty-three, he was studying law at Harvard. But homesickness for northeast Ohio and the lure of history and academia proved too strong. In 1969, dad received his Ph.D. from Ohio State, writing a dissertation on FDR's refugee policy towards German Jews. In the same year he graduated from OSU, he started his career as an assistant professor in the history department at Youngstown State.

During his thirty-seven-year tenure at YSU, dad went on to write twelve books, produce five documentaries, take a leading role in the Jewish community, and inspire generations of future teachers. From his immortalization of the experiences of local Holocaust survivors in 1979's *Amcha,* to his 2004 textbook on the Nazi genocide, dad's impact on the preservation of Holocaust memory is indisputable. The list of distinctions he received is truly imposing—six distinguished professorships from the university, the Brandeis Award, the Ohio Humanities Council's Richard Bjornson Lifetime Achievement Award for Service to the Humanities. Then, as a capstone, in 2000, he received an endowment from the Clayman Family of Youngstown to establish a Judaic Studies program at YSU.

The contributions in this volume are a fitting tribute to the research which my dad conducted over the course of his life. They reflect his own mastery of a number of fields, ranging from ancient history to modern U.S. history to the Holocaust. There are essays on the Holocaust (by Helen Sinnreich, Dennis Klein, and Rochelle Millen), ancient Israel (by Robert Miller and Raphal Frankel), Zionism (by Zev Garber and Gershon Greenberg), genocide (by Steven Jacobs), American Jewry (by Edward Alexander), and contemporary anti-Semitism (by Monty Penkower). The focus on the fate and response of the Jews during the 1930s (in the essays by Rafael Medoff and myself) is especially appropriate, given that dad's dissertation, which appeared in 1973 from Wayne State University Press as *No Haven for the Oppressed,* was one of the first studies to question the consensus on the powerlessness of American Jewry vis à vis the Roosevelt administration. The essay by Steven Leonard Jacobs, on Jewish influences on Rafael Lemkin's concept of genocide, speaks to dad's commitment to justice for all victims of human rights abuses.

There are so many professional anecdotes about dad's life and research that are relevant in this context, and yet one that stands out to me is more personal and touches less on dad's academic accomplishments and more on his selflessness. In March and April 1997, I was undergoing treatment for thyroid cancer, just at the time that dad was beginning to suffer with the symptoms of Parkinson's disease. Despite his illness, he drove to D.C. to take me back to Canfield in the same day so that I could recover. After a few weeks, he drove me back to Washington so that I could have my radiation treatment, returned home to Canfield, and then, a week later, once I was no longer glowing, he came back to D.C. as I was recuperating once again. He did this while he himself was suffering and in pain. He did things like this for all of us—for everyone in our immediate and extended family, for students, for members from many different communities in Youngstown. His model was action, not words or ideas, and heaven knows, we disagreed on plenty of political issues. But the fact remains that I'm a historian of the Holocaust and human rights because of his influence.

The last years of dad's life weren't kind or fair. I think we all envisioned that he would teach and publish until his last breath. Academia was that central to his life. He could lecture like few professors I've ever known, he cared deeply about his students and their success, and he wrote with a level of depth, humor, and sophistication that few in our profession can match. It is a tragedy that he did not have the opportunity to sit back and enjoy his golden years and bask in the glow as it were, but dad probably would never have wanted that. He wanted to leave an imprint, and he did. Countless generations will be able to read about his groundbreaking research on the Holocaust, begun at a time in the 1970s when there were only a handful of other scholars in the field. There are legions of former students who are now educators who will make sure that that history is taught. This book allows us to reflect on these contributions, from a man with an exceptionally difficult past who went on to do exceptional things. Through this book, we remember the body of Saul Friedman's life—not the bookends, but the body, the time not of his greatest suffering, but of his greatest achievement.

"God and the Asiatic Mode of Production"

Robert D. Miller
Catholic University of America

Saul Friedman was my first academic mentor, as an undergraduate at Kent State University in the mid-1980s. His emotional engagement with a distant past enthralled a young college student and opened the door to a career of historical research. Although my own field became Hebrew Bible and not Holocaust or Zionism, Saul Friedman was himself a historical polymath, engaging even the realm of political critique and social commentary. His 1967 essay in the *National Review*, "Riots, Violence, and Civil Rights," placed the blame for the conditions that led to Cleveland's Hough Riots of 1966 on the shoulders of nearly everyone: city administration, the federal government, social workers, and the African-American community as well. It is almost, but not quite (he offers paths forward in the essay), a Hobbesian view, and it is here that I would like to bring in the Hebrew Bible.

Was ancient Israel Hobbesian? Or, is the Hebrew Bible Hobbesian? The philosopher, Thomas Hobbes maintained, "During the time men live without a common power to keep them all in awe, they are in that condition which is called war; and such a war as is of every man against every man" (*Leviathan*, chap. 13) – "the war of all against all" (*Bellum omnium contra omnes*; *De Cive,* preface §14). The book of Judges, on which I have spent much of my career and which we do well to see as a treatise on leadership,[1] seems to agree.[2] The middle and end of the book of Judges repeat that, "There was no king in Israel, and everyone did what was right in their own eyes."

---

[1] Elie Assis, *Self-Interest or Communal Interest: An Ideology of Leadership in the Gideon, Abimelech, and Jephthah Narratives* (Vetus Testamentum Supplement 106; Leiden, 2005); Marc Z. Brettler, "The Book of Judges: Literature as Politics," *Journal of Biblical Literature*, Vol. 108 (1989): 406-412.

[2] W. J. Dumbrell, "'In those days there was no king in Israel; every man did what was right in his own eyes.' The Purpose of the Book of Judges Reconsidered," *Journal for the Study of the Old Testament*, Vol. 25 (1983): 28.

This is the problem framing the stories, and "what was right in their own eyes" is always "what was evil in God's eyes"—the progressive threefold deterioration of Israel into idolatry, violence, and immorality.

Yet Israel's political philosophy was altogether too communal for Hobbes (or for Bernard Mandeville's magic of competing private vices yielding a common good [*Fable of the Bees*]). The Hebrew Bible consistently presents a corporate, organic view of society. Individuals (Korah, Achan, David) are often treated as representatives for, or even as wholly identified with, groups of people. For this reason, the Ten Commandments are phrased in second-person singular pronouns, since the fate of the community rests on each individual (Joshua 7). Similarly, the prophets clearly hold that while few are guilty, all are responsible; if any in society practice social injustice (or idolatry), all may be held accountable (Hos 11:1-2; Isa 5:2; Jer 2:3, 7).[3]

Perhaps, then, the Hebrew Bible is closer to John Locke, who especially in his *Second Treatise on Government* held that social contracts mitigate self-interest as persons in a state of nature willingly come together to form a corporate entity. Indeed, "Covenant" has been called "the overriding and unifying category in … OT theology,"[4] "of fundamental importance in Old Testament Religion."[5] Others have said, "The idea of covenant is perhaps the most daring in the Bible and one of the most daring in all human history."[6] Yet while the equation of the biblical covenant with a social contract goes back to Spinoza and continues to have proponents today,[7] such a view of the

---

[3] The classic study is H. Wheeler Robinson, *Corporate Personality in Ancient Israel* (Philadelphia, 1964); see more recently Joel S. Kaminsky, *Corporate Responsibility in the Hebrew Bible* (Journal for the Study of the Old Testament Supplement 196; Sheffield, UK, 1995).

[4] G. Hasel, *Old Testament Theology* (Grand Rapids, Michigan, 1972), 20.

[5] G. W. Anderson, *The History and Religion of Israel* (1966; repr. Oxford, 1989), 35. Also André Chouraqui, "L'Alliance dans les Écritures," *Revue des Sciences Morales de Politiques*, Vol. 150 (1995): 5.

[6] Daniel J. Elazar, "Covenant and Community," *Judaism*, Vol. 49 (2000): 393.

[7] Baruch Spinoza, *Tractus Theologico-Politicus*, chap. 16; George Wesley Buchanan, "The Covenant in Legal Context," in *The Concept of the Covenant in the Second Temple Period*, ed. Stanley E. Porter and Jacqueline C. R. DeRoo (Journal for the Study of Judaism Supplement 71; Leiden, 2003), 28-35.

covenant either excludes the God that Israel considered essential to the institution, or includes God as a partner in the social contract (as Locke's kings would be), a degradation of God simply untenable in the biblical covenant.[8]

Moreover, Locke's integrally related concept of property, that property is the product of individuals through their labor (*Second Treatise on Government* 5.39-42; 11.138), is quite alien to Israelite thought. There was nothing like a market economy at any point in ancient Israel, nothing resembling capitalist economics.[9] Israelite philosophy of property is itself essentially political theory, and can best be understood when analyzed as such. In fact, Hebrew Bible theology of God is also political economics. This essay précises recent scholarship on the socio-economics of ancient, pre-exilic Israel using social anthropological methods. It adds to that scholarship recent theory on the "Asiatic Mode of Production." And finally, it shows that the socio-economic character of Israelite society provided a model for Israelite perceptions of "God's economics," for the nature of God and his relationship to Israel, both people and land.

There is a growing consensus among archaeologists and historians that pre-Exilic Israel functioned as a both a tributary state and a patronage society.[10] The archaeological evidence assembled by Avraham Faust,[11] along with legal texts like Deuteronomy 15 and

---

[8] David Novak, "Is the Covenant a Bilateral Relationship?" in *Reviewing the Covenant*, ed. Peter Ochs (Albany, New York, 2000), 84, 87.

[9] Roland Boer, "The Sacred Economy of Ancient 'Israel'," *Scandinavian Journal of the Old Testament*, Vol. 21 (2007): 35, 42.

[10] Andrew Dearman, *Property Rights in the Eighth-Century Prophets* (Atlanta, 1988), 9-52, 133-34; S. N. Eisenstadt and L. Roniger, *Patrons, Clients, and Friends* (Cambridge, UK, 1984), 48-49; Ronald A. Simkins, "Patronage and the Political Economy of Monarchic Israel," *Semeia,* Vol. 87 (1999): 128-29, 136-38; following Niels Peter Lemche, "Kings and Clients," *Semeia,* Vol. 66 (1994): 119-32; "Justice in Western Asia in Antiquity, or: Why no Laws Were Needed," *Chicago-Kent Law Review,* Vol. 70 (1995): 1695-1716; "From Patronage Society to Patronage Society," in *The Origins of the Ancient Israelite States,* ed. V. Fritz and P. R. Davies (Journal for the Study of the Old Testament Supplement 228; Sheffield, UK, 1996), 106-120; "The Relevance of Working with the Concept of Class in the Study of Israelite Society in the Iron Age," in *Concepts of Class in Ancient Israel,* ed. M. R. Sneed (South Florida Studies in the History of Judaism; Atlanta, 1999), 89-98

[11] Avraham Faust, *Israelite Society in the Period of the Monarchy* (Jerusalem, 2005, in Hebrew), 42-46, 113-16, 142-92, 208-236, 256-83, 299; "Ethnic Complexity in Northern Israel during

Leviticus 25, descriptive passages like Job 29, and prophetic texts Amos 3:9-12; 4:1; 6:1; Mic 3:1-3, 10; Isa 3:14-15, 10:1-3; Jer 22:13-19 suggest that the political economy of Israel and Judah resembled the model to be elucidated herein. As Faust has shown, the "tributary" model, at least that of Andrew Dearman, Norman Gottwald, and Marvin Chaney, is fully compatible with the "patronage" model of Niels Peter Lemche and Ronald Simkins.[12] Roland Boer treats the patronage system as the "Regime of Allocation" and the tributary system as the "Regime of Extraction" of one and the same overall system.[13] The textual (biblical and ancient Near Eastern) and archaeological evidence for the applicability of this combined model is provided in Faust's work, the others cited in footnotes 10 and 11, and most recently the comprehensive study of Emanuel Pfoh,[14] and will not be repeated here. It suffices to say only that the rent capitalism model of Bernhardt Lang[15] cannot describe more than the immediate vicinities of the major cities, and the Hebrew Bible shows no understanding of rent in the sense they describe.[16]

Iron Age II," *Palestine Exploration Quarterly,* Vol. 132 (2000): 17-18; "The Rural Community in Ancient Israel during Iron Age II," *Bulletin of the American Schools of Oriental Research,* Vol. 317 (2000): 26-29; "Residential Patterns in the Ancient Israelite City," *Levant,* Vol. 35 (2003): 95-97; "The Settlement of Jerusalem's Western Hill and the City's Status in Iron Age II Revisited," *Zeitschrift des Deutschen Palästina-Vereins,* Robert Cowley, Vol. 1121 (2005):102-108.

12 See Norman K. Gottwald, "A Hypothesis about Social Class in Monarchic Israel in the Light of Contemporary Studies of Social Class and Social Stratification," in *The Hebrew Bible in its Social World and in Ours*, ed. N. K. Gottwald (Atlanta, 1993): 153-56, 158; "Social Class as an Analytic and Hermeneutical Category in Biblical Studies," *Journal of Biblical Literature,* Vol. 112 (1993):5-9; *The Politics of Ancient Israel* (Louisville, Kentucky, 2001); Marvin L. Chaney, "Systemic Study of the Israelite Monarchy," *Semeia,* Vol. 37 (1986): 53-76; "Bitter Bounty," in *The Bible and Liberation,* ed. N. K. Gottwald and R. Horsley (Maryknoll, 1993), 250-63.

13 Boer, "Sacred Economy," 40-41.

14 Emanuel Pfoh, *The Emergence of Israel in Ancient Palestine* (London, 2009), 85, 123-38.

15 Bernardt Lang, "The Social Organization of Peasant Poverty in Biblical Israel," in *Anthropological Approaches to the Old Testament,* ed. B. Lang (Sheffield, UK, 1985), 114-27.

16 And the "Ancient Class Society" of Hans G. Kippenberg, "Die Typik antiker Entwicklung," in *Seminar: Die Entstehung der antiken Klassengesellschaft*, ed. H. G. Kippenberg (Frankfurt, 1977), 9-61, hardly fits the monarchic societies of ancient Israel and Judah with their royal courts and professional armies. The pros and cons of each model are thoroughly summarized in Walter Houston, *Contending for Justice* (2nd ed.; New York, 2006), 18-51.

Now in many ways, the combined tributary-patronage model of Faust, Gottwald, Dearman, and others is quite similar to what Karl Marx called the "Asiatic Mode of Production,"[17] a term he used for the structural elements of a specific type of pre-capitalist society. As both the most obscure and controversial of the "modes of production," it will be easier to describe its elements than to define the term. "Marx's view of Asian society and his theory of the Asiatic mode of production developed gradually over time, and his early views are not the same as those of his later years."[18] In 1931, a conference in Leningrad declared that Asiatic Mode did not exist, in all probability because the idea of an exploiting state that did not rest on private property was a bit awkward for Stalin.[19] The Asiatic Mode was significantly redefined by Karl Wittfogel,[20] and Wittfogel's iteration of the Asiatic Mode has been thoroughly discredited.[21] Neither Wittfogel's interpretation nor its refutation need detain us here, as the term "Asiatic Mode of Production" can easily be stripped back to its Marxist sense.[22] It has only in recent years begun to again to have some currency among economists and anthropologists,[23]

---

[17] This model was proposed for Israel already by A. –Ph. Lagopoulous, "Mode de production asiatique et modelés sémiotiques urbains," *Semiotica*, Vol. 53 (1985): 38-41.

[18] Kimio Shiozawa, "Marx's View of Asian Society and his 'Asiatic Mode of Production,'" *The Developing Economies*, Vol. 4 (1966): 301.

[19] Heinz Dieterich, "Some Theoretical and Methodological Observations about the Inca Empire and the Asiatic Mode of Production," *Latin American Perspectives,* Vol. 35 (1982): 130; Neil Davidson, "Asiatic, Tributary or Absolutist?" *International Socialism* online edition at http://www.isj.org.uk/?id=20 (2004): 3.

[20] Karl Wittfogel, *Oriental Despotism* (New Haven, Connecticut, 1957).

[21] Bruce Trigger, *Understanding Early Civilizations* (Cambridge, UK, 2003), 51-52. The state of the literature on the Asiatic Mode up to 1980 is surveyed in Frederic Pryor, "The Asian mode of production as an economic system." *Journal of Comparative Economics*, Vol. 4 (1980): 420-43.

[22] Or properly, "senses": the Asiatic Mode, as other non-capitalist modes, lacks singularity; Mike Donaldson, "'The Riddle of History Solved': Socialist Strategy, Modes of Production and Social Formations in *Capital*," *Journal of Australian Political Economy*, Vol. 70 (2012): 132, 136.

[23] Bruce McFarlane, Steve Cooper, and Miomir Jaksic, "The Asiatic Mode of Production - a new Phoenix (Part 1)," *Journal of Contemporary Asia,* Vol. 35 (2005): 283-318; Boer, "Sacred Economy," 32-33.

although some have rejected the term as an Orientalist symbol of Western neo-liberal imperialism.[24]

Whatever we decide to call this economic/political system, much of the serious scholarship on the Asiatic Mode integrates seamlessly into current thought about ancient Israelite economy. Biblical archaeologists and historians of ancient Israel have been reluctant to use the categories of political economics to define the supposedly contradictory elements of the complex Israelite social system, and the advantage of using the appellation, "Asiatic Mode of Production," itself a category of political economy, is that it renders these elements coherent parts of a specific and definable formation.[25] Furthermore, the term "tributary" is problematic, as one can only reasonably speak of "tribute" when describing relationships of subordination *between* societies.[26]

In what follows, scholarship on the Asiatic Mode is brought into the tributary/patronage models. The only comparable attempt to do so is that of Roland Boer (2007).[27] Yet Boer differs in several respects. He views the Asiatic Mode through Neo-Marxist Regulation Theory, which allows a great deal of particularist variation in the traditional idea of the mode of production.[28] This leads him to refine his version of the Asiatic Mode in the light of scholarship on the ancient Near East, largely Soviet scholarship, as he states.[29] But in so

---

24 Rebecca E. Karl, "The Asiatic Mode of Production," *Historein*, Vol. 5 (2005): 58-75. Kate Currie preserves the mode but removes the "Asiatic" from the name, in her "The Asiatic Mode of Production," *Dialectical Anthropology,* Vol. 8 (2007): 251-68.

25 Ernest Mandel, "Ten Theses on the Social and Economic Laws Governing the Society Transitional Between Capitalism and Socialism," *Critique,*Vol. 3 (1974): 5; Dieterich, "Some Theoretical and Methodological Observations," 111-12; Nicola B. Tannenbaum, "Galactic Polities, the Asiatic Mode of Production and Peasant-States," *The Australian Journal of Anthropology*, Vol. 4 (1993): 46-47. On the necessity of integrating also Greenwood's "Peasant State" into the model, see Tannenbaum, "Galactic Polities," 59.

26 Dieterich, "Some Theoretical and Methodological Observations," 126.

27 Boer, "Sacred Economy."

28 Boer, "Sacred Economy," 30; "A Titanic Phenomenon: Marxism, History and Biblical Society," *Historical Materialism,* Vol. 16 (2008): 148, 163. For Lenin's sharp critique of such theoretical eclecticism, see V. I. Lenin, *What is to be done?* (1902; New York, 1969; repr. 1992), 25.

29 Boer, "Sacred Economy," 29-38.

doing, he includes material from the whole of the ancient Near East, from the Sumerian period to the Persians, in explicit preference to ethnographic material from Asiatic Mode societies elsewhere in the world.[30] We can hardly assume that temple-city economics of Mesopotamia from any period were ever applicable in ancient Israel.[31] The average city in Mesopotamia was two thousand acres; those in Palestine were about twenty.

But there is a deeper theoretical problem here. In anthropological comparison, proximity of the cultures is all but irrelevant. Ontogenetic typology indicates which societies make the best comparands. In support of this use of ethnographic comparison, the skeptic should refer to the older discussions by I. J. Gelb and Avraham Malamat, who thoroughly defend the acceptability and utility of ethnographic analogy.[32] To agree with Norman Yoffee, "Societies do not form phyletic stages ... cross-cultural comparison can best proceed through analogy rather than homology."[33] But there is still validity in typologies. Julian Steward's dictum holds true that "there must be a typology of cultures, patterns, and institutions ... for formulating cultural regularities."[34] The sort of types needed allow the researcher "not to identify fossilized natural classes, but rather to deal with a series of sociocultural variables, which are seen as analytical categories, which can be combined and recombined into numerous societal constellations."[35] These types are not phyletic or phylogenetic but rather ontogenetic; they relate to the development of the

---

30 Boer, "Titanic Phenomenon," 159-60; "Sacred Economy," 33-34. Note phrases like "what we find in the Ancient Near East"; "Sacred Economy," 34.

31 Cf. Boer, "Sacred Economy," 36.

32 I. J. Gelb, "Comparative Method in the Study of the Society and Economy of the Ancient Near East," *Rocznik Orientalistyczny*, Vol. 41 (1980): 28-36; A. Malamat, "Tribal Societies," *Archives Européennes de Sociologie,* Vol. 14 (1973): 126-36; also Lemche, "From Patronage Society," 539.

33 Norman Yoffee, "The Decline and Rise of Mesopotamian Civilization," *American Antiquity,* Vol. 44 (1979): 7.

34 Julian Steward, "Cultural Causality and Law," *American Anthropologist*, Vol. 51 (1949): 3.

35 Yoffee, "Decline," 28.

particular economy and not to some evolutionary scheme into which the class itself might be placed.

Finally, nothing in the use of Marxian description to understand ancient Israel is meant to suggest any sort of determinism in history—dialectic, materialist, or otherwise. Actors in society can play on the multiple meaning of symbols, redefining situations in ways that they believe will favor their purposes.[36] Culture is "in continual flux…a pool of diverse resources, in which traffic passes between the literate and the oral, the superordinate and the subordinate, the village and the [comparative] metropolis; it is an arena of conflictual elements, which requires some compelling pressure…to take form as 'system.'"[37] We were simply mistaken that a culture's most important beliefs are consensual, agreed on by most of a society's members.[38] There were surely examples of resistance to the well-oiled economies of ancient Israel.[39]

No real private ownership of land existed in ancient Israel. This was Marx's insight;[40] and that it is antithetical to the real development of classes ensured its departure from orthodox Marxist thought.[41] Each "landowner" really only had usufruct rights over land that was owned by the state. This is clear from the Samaria Ostraca, which show that the state bureaucracy had the seigniorial rights over the farms of private individuals in the countryside.[42] Deuteronomy 21

---

[36] W. H. Sewell Jr., "Concept(s) of Culture," in *Beyond the Cultural Turn*, ed. V. E. Bonnell and L. Hunt (Studies on the History of Society and Culture 34; Berkeley, 1999), 51. For an assessment of recent misreadings of Marx that consider all life, work, and human activity to be totally subsuming by capital, see Donaldson, "Riddle," 136. For such a misreading, see Randall H. McGuire, *A Marxist Archaeology* (New York, 2002), 143

[37] E. P. Thompson, *Customs in Common* (New York, 1993), 6.

[38] Sewell, "Concept(s)," 54.

[39] The branch of Marxism to develop the strongest emphasis on individual agency as opposed to materialist determinacy has been North Korean *Juche*. See n.a., "What is Social History?" *Journal for the Study of the Juche Idea,* Vol. 82 (2011): 75.

[40] Karl Marx, *Grundrisse* (New York, 1973), 472; Letter to Friedrich Engels, June 2, 1853.

[41] Trotsky, however, had no problem with this; Leon Trotsky, *The Russian Revolution* (1932; Garden City, 1959), 4.

[42] Nili S. Fox, *In the Service of the King* (Monographs of the Hebrew Union College 23; Cincinnati, 2000), 204-235; Avraham Faust, "Household Economies in the Kingdoms of

(and 19:14; Josh 14:9; Prov 22:28; 23:10) and 1 Kings 21 attest only to the *allocation* of property, an allocation inherited within families.[43] It is an important legal notion, but we cannot understand private property ownership in modern terms as being practiced anywhere in the ancient world.

Now "the state" who owned the land really should be thought of as a polity that is a network of relations among powerful people and their followers.[44] That is, the state, which ultimately appears as a person, the King, was not primarily a territory but relationships between powerful and the less so.[45]

The nature of land ownership means that "tax" and "rent" would be merely two terms for the same thing.[46] And, as Marx knew, there was no such thing as tax beyond rent.[47] For the people on the land, those with usufruct rights, paying the rent to the legal landowner was the same thing as paying taxes to the state. Tax-rent included both material goods (1 Sam 8:15-17) and corvée labor (Micah 3:9-10).[48] The poorest of people in society, therefore, were

---

Israel and Judah," in *Household Archaeology in Ancient Israel and Beyond,* ed. A. Yasur-Landau, J. R. Ebeling, and L. B. Mazow (Culture and History of the Ancient Near East 50; Leiden, 2011), 268.

[43] Boer, "Sacred Economy," 40.

[44] Shiozawa, "Marx's Asiatic Mode," 314.

[45] R. Saks, *Human Territoriality* (Cambridge Studies in Historical Geography 7; Cambridge, 1986), 19-21; Tannenbaum, "Galactic Polities," 57. This does not appear to be true, however, for China under the Northern Song dynasty, a cultural otherwise quite comparable. See Nicolas Tackett, "The Great Wall and Conceptualizations of the Border under the Northern Song," *Journal of Song-Yuan Studies,* Vol. 38 (2008): 99-138.

[46] Umberto Melotti, *Marx and the Third World* (London, 1977), 54; Gottwald, "Social Class," 153-55.

[47] Karl Marx, *Capital* (New York: International Publishers, 1967), 3.791. See also Rosa Luxemburg, *The Accumulation of Capital* (1913; London, 1951), 443.

[48] Lagopoulos, "Mode," 42. For examples from pre-feudal Russia, see Bruce McFarlane, Steve Cooper, and Miomir Jaksic, "The Asiatic Mode of Production - a new Phoenix (Part 2)," *Journal of Contemporary Asia,* Vol. 35 (2005): 509, and 503-504 for Funan Kampuchea. Monumental architecture in 9th-century Israel and 8th-century Judah is probably testimony to this corvée.

not slaves but workers who could serve and then return home. Marx also had this correct.[49]

Villages themselves were largely self-sufficient, at least for agricultural and domestic crafts.[50] They passed surplus up to the state as their rent-tax (cf. Amos 5:11).[51] In the villages, the individual's relation to the land that he worked was mediated by means of the particular community, which was the elemental unit of production.[52] The community, not the individuals or even families within it, was collectively responsible to the state for rent/taxes.[53] While part of the surplus labor belonged to the higher community, the community had control over its internal affairs as long as it fulfilled those obligations.[54] The state was thus not all-powerful, even economically, and this Marx exaggerated, although he can hardly be blamed for the insufficiency of the data available to him.[55]

Locals groups "wanted" from the state law codes, economic integration, lines of communication, and defense; the state "wanted" from the villages their surplus, economic integration, and control of the use of force.[56] It was not in the interest of the state to manage

---

[49] Shiozawa, "Marx's Asiatic Mode," 305.

[50] Melotti, *Marx,* 54; Gottwald, "Social Class," 153-55; Marx, *Grundrisse,* 486.

[51] Shiozawa, "Marx's Asiatic Mode," 311. Regional storage systems in Iron II Dan, Hazor, Megiddo, and Lachish provide evidence; Robert D. Miller II, "Cities and Villages," in *Dictionary of the Old Testament Historical Books*, ed. Bill T. Arnold and H. G. M. Williamson (Downers Grove, 2005), 189.

[52] Shiozawa, "Marx's Asiatic Mode," 310; Boer, "Sacred Economy," 35-36. For examples from pre-colonial Swazi villages, see Carolyn Sachs and Christine Roach, "Women and Agricultural Production on Swazi Nation Land, research project report, USAID Office of Women in Development, Washington, 1983), 9.

[53] Davydd J. Greenwood, *The Political Economy of Peasant Family Farming* (Cornell University Rural Development Committee Occasional Papers 2; Ithaca, New York, 1973), 61-62.

[54] Lagopoulos, "Mode," 42; Greenwood, *Political Economy*, 37. Tannenbaum, "Galactic Polities," 57 provides ethnographic examples from Shan and Tai Long villages.

[55] Davidson, "Asiatic, Tributary or Absolutist?" 4.

[56] Greenwood, *Political Economy*, 38. For examples from Shan villages, see Nicola B. Tannenbaum, "From Repairing the Village/Repairing Country Ceremonies to Tree Ordinations," in *Inter-Ethnic Relations in the Making of Mainland Southeast Asia and Southwestern China*, ed. Yukio Hayashi and Aroonrut Wichienkeeo (Bangkok, 2002): 180, 188-89.

every affair of the peasantry, because then the villages would become too dependent.[57] "The relationship between peasant domestic groups, local communities and the state is seen as one of constant trade-offs: autonomy for protection, wealth for services, state authority for voluntary community support."[58]

The system was not based on coercion; peasants thought of themselves as part of the state.[59] The trade-off thus included cognitive elements, not just material: personal loyalty, a morality of fidelity, respect for elders, devotion to the house of David, etc.[60]

Village elders were responsible for organizing the village, distributing stores, and organizing corvée,[61] and they were compensated with rights to land ("from the state") and labor from the peasants (cf. *Amarna Letter* 100.4).[62] Such village elders were likely not chosen by the state, but the state rather tapped those with existing power and support.[63] Yet they were only minimally distinct from rest of peasants (as, e.g., Egyptian tombs of town elders are minimally different from commoners).[64] No one in the villages had access to specialized artistic items.

---

57 Shiozawa, "Marx's Asiatic Mode," 311; Greenwood, *Political Economy*, 38; Lagopoulos, "Mode," 42.

58 Greenwood, *Political Economy*, 39.

59 Greenwood, *Political Economy*, 67.

60 For ethnographic examples from the Swazi, see Philip Bonner, "Classes, the Mode of Production and the State in Pre-Colonial Swaziland," paper presented to the University of the Witwatersrand African Studies Institute, September 13, 1976. In this, we must perhaps move away from the sole emphasis on economic factors characteristic of Marxism, especially in its Stalinist manifestations, e.g., Enver Hoxha, "On the Intellectuals" (1958), in *Selected Works* (Tirana, 1975), 2.724; Hoxha, *Study Marxist-Leninist Theory Linking it Closely with Revolutionary Practice* (Tirana, 1971), 38, 43.

61 Faust, "Household Economies," 265.

62 Victor H. Matthews and Don C. Benjamin, *The Social World of Ancient Israel 1250-587 BCE* (Peabody, Massachusetts, 1993), 97-98; H. Reviv, *The Elders in Ancient Israel* (Trans. L. Plitmann; Jerusalem, 1989), 18, and *passim*; Shiozawa, "Marx's Asiatic Mode," 310; Greenwood, *Political Economy*, 37. Tannenbaum, "Galactic Polities," 51; and "Repairing," 178 give ethnographic examples from Shan and Thai headmen.

63 Tannenbaum, "Galactic Polities," 50, 56.

64 C. Schäfer-Lichtenberger, *Stadt und Eidgenossenschaft im Alten Testament* (Beihefte zur Zeitschrift für die Alttestamentliche Wissenschaft 156; Berlin, 1983), 290-96 distinguishes

All of these relationships—state to village, elder to peasant—were relations of patronage (cf. Job 29). The patron had a personal relationship with the client, envisioned as a parent-child relationship (Deut 15:1-18; Lev 25:35-43).[65] In fact, kin relationships were being replaced by patrons working directly with nuclear families.[66] Thus, while kinship language and concepts may have been applied to socio-political interactions in ancient Israel, we should define this as patronage when the real kinship relationships have been superseded. Ethnographically, this is a very durable system.[67] During periods of centralization, the peasant economy underwrites the state; during center collapse, peasants can take care of selves.[68]

Nevertheless, such a system is not static. There are both inherent changes— "development [that] arises from the contradictions inside a thing"[69]—and changes resulting from the particulars of Israelite history. From the start, there is some stratification in the Asiatic Mode. Technology continued to advance through the Iron Age, in what Marx called the Extension of the Hand and Extension of the Land; that is, ways to increase what one human could physically do and ways to make land more productive. Those peasants who had slightly better productivity to start with had the means to take advantage of the technological developments and

---

between judiciary elders and executive "men of the city," but others doubt such a distinction is possible; R. Neu, *Von der Anarchie zum Staat* (Neukirchen-Vlyun, 1992), 208-209.

65 Eisenstadt and Roniger, *Patrons,* 48-49; Tannenbaum, "Galactic Polities," 53, 56.

66 Simkins, "Patronage," 136-38. For extensive evidence that nuclear families were the norm in Iron Age Israel and Judah, see Miller, "Cities and Villages," 190-91.

67 Greenwood, *Political Economy*, 34, 68-69, where he notes the endurance of such systems for centuries in Spain, France, and Italy.

68 For examples from 9th-century A.D. Indonesia, see Janice Stargardt, "Hydraulic Works and Southeast Asian Polities," in *Southeast Asia in the 9th to 14th Centuries*, ed. David G. Marr and Anthony Crothers Milner (Singapore, 1987), 26.

69 Mao Zedong, "On Contradiction" (1937), *Selected Works of Mao Tse-Tung*, vol. 1 (Beijing, 1937), §1. And further, "In other words, the development of things should be seen as their internal and necessary self-movement, while each thing in its movement is interrelated with and interacts on the things around it. ... Does materialist dialectics exclude external causes? Not at all. It holds that external causes are the condition of change and internal causes are the basis of change, and that external causes become operative through internal causes."

thereby to improve their standard of living even more.[70] This was the beginning of a higher class, and it was first based on having more movable property.[71] The real poor lacked the resources to employ the new technology, and as their neighbors' production increased, the value of produce decreased, so the poor earned even less.[72]

Young people migrated to the cities throughout the Iron II period.[73] This urbanization[74] also contributed to social stratification, especially as Assyria imposed tribute in the West in 9th-8th centuries.[75] Allocation rights to suburban land began to be appropriated by the wealthy urbanites, as creditor latifundaries took custody of the encumbered lands, reducing former "users" to wage farmers (Micah 2:2-10), while in the inner circle, flattery of the despot and palace intrigue were constant.[76]

---

70 Shiozawa, "Marx's Asiatic Mode," 311, 315; Dieterich, "Some Theoretical and Methodological Observations," 116; Greenwood, *Political Economy*, 25.

71 Shiozawa, "Marx's Asiatic Mode," 312. For Swazi examples, see Mmantoa S. Kgaphola and Annemarie T. Viljoen, "Food habits of rural Swazi households: 1939–1999 Part 1," *Tydskrif vir Gesinsekologie en Verbruikerswetenskappe*, Vol. 28 (2000): 70.

72 McFarlane et al, "Asiatic Mode Part 2," 2nd page, 515; Greenwood, *Political Economy*, 25.

73 S. Bendor, *The Social Structure of Ancient Israel* (Jerusalem Biblical Studies 7; Jerusalem, 1996), 173-204.

74 This is not the best term: most "cities" were not urban—except for Mizpah and Tell Beit Mirsim, they had no industries, but were parasitical on the villages for their goods. See Miller, "Cities and Villages," 190.

75 William R. Domeris, *Touching the Heart of God* (Library of the Hebrew Bible/Old Testament Studies 466; New York, 2007), 52, 65. In the famous black obelisk of Shalmaneser, dated to 841, Israel's king Jehu brings to Shalmaneser. Adad-nirari received tribute from Israel in 805; Susan Ackerman, "Assyria in the Bible," in *Assyrian Reliefs from the Palace of Ashurnasirpal II,* ed. Ada Cohen and Steven E. Kangas (Hanover, NH: University Press of New England, 2010), 128-29; *ARAB* (*Ancient Records of Assyria and Babylonia*) 1.734-35, 739-40. The Israelite king Joash (798-783) also presented tribute to Adad-nirari, as recorded in the Tell Rimah Stele. King Menahem of Israel paid tribute to Tiglath-pileser (2 Kgs 15:18-20). Judah's king Ahaz is recorded as paying tribute faithfully to Assyria in 734 or 733; *ARAB* 1.801. The Rassam Cylinder includes tribute from Hezekiah of Judah in lines 55-58.

76 Faust, "Household Economies," 271; Trotsky, *Russian Revolution,* 94. McFarlane et al, "Asiatic Mode Part 2," 502, has examples from the Northern Song dynasty, and see Yoshifumi Tamada, "*Itthiphon* and *Amnat*," *Southeast Asian Studies,* Vol. 28 (1991): 455-66, for examples with Thai headmen. After these developments, the economic model of Boer becomes more applicable; see Boer, "Sacred Economy," 39-40.

Now nothing presented above is new. This essay has merely expanded the work of others on tributary-patronage economics in ancient Israel with scholarship on the Asiatic Mode of Production. What is noteworthy, however, is that Israel inscribed its conception of God according to this model.[77] Boer calls this "theological metaphorization of allocation," but in his very brief treatment focuses on Israel's clothing of the earthly economy with the language of the sacred.[78] Yet in several places, the Hebrew Bible presents a portrait of the divine-human relationship itself that is precisely the Asiatic Mode of Production.

To begin with, the land of Israel was explicitly not Israel's. It was God's land (Deut 17:2, 7). Not only did he reserve the right to remove Israel from that land, as in Isaiah 5 where God promises to uproot his "vineyard" Judah, but each individual—including the king—was seen as at most a steward of their land and at times a resident alien employed on that land (Lev 25:23-25, 29-31).[79] Lev 25:23 is most explicit, "You are but resident aliens under my authority." God reserved the right to redistribute the land within the Israelite community (Micah 2; Psalm 37:1-11).[80] Thus the complaint of the previously wealthy in Micah 2:5, "He changes the portion of my people! How he removes it from me!" The books of the prophets claim that those who will not provide for poor dispute God's legal claim to the earth and right to redistribute property as he decrees.

Furthermore, the individual's relation to God was mediated by means of the Israelite community. The community was collectively responsible to God. This is the corporate responsibility

---

77 Lagopoulos suggests this was the case, but does not develop the thought; "Mode," 54.

78 Boer, "Sacred Economy," 43.

79 Walter Brueggemann, *The Land* (Overtures to Biblical Theology 1; Philadelphia, 1977), 7; Norman C. Habel, *The Land is Mind* (Overtures to Biblical Theology 16; Philadelphia, 1995), 98, 107, and *passim*.

80 For discussion of this notion encoded in the "conquest" narratives, see Clive Beed and Cara Beed, "Economic Egalitarianism in Pre-monarchical Israel," *Faith & Economics*, Vol. 54 (2009): 83-105.

noted above. To be in this community is the solidarity the Hebrew Bible calls *ṣedaqah*: "right relationship."[81]

This "system" or "covenant" was not based on coercion; Israelites think of themselves as part of the covenanted community. Of course, there were promises of rewards and punishments, but the laws of the Sinai covenant were the secondary, response side of the relationship with God. They never gained "greater importance in the statements of faith" than God's actions held.[82] The law was "a logical extension of the election," the means "by which the meaning and implications of election were concretely stated."[83] But the rewards and punishment are never presented *outside* of the context of covenant relationship. The law was given to an Israel *already* elect. The relationship, furthermore, is independent of the fulfilment of the obligations, and yet "presupposes or demands the positive response from the other party" (Deut 6:24-25; Mic 6:1-8; Jer 2:4-13).[84]

The Israelite king was in many ways envisioned as a large-scale village elder. He is *primus inter pares*, never "exalting himself above his brothers" (Deut 17:19-20). He was responsible for administering God's justice in the real world, and for little else (Proverbs 29:4, 12, 14; Psalm 72; Deut 10:14-19).[85] What Psalm 72 says about the king with regard to working justice is said of God elsewhere in the Hebrew Bible, and a king who does not help poor is not God's king.

All of these relationships—God to people, king to commoner—were relations of patronage.[86] The king and other

---

[81] Henning Graf Reventlow, *Eigenart des Jahweglaubens* (1973; repr. Biblisch-Theologische Studien 66; Neukirchen-Vluyn: Neukirchener Verlag, 2004), 33, 35; Pavel Keřkovský, "Biblical Language of Law," *Communio Viatorum,* Vol. 48 (2006): 21.

[82] Josef Schreiner, "The Development of the Israelite Credo," *Concilium*, Vol. 10.2 (1966): 17; Kevin G. O'Connell, "Grace in the Old Testament," *Scripture,* Vol. 20 (1968): 43.

[83] Dale Patrick, "Moral Logic of Election," *Encounter*, Vol. 37 (1976): 204

[84] Paul Kalluveettil, "Covenant Reality in the Hebrew Society," in *Indian Church in the Struggle for a New Society* (Bangalore, 1981), 51; John E. Harvey, *Retelling the Torah* (Journal for the Study of the Old Testament Supplement 403; London, 2004), 12.

[85] Houston, *Contending*, 135-53.

[86] Houston, *Contending*, 123-26.

powerful people were called to assume the patron's role vis-à-vis the poor (Exod 22:24-26). God was envisioned as the ultimate patron (Psalm 82).[87] The moral commitment of God to his servants was based on personal relationship. But this relationship was much of the time not seen in kinship terms, and this is one way to understand the elusive concept of *khesed. Khesed* is the benevolence of a unique superior helping one unable to do something necessary.[88] It is the patronage of God that the powerful in Israel were expected to practice themselves. Thus, Hosea uses the term ubiquitously but never with reference to God's *khesed*, only with a demand that Israel practice *khesed*. Yet, in the Bible overall the phrase "'abounding in (Heb. *rab*) *khesed*' is used only in reference to God."[89] Israel maintains that duties of one person to another, then, are prior to individual rights.

I do not deny that some of the biblical tradition interrogates the prevailing economic paradigm of ancient Israel.[90] The Sabbath legislation, in particular, is "a principal of anti-economy lodged at the heart of the West's cultural, philosophical, and monetary economies."[91] Nevertheless, as this essay has shown, Israel's conception of its relationship with God owes a great deal to its own economy, to the Asiatic Mode of Production.

---

87 Houston, *Contending*, 204-215.

88 Tannenbaum, "Galactic Polities," 53, uses the term "benevolence" in an identical fashion to speak of human patronage.

89 Katharine Doob Sakenfeld, "Love (Old Testament)," *Anchor Bible Dictionary* (Garden City, 1992), 4.375-80. When the Hebrew Bible refers to God as "father," therefore, it is far from sentimentalism. The concept is in part economic.

90 Timothy Gorringe, "Idolatry and Redemption: Economics in Biblical Perspective," *Political Theology*, Vol. 11 (2010): 367-82.

91 Kenneth Reinhard and Julia R. Lupton, "Revelation: Lacan and the Ten Commandments," *Journal for Cultural and Religious Theory*, Vol. 2, No. 1 (2000) online article at http://www.jcrt.org/archives/02.1/reinhard_lupton.shtml.

"Some Ancient Geographic Texts Relating to the Land of Israel"

Rafael Frankel
Haifa University

I met Saul Friedman for the first time in Israel when he accompanied his son on a field trip that I guided. Later he invited me to give a lecture at Youngstown State University and I want to take this opportunity to thank him for that kind invitation.

My contribution to the *Gedenkschrift* is in a way a continuation of the trip. I will not add to the vast research that has been devoted to the historical geography of ancient Israel.[1] Instead I will present the reader with a selection of descriptions of the country and places in it from the works of two ancient writers, Pliny the Elder and Josephus Flavius. The most important are detailed descriptions of the country. That of Pliny (**P1**) is remarkable for the degree of detail and accuracy. His description of the river Jordan is almost certainly the most vivid in ancient literature. The attached map includes nearly all the places Pliny mentions. Josephus's description (**J1**) is particularly useful because it defines the extent of the various districts by specifying border points "from x to y," and the attached map includes mainly these, Both writers give a list of the toparchies of Judaea; for an explanation of the differences see note at the end of **J1**

Pliny the Elder (Gaius Plinius Secundus. 23/4-79 CE), the Roman writer had a long military and legal career. It has been suggested that he served in the Roman army that suppressed the Jewish revolt; his detailed and vivid descriptions of Israel make that very probable. His nephew, Pliny the Younger, described how he died investigating the eruption of Vesuvius that destroyed Pompeii and also enumerated the many books that he wrote. However, the

---

[1] See the pioneering work of Smith (1894) that is still relevant today. For the early periods see Aharoni (1967) and Aharoni et al. (2011) and for the later periods Avi-Yonah (1966) and (1976) and Tsafrir et al. (1998). For a detailed bibliography of place names in Talmudic literature, see Reeg (1989).

only one to survive is the encyclopedic *Naturalis Historia – Natural History* -NH from which I quote here.

Josephus Flavius (Joseph ben Matityahu 37/8-c.100 CE) of a priestly family was governor of Galilee and commander in the revolt against the Romans in that region, but was captured and from then on accompanied Vespasian the future emperor. He settled in Rome, where he received Roman citizenship and was granted a pension and housing. He wrote four books *The Jewish War* JW (appeared 75-79 CE), *Jewish Antiquities* JA (appeared 93-94 CE) *The Life* L, and *Against Apion* AA, both probably later.

Pliny and Josephus lived and wrote at the same time, both in Rome, and although they do not mention one another, they almost certainly knew of each other and were probably acquainted.

In almost all cases I have followed the Loeb translations. As regards place names. in the case of Pliny I have usually given the Latin names as in the text with other names in brackets, Hebrew/Aramaic names in ordinary font, and Arabic names in italics, whereas in the case of Josephus I have not given the Greek but the names as they are in the Loeb translation. As regards identifications, I have usually followed Avi-Yonah (1966; 1976).

Pliny

P1: HN V XIV- XVII (#68- 76)

XIV "At **Ostracine (Ras *Straki*) is** the frontier of Arabia.65 miles from **Pelusium.** Then begins **Idumea** and **Palaestina** at the point where **Lake Serbonis (*Sabkhat el Bardawil*)** comes into view. This lake is recorded by some writers as having measured 150 miles round – Herodotus gave it as reaching **Mount Casius (*el Kas*)**. But it is now an inconsiderable fen. There are the towns of **Rhinocolura (*el Arish*)** and inland **Rhaphea, Gaza** and inland **Anthedon** and **Mount Argaris**, Further along the coast is the region of **Samaria,** the free town of Ascalo **(Ashkelon**), **Azotus (Ashdod)** and the two towns named **Iamnea (Yavneh),** one of them inland, and the Phoenician city of **Iope (Jaffa).** This is said to have existed before the flood. It is situated on a hill and in front of it is a rock on which they point out marks made by the chains with which Andromeda was fettered; here there is a cult of the legendary goddess

Ceto. Next **Apollonia** and the **Tower of Straton,** otherwise **Caesarea,** founded by King Herod but now called **Prima Flavia,** established by the Emperor Vespasian. This is the frontier of **Palaestina,** 189 miles from the confines of **Arabia**. After this comes **Phoenicia** and inland **Samaria:** the towns are **Neapolis (Nablus)** formerly **Mamortha, Sebaste** on a mountain and on a loftier mountain **Gamala**.

XV Beyond **Idumea** and **Samaria** stretches the wide expanse of **Iudaea.** The part of **Iudaea** adjoining **Syria** is called **Galilaea** and that next to **Arabia** and **Aegyptus Peraea. Peraea** is covered with rugged mountains and is separated from the other parts of **Iudaea** by the river **Iordanes (Jordan).** The rest of Iudaea is divided into ten toparchies in the following order: **Hiericus (Jericho),** which has numerous palm-groves and springs of water, **Emmaus, Lydda, Joppa, Acrebitenum (Acrabetta/Acraba), Gophna, Thamna, Beth-Leptephenen (Betholetepha/*Beit Nattif*),** the **Hills,** the district that formerly contained **Hierosolyma (Jerusalem),** by far the most famous city of the East and not of **Judaea** only, and **Herodium** with the celebrated town of the same name.

The source of the river **Iordanes** is the spring of **Panias** from which **Caesarea** described later takes its name. It is a delightful stream, winding about as far as the conformation of the locality allows and putting itself at the service of the people who dwell on its banks, as though moving with reluctance towards that gloomy lake, the **Asphalt Lake (the Dead Sea)** which ultimately swallows it up, its much –praised waters mingling with the pestilential waters of the lake and being lost. For this reason at the first opportunity afforded by the formation of the valleys it widens out into a lake usually called the **Sea of Gennesareth**. This is 16 miles long and 6 broad, and is skirted by the pleasant towns of **Iulias (Bethsaida)** and **Hippo (Suseita)** on the east, **Tarichea (Migdal)** on the south (the name of which place some people also give to the lake), and **Tiberius** with its salubrious hot springs on the west. The only product of the **Asphalt Lake (the Dead Sea) is** bitumen, which gives it its name. The bodies of animals do not sink in its waters, even bulls and camels floating; this has given rise to the report that nothing at all can sink in it. It is more than 100 miles long and fully 75 miles broad at the broadest part but only 8 miles at the narrowest. On the east it is faced by **Arabia of the Nomads** and on the south by **Machaerus,** at one time next to **Hierosolyma (Jerusalem)** the most important fortress in **Iudaea**. On the same side is a hot spring possessing medicinal value, the name of which, **Callirhoe,** itself proclaims the celebrity of its waters. On the west side but out of range of the noxious exhalations of the coast, is the solitary tribe of the Essenes which is remarkable beyond all the other tribes in the whole world as it has no women and has renounced all sexual desires, has no money and has only palm-trees for company. Day by day the throng of refugees is recruited to an equal number by numerous accessions of persons tired of life and driven thither by the waves of fortune to adopt their manners. Thus through thousands of ages (incredible to relate) a race in which no one is born lives on forever: so prolific for their advantage is other men's weariness of life.

Lying below the Essenes was formerly the town of **Engada (Engedi),** second only to **Hierosolyma (Jerusalem)** in the fertility of its land and in its groves of palm-trees, but now like **Hierosolyma (Jerusalem)** a heap of ashes. Next comes **Masada** a fortress on a rock itself also not far from the **Asphalt Lake (Dead Sea).** This is the limit of **Judaea**

XVI Adjoining **Iudaea** on the side of **Syria** is the region of Decapolis, so called from the number of its towns though not all writers keep to the same towns in the list. Most however include **Damascus** with its fertile water-meadows that drain the river **Chrysorroa, Philadelphia (Rabat Ammon), Rhaphana** (all these three withdrawn towards **Arabia**), **Scythopolis (Bet Shean),** formerly **Nysa** (after Father Liber's nurse whom he buried there) where a colony of Scythians are settled, **Gadara** past which flows the river **Hieromice (Yarmuk)**, **Hippo (Suseita)** mentioned already, **Dion. Pella,** rich with its waters, **Galasa, Canatha.** Between and around these cities run tetrarchies each of them equal to a kingdom, and they are incorporated into kingdoms – **Trachonis. Panias** (in which is **Caesarea** with the spring mentioned above), **Abila, Arca, Ampeloessa,** and **Gabe**

XVII From this point we must go back to the coast to **Phoenice.** There was formerly a town called **Crocodilon,** and there is still a river of that name, and the cities of Dora and **Sycamini** of which only the memory exists. Then comes Cape **Carmelum** and on a mountain the town of the same name formerly called **Acbatana.** Next are **Getta, Geba,** and the river **Pacida** or **Belus,** which covers its narrow bank with sand for making glass; the river itself flows out of the marsh **Cendebia** at the foot of Mount **Carmel.** Close to the river **Ptolemais (Akko/Acre),** a colony of the Emperor Claudius formerly called **Acce,** and then the town **Ecdippa (Achzib)** and the **White Cape.** Next **Tyros (Tyre),** once an island separated from the mainland by a very deep sea-channel 700 paces wide but now joined to it by the works constructed by Alexander when besieging and formerly famous as the mother-city from which sprang the cities of Leptis**,** **Utica,** and the great rival of Rome's empire in coveting world-sovereignty **Carthage,** and also **Cadiz,** which was founded outside the confines of the world. But the entire renown of Tyre now consists in a shell-fish and purple dye. The circumference of the city including Old Tyre on the coast measures 19 miles, the actual town covering 2 3/4 miles. Next are **Sarepta [Sarafand]** and **Ornithon** and the mother-city of **Thebes** in Boeotia, **Sidon,** where glass is made.

P 2:NH IX IV # 11

"The skeleton of the monster to which Andromeda in the story was exposed was brought by Marcus Scaurus from the town of **Ioppe (Jaffa)** in **Iudaea** and shown at **Rome---"**

P3: NH XII LI #109

"A tree found in Egypt is the henna ---The best is made from the tree grown at Canopus on the banks of the Nile, the second best at **Ascalon** in **Iudaea** ----

P4: NH XII LIV # 111

"But every other scent ranks below balsam. The only country in which this plant has been vouchsafed is **Iudaea,** where formerly it grew in only two gardens both belonging to the king---- this variety of shrub was exhibited to the capital by the emperors Vespasian and Titus---the Jews vented their wrath upon this plant as they also did upon their own lives but the Romans protected it and there have been pitched battles in defense of the shrub----"

P5:NH XIII VI # 26

"But Judaea is even more famous for its palm-trees the nature of which will now be described ----"

P6: NH XIII IX # 44

" But not only are these trees[caryotae dates] abundant and bear largely in **Iudaea,** but also the most famous are found there and not in the whole country but especially in **Hiericus (Jericho),** although those growing in the valleys of **Archelais** and **Phaselis** and **Livias** in the same country are also highly spoken of."

Josephus Flavius

J1:JW III #35-58

"**Galilee** with its two divisions known as **Upper** and **Lower Galilee** is enveloped by **Phoenicia** and **Syria**. Its western frontiers are the outlying territory of Ptolemais and **Carmel,** a mountain once belonging to **Galilee** and now in **Tyre**: adjacent to Carmel is **Gaba** the "city of cavalry" so called from the cavalry who on their discharge by King Herod settled in this town. On the south, the country is bounded by **Samaria** and the territory of **Scythopolis** up to the waters of **Jordan;** on the east by the territory of **Hippos, Gadara,** and **Gaulanitis, the** frontier-line of **Agrippa's kingdom;** on the north **Tyre** and its dependant district mark its limits. **Lower Galilee** extends in length from **Tiberius** to **Chabulon (Cabul),** which is not far from **Ptolemais** on the coast ; in breadth from a village in the Great Plain called **Xalot (Chislot-Tabor, *Iksal*)** to **Bersaba (Beer Sheba).** At this point begins **Upper Galilee, which** extends in breadth to the village of **Baca (Buqeia/Peqi'in),** the frontier of Tyrian territory; in length it reaches from the village of **Thella (Tuleil)** near the Jordan to **Meroth (Marus).**

With this limited area and although surrounded by such powerful foreign nations, the two Galilees have always resisted any hostile invasion, for the inhabitants are from infancy inured to war and have at all times been numerous; never did the men lack courage nor the country men. For the land is everywhere so rich in soil and pasturage and produces such variety of trees, that even the most indolent are tempted by these facilities to devote themselves to agriculture. In fact, every inch of the soil has been cultivated by the inhabitants; there is not a parcel of wasteland.

The towns, too, are thickly distributed. And even the villages, thanks to the fertility of the soil, are all so densely populated that the smallest of them contains fifteen thousand inhabitants.

In short, if Galilee in superficial area must be reckoned inferior to Peraea, it must be given the preference for its abundant resources: for it is entirely under cultivation and produces crops from one end to the other, whereas Peraea, though far more extensive, is for the most part desert and rugged and too wild to bring tender fruits to maturity, However, there too, there are tracts of finer soil which are productive of every species of crop; and the plains are covered with a variety of trees, olive, vine and palm being principally cultivated. The country is watered by torrents descending from the mountains and by springs which never dry up and provide sufficient moisture when the torrents dwindle in the dog-days.

Peraea extends in length from **Machaerus** to **Pella,** in breadth from **Philadelphia** to the **Jordan**. The northern frontier is **Pella, which** we have just mentioned; the western frontier is the **Jordan;** on the south, it is bounded by the land of Moab; on the east by Arabia Heshbonitis, Philadelphia**,** and **Gerasa.**

The province of **Samaria** lies between **Galilee** and **Judaea**; beginning at the village of Ginaea **(*Jenin*?)** situated in the Great Plain it terminates at the toparchy of **Acrabatane.**

Its character differs in no wise from that of Judaea. Both regions consist of hills and plains, yield a light and fertile soil for agriculture are well wooded and abound in fruits, both wild and cultivated; both owe their productiveness to the entire absence of dry deserts and to a rainfall for the most abundant. All the running water ha a singularly sweet taste; and owing to the abundance of excellent grass the cattle yield more milk than in other districts. But the surest testimony to the virtues and thriving conditions of the two countries is that both have a dense population

On the frontier separating them lies the village called **Anuath Borcaeus** (***Berqit***) the northern limit of **Judaea;** its southern boundary if one measures the country lengthwise is marked by a village on the Arabian frontier which is called by the Jews **Iardan**

(Arad ?). In breadth it stretches from the river **Jordan** to **Joppa.** The city of **Jerusalem** lies at its very centre for which reason the town has sometimes not inaptly been called the "navel" of the country. **Judaea** is moreover not cut off from the amenities of the sea because it slopes down towards the coast on a ridge extending as far as **Ptolemais.** It is divided into eleven districts among which **Jerusalem** as the capital is supreme dominating all the neighborhood as the head towers above the body ; in the case of the other minor districts the divisions coincide with the toparchies: **Gophna** is the second, then come **Acrabeta, Thamna, Lydda Emmaus, Pella, Idumaea, Engaddi, Herodion,** and **Jericho**, To these must be added **Jamnia** and **Joppa,** which have jurisdiction over the surrounding localities, and lastly the territories of **Gamala, Gaulanitis, Batanaea,** and **Trachonitis** which form moreover part of **Agrippa's kingdom.** That kingdom beginning at **Mount Libanus** and the sources of the **Jordan** extends in breadth to the lake of **Tiberius** and in length from a village called **Arpha** to **Julias.** **I**t contains a mixed population of Jews and Syrians. Such in briefest possible outline is my description of the country of the Jews and of their neighbors."

Note: In the Loeb edition of JW III-IV there are two important explanatory notes from which I will quote here verbatim:-

1] Regarding the difference between the lists of toparchies in Pliny and Josephus:-

p.20 n. a "Pliny (HN V14 #70) mentions the division of Judaea into ten toparchies: he omits Idumaea and Engaddi inserts Joppa (incorrectly) and substitutes (correctly) for Pella Betholethephene (=Betheptepha JW IV # 445))

2] Regarding Agrippa's Kingdom etc.

p. 21 n. c " Josephus here appends to the four main provinces of Jewish territory (1) the only maritime towns whose population was predominantly Jewish (3) Agrippa's kingdom in the north also containing a large Jewish element"

J2 JW III 514 -515

"After issuing from this grotto the **Jordan** whose course is now visible intersects the marshes and lagoons of **Lake Semechonitis** then traverses another hundred and twenty stades, and below the town of **Julias cuts** across the **Lake of Gennesar,** from which after meandering through a long desert region ends by flowing into **Lake Aspheltitis**

J3:JW II # 188-190

Ptolemais is a maritime town in **Galilee** built at the entrance to the Great Plain and encompassed with mountains. To the east at a distance of 60 stades is the Galilean range ; to the south 120 stades off lies **Carmel** ; to the north is the highest chain of all called by the natives **"Ladder of the Tyrians,"** 100 stades away. At a distance of about two stades from the town runs the diminutive river **Belus; on** its banks stands the **tomb of Memnon,** and close to it is a very remarkable region a hundred cubits in extent. It consists of a circular basin which produces vitreous sand---"

For other detailed descriptions in Josephus' works see:
Jerusalem including the temple: - JW V iv-v 1 #136-247;
Masada JW VII vii # 280-303
Dead Sea JW IV I viii # 476-455
Caesarea JW I xxi #408-416; JA XV # 331-341
Jericho and surroundings JW IV # 451-471

Sidon
Sarepta
Tyrus
Panias
Caesarea
Galilaea
Ptolemais
Iulias
Tarichea
Tiberias
Hippos
Phoenice
Dora
Caesarea
Decapolis
Scythopolis
Pella
Samaria
Sebaste
Neapolis
Palaestina
Apollonia
Iope
Philadelphia
Gophna
Archelais
Livias
Peraea
Emmaus
Thamna
Herodium
Anthedon
Gaza
Iudaea
Callirroe
Machaerus
Engadia
Masada
Sirbonis Lacus
Rhinocolura
Pelusium
Ostracine

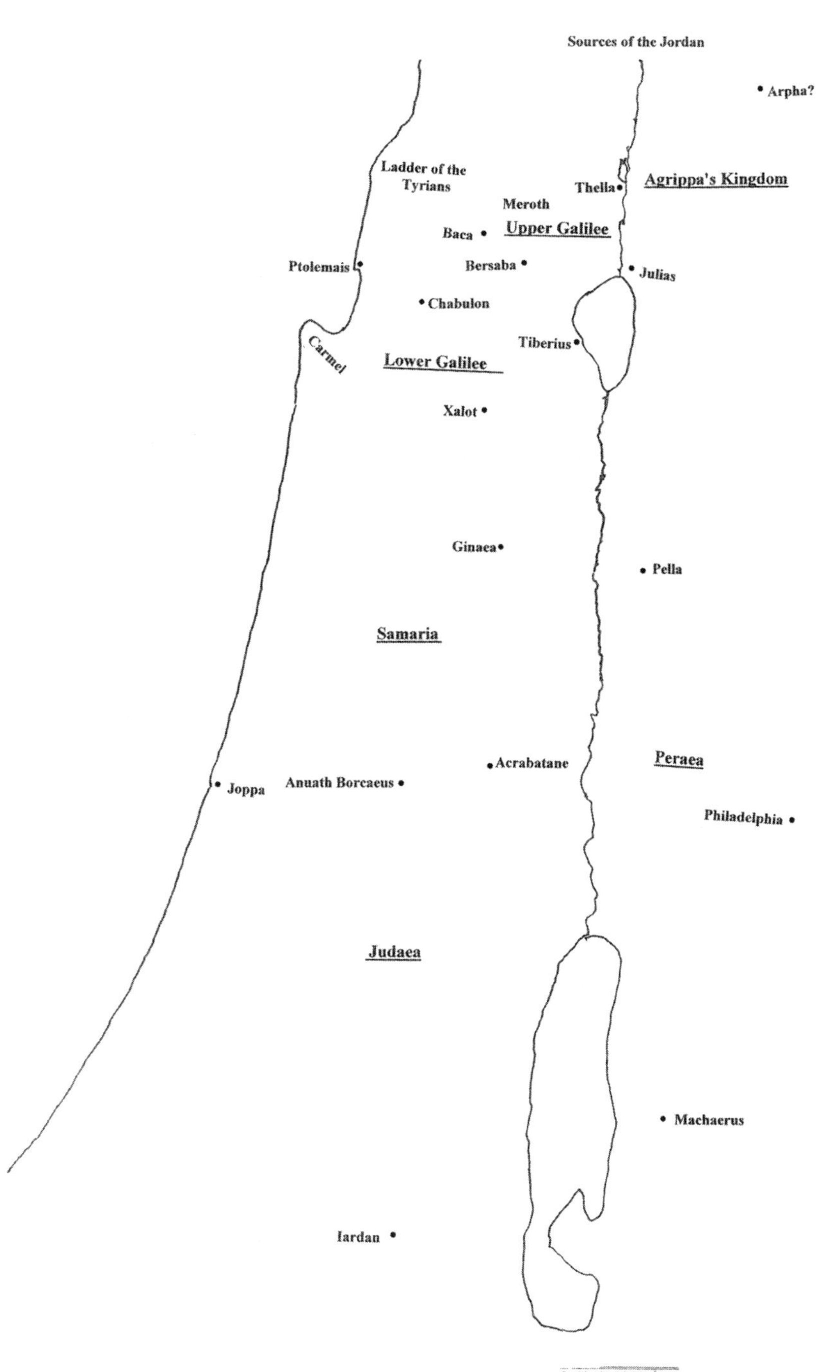
Sources of the Jordan
Arpha?
Ladder of the
Tyrians
Thella
Agrippa's Kingdom
Meroth
Baca
Upper Galilee
Ptolemais
Bersaba
Julias
Chabulon
Carmel
Tiberius
Lower Galilee
Xalot
Ginaea
Pella
Samaria
Acrabatane
Peraea
Joppa
Anuath Borcaeus
Philadelphia
Judaea
Machaerus
Iardan

Bibliography

Aharoni, Yohanan, 1967.*The Land of the Bible A Historical Geography,* London

Aharoni, Yohanan. Michael Avi-Yonah, Anson F. Rainey R. Steven Notley Ze'ev Safrai 2011 *The Carta Bible Atlas,* Jerusalem

Avi-Yonah, Michael, 1966 *The Holy Land from the Persian to the Arab Conquest (536 BC-Ad 640 A Historical Geography,* Grand Rapids

Avi-Yonah, 1976 Michael *Gazetteer of Roman Palestine.* Qedem Monographs of the Institute of Archaeology, The Hebrew University of Jerusalem no, 5 Jerusalem

Josephus Flavius 1926.*The Life* [L], *Against Apion* [AA] H.St.J. Thackeray (trans.) Cambridge Mas. /London, Loeb Classical Library

Josephus Flavius 1927-1928 *The Jewish War* [JW] (in Greek VII books) H.St.J. Thackeray (trans.) Cambridge Mas. /London, Loeb Classical Library 3 vols.

Josephus Flavius *Jewish Antiquities* [JA] (in Greek XX books) H.St.J. Thackeray. Ralph Marcus Allen Wikgren, Louis H. Feldman (trans.) Cambridge Mas./London, Loeb Classical Library 1930 -1965 9 vols.

Pliny/Plinius: Gaius Plinius Secundus, *Naturalis Historia* [NH] (in Latin XXXVI books) H. Rackman, W. H. S. Jones and D. E. Eichholz (trans.) Cambridge Mas./London, Loeb Classical Library 1938-1962 10 Vols.

Reeg, Gottfried 1989 *Die Ortsnamn Israels nach der rabbinischen Literatur,*Dr. Ludwig Reichert Verlag, Weisbaden

Smith, George Adam 1894.*The Historical Geography of the Holy Land* London etc, 1894

Tsafrir, Yoram, Leah Di Signi, Judith Green 1998 *Tabula Imperii Iudaea Palaestina: Eretz Israel in the Hellenistic, Roman & Byzantine Periods, Maps and Gazetteer* Israel Academy of Sciences and Humanities, Jerusalem

"The Story of *The Eternal Road*"

Jonathan C. Friedman
West Chester University

In January 1937, an obscure play opened on Broadway. Its name was *The Eternal Road.* Part biblical pageant, part anti-Nazi protest, *Road* was the brainchild of writer Franz Werfel, composer Kurt Weill, and director Max Reinhardt. In academic circles, the play is relatively well known, but it disappeared from public memory rather quickly after its five month run, mostly because it was a financial disaster. Although its 153 performances at the Manhattan Opera House played to full houses, the show (in its time) ran up the largest deficit in Broadway history. Producer Meyer Weisgal dubbed the play one of the theater's most brilliant money-losers ever. However, the significance of *Road* lies elsewhere—in its singular moment of expression of Jewish pride by several colorful, albeit complicated, *dramatis personae.*

The play offers an especially interesting point of departure for a discussion of the empowering role of theater as a mechanism of protest and collective self-respect. According to historian Atay Citron, "the idea of employing theatre as a weapon in the struggle against Nazism seems naïve and pathetic after the Holocaust. In the fall of 1933, however, there was reason to believe that an intensive anti-Nazi propaganda campaign could make a difference."[1] *Road* was but one of fourteen protest plays and pageants written by Jewish and non-Jewish émigrés after 1933.

The more intriguing issue for me is where to situate *Road* within the broader context of the life work of its principal creators. To what degree was it a departure from, or a continuity within, the aesthetic approaches of Reinhardt, the Austrian-born *parvenu*, Werfel,

---

[1] Atay Citron, "Art and Propaganda in the Original Production of *The Eternal Road,"* in Helmut Loos and Guy Stern, eds., *Kurt Weill: Auf dem Weg zum Weg der Verheissung* (Freiburg, 2000). See also his, "Pageantry and Theater in the Service of Jewish Nationalism in the United States, 1933-1946" Diss. (New York University, 1989).

the would-be Catholic from Prague, and Weill, the left-leaning social critic (and, of the three, the only native born German)? To what extent did the three artists project their conflicts with, and corresponding concepts of, "Jewishness" onto the text and performance of the play? What was the interplay of external and intrinsic factors that helped to bring *Road* into existence? If Hitler had never come to power, would there have been an *Eternal Road?*

In describing the project he was undertaking, Reinhardt mused that "whenever the Jews were in crisis, they returned to their holy books…and looked to the past to hope for the future." He added, to deflect charges that he was creating propaganda, that "the books of the Bible…are hallowed artwork of incomprehensible, mystical greatness."[2] Werfel offered his own take on the play: "All I have tried to do is to bring out the truth—the tolerance, the love, and by all means the culture that is in the Bible. We need more peace and friendship."[3] *Road* was the only occasion in which Reinhardt, Werfel, and Weill joined together to issue a condemnation, in the only language and forum they knew, of the Nazi assault on Jewish civilization. Yet their play was more than mere anti-Nazi tableau, and certainly more than either a bloated, technical wonder or a box office bomb. It was a remarkable tribute to Jews throughout history in all their various and conflicting incarnations.

On a broad continuum of Jewish identity, it would appear on the surface that Reinhardt, Werfel, and Weill had a great deal in common. Products of the German world of *Bildung* and letters, as well as the modern-Jewish world of secularism and humanitarianism, the three artists did not represent the kind of Jewishness reflected in the shtetls of Eastern Europe or the orthodox shuls of the west. Still, there were vast differences between them. Werfel came closest of the three to converting to Christianity. In deference to his moderately anti-Semitic wife, Alma, he officially seceded from the Jewish community, although he never officially converted, and he

---

[2] Max Reinhardt, "Konzept für eine Rede," in Edda Fuhrich Leisler and Gisela Prossnitz, *Max Reinhardt in Amerika* (Salzburg, 1967).

[3] Victoria Powell, "Notes for public lectures on the 'Eternal Road,'" Weill-Lenya Research Center, New York City, (hereafter, WLRC): n.p.

consistently sought ways of reconciling Judaism with Christianity and vice versa. In confronting his crisis of conscience, Werfel once maintained that he was a "Jew in the flesh and a Christian in spirit" and that he would be "happiest in a world that comes closest to the period of primitive Christianity."[4] Weill's Jewishness manifested itself as passionate socialism, and Reinhardt was perhaps the most conflicted of the three. For his part, Weill, the son of a cantor: "...began to think of the Jewish historical experience...primarily as a universal lesson, 'never to forget' the enormity of humankind's mindless capacity for cruelty...but also a remarkable resilience that enables survivors of good will to follow the dictates of their God-given creative potential."[5] A prodigy at the piano, Weill was writing music at the age of twelve, and by 1916 he had written a composition for Jewish weddings (*Mi Addir: Jüdischer Trauungsgesang*) as well as a lengthier song cycle (*Ofrahs Lieder*) based on five poems of the medieval Jewish writer, Judah HaLevi.[6] Christian Kuhnt argues that Weill was more sympathetic to Zionism and Judaism as a religion than many have previously believed, but that by the mid 1920s, he had become disenchanted with both, as revealed in a letter to his mother:

> ...I searched for a community, and I thought I found it in Jewish society, but I have grown to despise Jewish circles. Communicating with them is impossible for me. Jews, both assimilated and Zionist, are impossible in every way. What remains

---

[4] Cited from Alma Mahler-Werfel's *Mein Leben* (Frankfurt am Main, 1960): 220f., and Peter Jungk, *Franz Werfel: A Life in Prague, Vienna, and Hollywood* (New York, 1990): 129.

[5] "*The Eternal Road* and Kurt Weill's German, Jewish, and American Identity: A Discussion with Kim H. Kowalke, Jürgen Schebera, Christian Kuhnt, and Alexander Ringer," *Theater*, vol. 30, no. 3 (2000): 95.

[6] The five Hebrew poems were translated into German: "In meinem Garten steh'n zwei Rosen," 'Nichts ist die Welt mir," "Er sah mir liebend in die Augen," "Denkst du des kühnen Flugs der Nacht," and "Nur dir, fürwahr, mein stolzer Aar." See Peter Andraschke, "Einige Bemerkungen zu Kurt Weills Liedern," in Helmut Loos and Guy Stern, eds., *Kurt Weill: Auf dem Weg zum Weg der Verheissung* (Freiburg, 2000): 66.

> is only this: Very gradually, out of one's own human development, we must find our way back to our childhood faith.[7]

As for Reinhardt, he was fascinated by Catholic ritual, and his plays tended either to be light diversions from Shakespeare, or ponderous masses on a huge scale. His often detached criticism of Nazi anti-Semitism and past history of embracing purely non-Jewish themes made him an unlikely candidate to carry the banner of Jewish resistance to Hitler. In Gottfried Reinhhadt's biographical account, his father "considered his own Jewishness a purely personal matter. He felt no particular solidarity with his fellow believers. He could not bring himself to take his ancestry as seriously as Hitler did. Nonetheless, according to Leonhard Fiedler, despite Reinhardt's fascination with Christian traditions and worldly themes, he never thought of converting, and he began the draft of his never finished memoirs with the declamation "Ich bin ein Jude—I am a Jew."[8] Reinhardt's sense of himself as a Jew was cryptic and often contradictory. In Gottfried's memory, his father resented "...being made to belong to a 'people' whose existence he doubted. A nation of Jews in Palestine he thought a utopia bereft of any attraction for him."[9] At the same time, Gottfried claims that his father "had a penchant for Eastern European Jews. One can put it this way: if Jewishness must be emphasized (which he did not recommend, especially in politics), then let it be the genuine kind!"[10] After Hitler came to power, Reinhardt senior had this to say: "My work on the stage has always been my chief calling...The new Germany wishes, however, members of the Jewish race, to which I naturally and unreservedly belong, to have no influential position...A true theater of the arts could never function

---

[7] Letter cited by Schebera in "*The Eternal Road* and Kurt Weill's German, Jewish, and American Identity,": 89.

[8] Leonhard Fiedler, "*The Eternal Road*: Max Reinhardts Weg," in Helmut Loos and Guy Stern, eds., *Kurt Weill: Auf dem Weg*: 168.

[9] Gottfried Reinhardt, *The Genius*: 244.

[10] Gottfried Reinhardt, *The Genius*: 245.

under these current circumstances..."[11] It is evident from these brief, but illuminating statements from Werfel, Weill, and Reinhardt that the three never escaped or ignored their Jewishness, but rather actively engaged it, forging distinct and new possibilities of identification for Jews in the modern world.

Preproduction

Within months of the Nazi seizure of power, Reinhardt and Weill had fled Germany. Werfel remained in Vienna. It was upon the occasion of Reinhardt's dismissal that a little-known member of the Zionist Organization of America by the name of Meyer Weisgal decided to fly to Europe and enlist the director in a project he had been developing. Weisgal, a Polish Jew from the town of Kikl who had come to the United States at the turn of the century, was in the midst of producing a Bible pageant at the Chicago World's Fair entitled *Romance of a People.* Imagining an even larger spectacle for Broadway that would serve as a vigorous Jewish response to Nazi persecution, Weisgal (an irrepressible shnorrer in the words of historian Stephen J. Whitfield), flew to Paris in November 1933 to meet Reinhardt.[12] Once in Paris, Weisgal sought out Pierre van Paassen, a friend from his days in Toronto who worked as the Paris correspondent of *The Toronto Star.* Using his contacts, Paassen was able to arrange a meeting with Reinhardt, and he accompanied Weisgal to the Théâtre Pigalle, where a production of *Fledermaus* was underway. Weisgal had exactly ten minutes to make his case to the director.[13]

"*Dieses Schauspiel muss Hitler unsere Antwort geben*" (This spectacle must be our answer to Hitler)," Weisgal pleaded in broken German.[14] He later looked back on this naïve declaration with

---

11 "An die Nationalsozialistische Regierung Deutschlands," Oxford, England, 16 June 1933, *Max Reinhardt Schriften: Briefe, Reden, Aufsätze, Interviews, Gespräche, Auszüge aus Regiebüchern,* ed. Hugo Fetting (East Berlin, 1974): 223, 224.

12 Stephen J. Whitfield, "The Politics of Pageantry," *American Jewish History,* vol. 84, no. 3 (1996): 221-251.

13 Meyer Weisgal, *...So Far: An Autobiography* (New York, 1971): 66, 67, 117.

14 Weisgal, *...So Far*: 117.

amazement: "We did not dream then of the coming unbelievable horror, or I would not have used such language, which in retrospect sounds almost flippant."[15] Listening to the pitch, Reinhardt said little, but as the minutes passed, he warmed to the project and eventually asked: "Who will write the book? Who will compose the music?" Weisgal deferred to the director on these questions, whereupon Reinhardt suggested Franz Werfel as playwright, Kurt Weill as composer, and Norman Bel Geddes as designer. The latter had already developed a reputation as a world-class stage designer with grandiose, some would say excessive, visions. His gutting of the Century Theater for Reinhardt's production of the play, *The Miracle,* to make room for a cathedral measuring 200 feet long, 120 feet wide, and 110 feet high, prefigured his approach to *Road.*[16] Upon hearing the names thrown out by Reinhardt, Weisgal, in his words, "swallowed hard, thinking of the remainder of my $10,000 kitty," but he agreed to draft Werfel and Weill into the project and to hold a preliminary meeting in Reinhardt's castle in Salzburg sometime during the following summer. The two also decided on New York City as the staging ground for the play, over London and Paris.[17]

New York was an obvious, and yet not-so obvious choice. Home to the largest Jewish community in the world (by 1930, some 1.83 million), New York had a built-in audience that would be receptive to such a show. But this amounted to preaching to the converted. The challenge was to reach out to non-Jews while minimizing the risk of inflaming native anti-Semitism. According to Reinhardt's son Gottfried, "...the manifest speculation on anti-Hitler sentiment by a New York Jewish audience did not sit well with him."[18] Yet in a letter to Gottfried, Reinhardt the elder seemed less concerned about the responses from his prospective milieu and more worried about the overall quality of the project's artistry:

---

[15] Weisgal, ...*So Far*: 117.

[16] See David Drew, "Reinhardt's Choice: Some Alternatives to Weill," in Helmut Loos and Guy Stern, eds., *Kurt Weill: Auf dem Weg*: 237-254.

[17] Weisgal, *So Far*: 117, 118.

[18] Gottfried Reinhardt, *The Genius*: 245.

> ...From what I have heard, it appears to end with the Jews finding a haven in America, after taking us from the creation of the world via the dance around the golden calf to every well-known alpine peak of kitsch. An opportunity for De Mille which, alas, I could not seize for all De Millions in the world...You must not be so silly as to believe that the Jewish theme is a stumbling block for me. I have always been staunch in my Jewish convictions. I am even a pious Jew and would be happy if I could help my brethren with what little I have to offer. But I don't believe that they can be helped with scorn or rose-colored trash. At my suggestion, Werfel[19] is now writing an oratorio and Weill is supposed to compose it. Should it really come to a production, it will be a work of art. I, at least, am convinced of that, for the first chapters of the *Road of Promise* Werfel read to me were grandiose and deeply moving. Whether it will make money is admittedly another question.[20]

On 4 August 1934, Reinhardt gathered Weill, Werfel, Weisgal, and Rudolf Kommer (Reinhardt's business manager) at Schloss Leopoldskron for a review of an early draft of the play, which Werfel had entitled *Der Weg der Verheissung—The Road of Promise.* As a gathering of Jews in the former residence of an Archbishop in full view of Hitler's chalet in Berchtesgaden, the meeting at Leopoldskron was nothing if not ironic. For his part, Weisgal was pleased with the draft manuscript although he disliked the play's "Christian" ending that featured a messiah appearing out of the ruins of the Temple. He recounts in his memoirs:

> The mystic strain in [Werfel] which might have identified with Chassidism he transferred to the Catholic Church...I spent a whole night walking with Werfel in the garden and explaining to him...that this was a Jewish play—that and nothing else. It was our history, the history of his and my people, that had to be portrayed—not some alien or abstract concept. Remote as he

[19] Werfel, like Reinhardt, had misgivings early on about the project. "I find anything truly creative a hundred times easier...It's a grotesque idea to think that these gigantic world tragedies of Jacob, Joseph, and his brothers...could be thrown together in a hurry...I'm still not certain if I want to take it on." Jungk, *Franz Werfel*: 150.

[20] Gottfried Reinhardt, *The Genius*: 247.

> was from Judaism, there was enough of the poet in Werfel to grasp the idea even through my barbarous German.[21]

Gottfried Reinhardt cites Alma's take on the controversy: "After [Franz] had finished, one of these gentlemen walked over to Werfel and said: 'That was very beautiful, Herr Werfel, but you must write an angrier god—a god of vengeance!'"[22] In her own diary, Alma wrote: "Poor Werfel has gotten himself into this senseless mess...Without Jesus Christ, the play cannot be brought to conclusion, and the Jews will not permit Jesus in the play."[23] Weisgal had second thoughts about Weill, too: "...he had shaken himself free of Jewish life...[and] did not appear to me the most suitable choice of composer for the score of a biblical pageant; but I had given Reinhardt a free hand, and his instinct turned out to be right."[24] Despite these misgivings, the Leopoldskron meeting propelled the musical drama forward. The play was set to debut in New York sometime between February and October 1935.[25]

Werfel divided his drama into four acts with two distinct but interweaving storylines. The leading action was to take place in a small synagogue during a pogrom (plot line A), with a rabbi distracting his fearful congregation with stories from the Hebrew Bible (plot line B). In Act One, Werfel set out the drama of the synagogue and the first of the biblical tales—Abraham, Isaac, Jacob, and Joseph. In Act Two, he focused entirely on the story of Moses. Act Three covered the period of the Kings (Saul, David, and Solomon), while Act Four concluded with the Major Prophets (Isaiah and Jeremiah), the destruction of the temple in 586 B.C., and the fate of the Jews huddled inside the small synagogue. Each line of dialogue was to have four major beats, with the number of syllables varying

---

21 Weisgal, ...*So Far*: 120.

22 Gottfried Reinhardt, *The Genius*, 251, and Atay Citron, "Pageantry and Theatre,": 149.

23 Alma Mahler, *Mein Leben*: 216.

24 Weisgal, ...*So Far*: 120.

25 Sub-contract Reinhardt to Verlag Heugel, Salzburg, 17August 1934, WLRC, Series 47: 1.

from nine to twelve, creating a "chanting" effect to the words as they were delivered.[26]

The composition itself was the product of intense research on Weill's part. He compiled two hundred synagogue melodies he remembered from his childhood and verified their authenticity at the Bibliothéque Nationale in Paris. The music was to have a notably Western European slant, and for ears accustomed to American synagogue arrangements, with their primarily Eastern European orientation, the result was often confusing, even more so when Weill interjected contemporary melodies. Atay Citron contends that in preparing the score, Weill was thinking more in "central European Christian" terms.[27] According to writer David Schiff, however, while "the music of the German synagogue echoed…Schubert and the harmonies of Mendelssohn, [it] had its own historic integrity…Although it never sounds Jewish… [it] is in fact a musical reliquary for a vanished liturgical tradition. [Weill's] use of important German-Jewish melodies is pervasive and…dramatically apt, with themes from the Shavuot and Yom Kippur services matched to crucial events in the play. Audiences today will notice melodic warmth uncharacteristic of earlier Weill…without recognizing that this new feel derives from carefully borrowed materials."[28]

Although there were the inevitable conflicts over libretto and music, venue selection (Reinhardt never really liked the Manhattan Opera House), and Bel Geddes' appetite for demolition, production of the play continued apace. Reinhardt's arrival in New York in September 1935 moved things along, and the cast, once assembled, counted fifty-one principals, thirty-six dancers, forty-eight chorus members, and 180 extras. Among the stars were Broadway standards like Sam Jaffe, and future Hollywood names such as Sidney Lumet and Dick van Patten. It appeared that an opening was just around the corner when Bel Geddes' production team hit bedrock and then water

---

[26] Franz Werfel, *The Eternal Road: A Drama in Four Parts,* (New York, 1936): vii.

[27] Atay Citron, "Art and Propaganda in the Original Production of *The Eternal Road,*" in Loos and Stern, *Kurt Weill: Auf dem Weg*: 211.

[28] David Schiff, "On the Road toward Hope: Kurt Weill's Celebration of the Jews," *New York Times,* 27 February 2000.

during its facelift of the Opera House, flooding the entire theater and forcing an abrupt halt to the rehearsals. Then, in February 1936, all the money ran out, and the show appeared truly doomed. It was only saved by a last minute injection of cash from Broadway producer Crosby Gaige. Once production resumed, the consensus was that the massive, acre-size set had to be seen through to completion, and when it was, after all the melodrama, Weisgal's pageant, no longer entitled *The Road of Promise* but appropriately *The Eternal Road*, opened on 7 January 1937.[29]

On the night of the premiere, New York's social elite turned out in droves to witness five hours of beauty, chaos, and history. The play nearly did not go on at first as fire fighters converged on the theater and told Weisgal, who was backstage, that the play could not continue in the presence of so many lit candles and in the absence of a fire curtain. Weisgal quickly phoned Rabbi Stephen Wise, informed him of the situation, and asked him to track down one of his close friends, Mayor Fiorello La Guardia. Wise luckily found La Guardia on a call with the fire department (a hobby of his), and the mayor agreed to race over to the Opera House to break the standoff. No one knew what to expect when the lights dimmed at 8:43 p.m. The darkened theater was illuminated only by a combination of flickering electric lights and real candlelight.

The Play

A *shofar* sounded. Offstage the audience could hear the trampling of thousands of feet—"the noise of a great human mass setting out upon its way and drawing nearer."[30] The noises were to grow in strength and speed, "as if in flight before pursuers." Sounds then arose of "breathless terror, of panting, of moaning cries." On the lowest stage level, lights and lanterns swarmed visibly, while out of the darkness, the *almemor* or rabbi's podium emerged from blackness. A congregation of old men stood around the raised table as a crowd of Jews fleeing their

---

[29] Rehearsals resumed on 29 November 1936 with December 30 set as the opening. That date was postponed to January 4, 1937, then ultimately to January 7. See Citron, "Pageantry and Theatre,": 199.

[30] Franz Werfel, *The Eternal Road: A Drama in Four Parts*: 3.

attackers pushed its way into the synagogue from stage right. The first scene setting the drama inside the synagogue had begun.

These sequences, removed both in time and in space from the biblical stories, served the dual purpose of political commentary and biblical criticism. For scholars of modern Jewish history, the synagogue tableau was a revealing window into the psyches of Werfel and Reinhardt. A Rabbi led the singing and reciting, but he was surrounded by more complex characters in perpetual struggle with themselves and their religion. These characters, reminiscent of the "Four Sons" of Passover, included the Pious Man, the Rich Man, the Estranged One (and his son), the Young Man, and the Adversary.

The Rich Man represented the court Jew, blinded by a faith in material status and connections to the king. "Did I not give money whenever I was asked?" he lamented early on, only to be hit by sarcasm from the Adversary.[31] At the same time, the Estranged One symbolized the failed assimilated Jew:

> Long, long ago I had forgotten this community into which I was born…For I had become wholly at one with the people of this land. I was wholly contented so and did not wish to be reminded of you and of the past…I would not have come back, had not the people recognized me by my face…[32]

The Adversary, meanwhile, offered comic relief through a cynical voice that evoked the image of *Pesach's* "Evil Son:" "The feeblest beast has claws and teeth for self-defense," he averred, "…We have memory and law…admirable weapons…"[33] An ensuing harangue between the Adversary and members of the congregation, found in Reinhardt's promptbook, was edited for the final version of the play. In a retort that survived the final cut, the Adversary howled: "…The trouble is you're living too much in the past, too much by reflected glory. You dream about your magnificent traditions, and you peddle

[31] Franz Werfel, *The Eternal Road*: 6.

[32] Franz Werfel, *The Eternal Road*: 6, 7.

[33] Franz Werfel, *The Eternal Road*: 9.

second hand clothes."[34] The below dialogue, however, appears to have been cut from the scene:

> [Estranged One]...I was bound to this community by nothing but the accident of my birth. I could not live, I could not work, despised for something which I was in no way to blame...I believed I had strength and the right to create a community for myself.
>
> [Adversary]...And now you find the doors shut right in your face...
>
> [First Pious Man]...Our community does not close its doors in the face of the prodigal.
> [Estranged One]...Even now I still believe that one should not seclude oneself in sects that merely challenge the hatred of other sects. I believe that we should become one with the people of this country.[35]

It is possible that the dialogue was removed because it was lyrically clunky, or because it took too much attention away from the Moses sequence. But, as before, the verses illustrated the more interesting discourse about Judaism that Werfel seemed to be having with himself through his various characters. A line in the scene uttered by the Adversary is especially revealing: "...We cling to our race, yet we change our names to hide that we are Jews...and [the excised line] your young people marry aliens and try to forget that they have ever heard of Israel."[36] This statement, which remained in the revised script, although in edited form, served as a bridge to an inserted sequence dealing with the presence of a non-Jewish maiden in the synagogue (the Alien Girl) and her romance with a young Jewish man.

---

[34] Reinhardt *Regiebuch* for *The Eternal Road*, Max Reinhardt Collection, State University of New York at Binghamton (hereafter MR-SUNY), R3244, Part Two: 4, 5.

[35] Reinhardt *Regiebuch*.

[36] Reinhardt *Regiebuch*. See also Final Revised Script of the play, 10 January 1937, in the Franz Werfel Collection, University of California at Los Angeles (hereafter, FWC), Box 17, File, "The Eternal Road," Act Two: 6, 7.

Werfel clearly wanted some commentary on Jewish-Gentile relations in the play and therefore incorporated the Biblical story of Ruth to accentuate the romantic subplot between the Young Man and the Alien Girl. Reinhardt and Werfel expanded the romance in later drafts to include the following verses:

> [Alien Girl]...I'm not an alien anymore! I love everything that surrounds him. I love this house and its customs. I love the Holy Book. After all, it is our Holy Book too...But never was it so alive to me as here now when you read it and make its figures appear among us. To follow him I left everything behind—my home, my parents, my brothers, and sisters. His God is my God. I cannot live unless I am with him.
>
> [Young Man]...I am bound to this girl for life, and only death can part us. If you insist, we will...leave this house...
>
> [Fanatic]...But it is also written 'Neither shalt thou make marriages with them!'"
>
> [First Pious Man]...The union of these two has been severely tested, and will have to undergo further tests...If God does not desire this union, it will not hold. It is not for us to anticipate his will.[37]

The courtship between Ruth and Boaz followed this discussion, and the rhetoric from the congregation softened as a result:

> [A Woman's Voice]...O Ruth, in the midst of your happiness do not forget us...
>
> [The Alien Girl]...Take me to the other women that I may become as one of them...
>
> [The Pious Man]...From Ruth, the stranger, sprang David and will spring the Messiah...[38]

---

[37] The text was more expansive in Reinhardt's promptbook than it was in the final revised version of the script. Reinhardt, *Regiebuch,* MR-SUNY, Pt. 3: insert 26, and Final Revised Script of the play, 10 January 1937, FWC, Box 17, File, "The Eternal Road," Act Three: 3.

[38] Franz Werfel, *The Eternal Road*: 93.

Although a cliché, the romance was nevertheless enlightening: a naysayer like the Adversary was beyond the pale, but intimate relationships between Jews and non-Jews were within the realm of acceptable behavior (or what Werfel and Reinhardt perceived would be tolerated as acceptable behavior by their audience.) The focus on Ruth, a non-Jew initially, over other important biblical figures, such as Deborah, Samson, Daniel, and Esther, was an extension of this conscious decision to promote interfaith relations. But Ruth was more than just a symbol of strength through diversity. She was truly the linchpin in Werfel's overarching humanist message, even if this message occasionally blurred the line between Judaism and Christianity.

As a way of balancing out his none-too-subtle defense of intermarriage, Werfel injected the first overtones of Zionism in passages during the story of David as king of Israel. The Pious Man declared: "They built the high seat of the king in the city that he has won, in the holy city…" "Yerushalayim!" Shouted David, followed by a response in unison by the congregation. "O city of our fathers…why have we lost you?...We mourn for you…we long for you…Behold the glory of Zion…Next year in Yerushalayim…"[39] During the play's finale, which resolved the synagogue drama with the forced expulsion of the congregation, all of the biblical and synagogue characters marched in processional up the five levels of the stage to the choir of angels. The final song had a decidedly Zionist thrust, Werfel's attempt to maintain equilibrium between his pseudo-Christian imagery and the more nationalist vision of producer Weisgal:

> When the Lord brings back the redeemed to Zion,
> Then shall we be like unto dreamers…
> In sorrow, we strewed the seed in earth,
> Now bind we our sheaves with the blessed.[40]

[39] Franz Werfel, *The Eternal Road*: 106.

[40] Franz Werfel, *The Eternal Road*: 144.

Around two in the morning, the play ended, and despite fears of a critical savaging, the initial press was favorable (mainly due to the numerous reporters who left to meet their deadlines at midnight). Five months later, the play was gone from Broadway, never to be staged again, until a production company in Chemnitz, Germany decided to revive it in 2000. The new version was another one of many ironies—translated back into German, it featured a different time frame (the 1930s rather the 18th century) and a different hero—the Adversary, who comes back to the synagogue and sacrifices himself to save the rabbi from being shot by a Nazi thug. In addition, the play revealed a disjunction between the American and German press over the issue of Jewish identity; while American reviews generally had problems with the style and form of the play, many German reporters fixated on the question of whether its creators were authentically Jewish. Michael Horst, writing for the *Berliner Morgenpost,* wrote that Weill "thought in exile about [his] Jewish heritage…driven out by the Nazis, robbed of the cultural mother earth of central Europe, which [he] had to thank for [his] artistic existence."[41] In his review for the *Frankfurter Rundschau,* Hans-Klaus Jungheinrich proclaimed Hitler was an involuntary Zionist and insisted that without Nazism, composers like Weill and Schönberg would never have jettisoned their German and Austrian identities.[42] This is perhaps the most tragic aspect of the play's revival; it failed to educate ordinary Germans about the spectrum of Jewish thought and belief before the Nazi dictatorship. This undifferentiated juxtaposition of either German or Jewish, rather than the blurred world of both, contrasted with the approach of most American writers. In the end, according to writer Tamara Levitz, "German critics let their remarks become blinded by their feelings of love for, nostalgia about, alienation from, or hostility toward the Jew…"[43] David Schiff, writing for the

---

[41] Michael Horst, "Jehova in Hollywood: Chemnitz, Erstaufführung von Weills *Weg der Verheissung,*" *Berliner Morgenpost,* 15 June 1999, and Tamara Levitz, "Either a German or a Jew: The German Reception of Kurt Weill's *Der Weg der Verheissung,*" *Theater,* vol. 30, no. 3 (2000): 99.

[42] Hans-Klaus Jungheinrich, review from the *Frankfurter Rundschau,* 15 June 1999, and Levitz, "Either a German,": 104.

[43] Levitz, "Either a German,": 103.

New York Times, went further, saying that "in the absence of a Jewish audience, the work became a pawn in the battle over the German past."[44]

Part of the thrust of this essay has been to reorient the discussion about German-Jewish identity toward a model that embraces both continuity and diversity. Reinhardt, Werfel, and Weill stood along a broad spectrum of the Jewish self. Their values were unique products of their personal circumstances and inclinations, and while we cannot suppose alternative histories in the absence of Hitler, we cannot at the same time deny that the three grappled with the uneasy fusion of Germanness and Jewishness throughout their lives and were not given the opportunity to resolve the union or see it evolve because of external political developments. *The Eternal Road* might not have been destined for commercial or artistic success, and it might not have ever happened without the Nazi rise to power. But this is not to suggest impossibility, particularly with respect to the latter. The assumption that such a project would have been more predictable from an overtly Zionist or ultra-orthodox camp reveals gross ignorance about the continuum of modern Jewish thought. Stephen J. Whitfield has argued that the play offered a small remedy to the sense of powerlessness that pervaded the Jewish experience.[45] At some point, it also reflected the convergence of numerous points along a decidedly Jewish continuum that emphasized the importance of art, obligations to ancestral roots, and the sacredness of humanity.

---

[44] David Schiff, "On the Road Toward Hope."

[45] Stephen J. Whitfield, "The Politics of Pageantry,": 221.

"Reflections on American Jewish Political Power in the 1940s: What New Research Reveals About Saul Friedman's Thesis"

Rafael Medoff
David Wyman Institute for Historical Studies

As the author of one of the first books about America's response to the Holocaust, *No Haven for the Oppressed*, professor Saul Friedman was an obvious choice to serve as one of historians consulting the American Jewish Commission on the Holocaust. The commission was a group of historians and Jewish organizational leaders who came together in 1981, under the chairmanship of former Supreme Court Justice Arthur Goldberg, to examine the U.S. Jewish community's response to the Nazi genocide. Ultimately the project imploded over the sharply different views of the commissioners and their research staff on some of the historical issues at stake. Subsequently a number of the essays composed by the consulting historians were published as book, *American Jewry During the Holocaust*, edited by commission director Seymour Maxwell Finger.[1]

Friedman's contribution, although unfortunately relegated to the volume's final appendix, was one of the most insightful and thought-provoking essays in the book. "The Power and/or Powerlessness of American Jews, 1939-1945," explored the claim that American Jews possessed insufficient political leverage to influence U.S. government policy toward European Jewry. That assertion, put forward by some Jewish leaders at the time, is still often heard in public discussions about American Jewry and the Holocaust.

Professor Friedman acknowledged that intra-Jewish disunity, rising antisemitism, and lopsided support for President Franklin Roosevelt and the Democratic Party hampered American Jewry's political effectiveness to some extent. But does that mean Jews were helpless? The Jewish community, after all, was wealthier, better

[1] Seymour M. Finger, *American Jewry During the Holocaust* (New York, 1984).

organized, and had much greater access to the halls of power in Washington than, for example, African-Americans or Polish Americans, yet those two groups successfully flexed political muscle during the war. Threats by black leaders to stage a mass march on Washington persuaded Roosevelt to issue an executive order banning racial discrimination in federal hiring. Rumblings in the Polish community about possible defections to the Republicans in the 1944 presidential race convinced Roosevelt to postpone concessions to the Soviet Union on Poland until after the election.

As Friedman looked more closely at the record of American Jewish responses to the Shoah, he found a number of instances in which the intervention of Jewish leaders, organizations, or advisers to the president did indeed influence U.S. policy. In 1936, for example, an appeal from Rabbi Stephen S. Wise persuaded Roosevelt to pressure the British to hold off on the intended closure of Palestine to Jewish immigrants. (As a result, 50,000 more European Jews found haven in the Holy Land before the British White Paper of 1939.) In 1943, protests by Jewish leaders and presidential advisers scotched an Anglo-American plan to ban all public discussion of Palestine until after the war. In 1944, Zionist activists successfully lobbied the Republican Party to include a pro-Jewish statehood plank into its party platform, which the Democrats then had to match—a milestone in the effort to achieve a bipartisan American consensus in support of Zionism. "The list of achievements by a supposedly powerless minority is impressive," Friedman noted.[2]

In one case, however, there was much more to the story than Friedman realized. One of the examples he cited was President Franklin Roosevelt's creation, in January 1944, of the War Refugee Board. Friedman attributed FDR's action to the intervention of Treasury Secretary Henry Morgenthau, Jr. But subsequent research by other scholars, including David S. Wyman and this author, utilizing archival resources that were not available at the time Prof.

---

[2] Sonja Schoepf Wentling and Rafael Medoff, *Herbert Hoover and the Jews: The Origins of the "Jewish Vote" and Bipartisan Support of Israel* (Washington, D.C, 2012), 102-103, 132-135; Saul S. Friedman, "The Power and/or Powerlessness of American Jews, 1939-1945, in Finger, *American Jewry*, 14.

Friedman was writing, has revealed the much more complicated circumstances that led to the board's establishment.

Soon after the Allies confirmed, in December 1942, that the mass murder of Europe's Jews was underway, American Jewish organizations began urging the Roosevelt administration to take concrete steps to rescue refugees. The Joint Emergency Committee for European Jewish Affairs, a coalition of the major Jewish groups, put forward an eight-point rescue plan in early 1943 that called for such steps as food shipments to starving Jewish communities, pressure on neutral countries in Europe to admit refugees, and negotiations with Axis satellite regimes for the release of Jews from their territory. The Roosevelt administration's position, however, was that nothing could be done to aid the Jews except to win the war.

Dissident rescue advocates known as the Bergson Group (after their leader, Peter Bergson) began organizing protests, independent of the established Jewish organizations, to challenge the Allies' refugee policy. In public rallies, newspaper advertisements, and meetings with members of congress and administration officials, the Bergsonites argued that it was possible to rescue at least some Jews without hampering the war effort. In the summer of 1943, the Bergson Group began focusing its efforts on pressuring the Roosevelt administration to establish a new government agency whose sole purpose would be to rescue the Jews. The centerpiece of this campaign was the introduction, in November 1943, of a congressional resolution calling for such an agency. The lead sponsors were Representatives Will Rogers, Jr. (D-California) and Joseph Baldwin (R-New York) in the House, and Guy Gillette of (D-Iowa) in the Senate.

Rep. Sol Bloom, chairman of the House Committee on Foreign Affairs and a staunch supporter of the Roosevelt administration's refugee policy, tried to stall the resolution by insisting that it be the subject of hearings. His action was unusual because hearings normally are reserved for legislation, not resolutions, since a resolution is only a recommendation rather than a law.

Much to the administration's chagrin, the Gillette-Rogers resolution attracted bipartisan support. Prominent Democrats and

New Dealers such as 1928 presidential candidate Al Smith and American Labor Party leader Dean Alfange endorsed the measure. So did prominent Republicans such as 1940 presidential nominee Wendell Willkie, New York City mayor Fiorello La Guardia, and newspaper publisher William Randolph Hearst. La Guardia traveled to Washington to testify in support of the resolution, and Hearst repeatedly published sympathetic editorials and news articles in his chain of thirty newspapers nationwide.

Rep. Bloom countered by bringing in the most important American Jewish leader of the era, Rabbi Stephen S. Wise, who asserted in his testimony that the resolution was "inadequate" because it made no reference to settling refugees in Palestine. The Bergsonites and Rep. Rogers had deliberately omitted Palestine from the text because some members of Congress would not support a resolution challenging British policy in Palestine. "I understand that there are differences of opinion in Jewish circles," a frustrated Rogers wrote to Wise and other Jewish leaders afterwards. "But sincerely, gentlemen, those differences should be forgotten when a case of rescue is concerned."

In the end, a blunder by Rep. Bloom and Assistant Secretary of State Breckinridge Long spoiled the administration's strategy for blocking the resolution. On November 26, testifying before the House foreign affairs committee as to why a separate rescue agency was unnecessary, Long declared: "[W]e have taken into this country since the beginning of the Hitler regime and the persecution of the Jews, until today, approximately 580,000 refugees." Long's testimony was given behind closed doors, but wavering congressmen subsequently asked him to release it publicly, because they believed his remarks would justify their decision to shelve the rescue resolution. Long, with Bloom's support, agreed to do so.

Long's statistics made the front page of the *New York Times* and seemed to sway key members of Congress against the resolution—until a few days later, when his figures were exposed as false. The actual number of refugees admitted was not more than 250,000, and many of them were not Jews. Long's errors set off a firestorm of criticism from the media, mainstream Jewish organizations, and members of Congress. The controversy deeply embarrassed the administration and provided additional momentum to the campaign for U.S. rescue action.[3]

While the battle over rescue was raging in the halls of Congress, another struggle was underway behind the scenes, at the Treasury and State departments. Here is where Treasury Secretary Morgenthau's role, as noted by Prof. Friedman, came into play. Aides to Morgenthau discovered that senior State Department officials had been deliberately obstructing opportunities to rescue Jewish refugees, blocking the transmission of Holocaust-related information from Europe to the United States, and trying to cover up evidence of their actions.

State Department officials took these steps because they feared the rescue of large numbers of Jews would put pressure on the United States to open its doors to them. As one official privately explained: "There was always the danger that the German government might agree to turn over to the United States and to Great Britain a large number of Jewish refugees. In the event of our admission of inability to take care of these people, the onus for their continued persecution would have been largely transferred from the German government to the Allied nations."[4]

On Christmas Day 1943, a senior Morgenthau aide, Josiah E. DuBois, Jr. composed an eighteen-page report which he titled "Report to the Secretary on the Acquiescence of This Government in the Murder of the Jews." In careful, detailed language, DuBois exposed the State Department's record of obstruction. The report's searing conclusion: State Department officials "have been guilty not only of gross procrastination and willful failure to act, but even of willful attempts to prevent action from being taken to rescue Jews from Hitler...Unless remedial steps of a drastic nature are taken, and taken immediately...to prevent the complete extermination of the

---

[3] See "Establishment of a Commission to Effectuate the Rescue of the Jewish People of Europe," in *Problems of World War II and Its Aftermath - Part 2: The Palestine Question, Problems of Postwar Europe* (Washington, D.C., 1976), 15-249 (La Guardia's testimony is 147-156; Wise's testimony is 217-243); Rogers to Goldstein, Monsky, and Wise, 8 February 1944, A364/1954, Israel Goldstein Papers, Central Zionist Archives, Jerusalem.

[4] David S. Wyman, *The Abandonment of the Jews* (New York, 1984), 99.

Jews [in Hitler Europe], this Government will have to share for all time responsibility for this extermination." DuBois pressed Morgenthau to bring the matter directly to the president, adding that if he did not act, DuBois would resign in protest and publicly expose the scandal.[5]

All this took place at the same time the controversy over Breckinridge Long's testimony was exploding on Capitol Hill and the rescue resolution was advancing in the Senate. The chairman of the Senate Foreign Relations Committee, Tom Connally of Texas, an administration loyalist, initially prevented the resolution from coming up for a vote. But just before Christmas, Connally took ill and his replacement, Senator Elbert Thomas of Utah—a staunch Bergson supporter—immediately placed the resolution before the committee. "It is not a Jewish problem alone," the Senators wrote in their preamble. "It is a Christian problem and a problem for enlightened civilization. We have talked; we have sympathized; we have expressed our horror; the time to act is long past due." The resolution passed unanimously.[6]

A vote on the resolution by the full Senate was scheduled for 24 January 1944. Knowledgeable observers expected it to pass. Capitol Hill lobbyist Dorothy Detzer, in her memoirs, recalled that a poll of both houses of Congress in mid-January 1944 found "a sufficient margin of votes to insure passage" of the rescue resolution.[7]

Morgenthau and his aides were well aware of what was happening on Capitol Hill. In a January 13 staff meeting, Morgenthau aide Ansel Luxford pointed out that FDR's supporters in Congress feared "that it will be a blow to the Administration to have this thing thrown out onto the Floor of the House and debated on the basis that it will be debated. It will not be any pleasant thing."[8]

---

5 Rafael Medoff, *Blowing the Whistle on Genocide: Josiah E. DuBois, Jr. and the Struggle for a U.S. Response to the Holocaust* (West Lafayette, Indiana, 2009), chapters 3 and 4.

6 *Congressional Record - Senate*, 78th Congress, 1st Session, 9305.

7 Dorothy Detzer, *Appointment on the Hill* (New York, 1948), 242.

8 Morgenthau Diaries (hereafter MD) 693, pp.188-211, Franklin D. Roosevelt Library and Archives, Hyde Park, NY.

Oscar Cox of the Lend-Lease administration, who aided the rescue advocacy effort behind the scenes, met with Secretary Morgenthau and his staff on January 15 to discuss the resolution. "Most of the people who know about the resolution feel that when it gets to the Floor [of the Senate] two things will probably happen. One element thinks the resolution will be passed; the other that in the course of debate State Department's position will be ripped open in that [Assistant Secretary of State] Breckinridge Long's testimony will be attacked in the specific context that his figures were wrong, in that his facts were wrong...[I]t will be a direct attack on the Administration, including the President, for having failed to act in this kind of an important situation..."[9]

Later in the discussion, Morgenthau told his staff that if they were to approach FDR to create a rescue agency, "our strongest out is the imminence of Congress doing something. That is our strongest out. Really, when you get down to the point, this is a boiling pot on [Capitol] Hill. You can't hold it; it is going to pop, and you have either got to move very fast, or the Congress of the United States will do it for you."[10]

It was in this context, with the resolution poised to come before the full Senate, that Morgenthau acted. The growing congressional pressure for rescue gave Morgenthau the ammunition he needed to confront the president. The clamor on Capitol Hill, combined with news coverage of the controversy, the Bergson Group's ongoing newspaper ads, and evidence of increased public sympathy for Europe's Jews, created the atmosphere necessary to force the president's hand. Morgenthau went to President Roosevelt on 17 January 1944, presented him with a summary of the DuBois report, and urged him to pre-empt Congress by unilaterally establishing a rescue agency. Roosevelt agreed. Within days, he announced the establishment of the War Refugee Board.

Leading newspapers at the time acknowledged the connection between the Bergson Group's congressional resolution and the

---

[9] MD 694, 88-90, 94-97.

[10] MD 694, 88-90, 94-97.

creation of the War Refugee Board. An editorial in the *Christian Science Monitor*, for example, called the creation of the Board "the outcome of pressure brought to bear by the Emergency Committee to Save the Jewish People of Europe [the Bergson Group], a group made up of both Jews and non-Jews that has been active in the capital in recent months." Likewise, an editorial in the *Washington Post* noted that the Bergson Group's "industrious spadework" was one of the forces that made it "entitled to credit for the President's forehanded move [in creating the Board]."[11]

Subsequent internal Treasury Department discussions further confirmed the link between the Bergson Group's efforts on Capitol Hill and Morgenthau's approach to the president. For example, on 8 March 1944, recalling the events leading up to the creation of the Board, Morgenthau remarked to his staff: "[T]he thing that made it possible to get the President really to act on this thing—we are talking here among ourselves—was the thing that—the resolution at least had passed the Senate to form this kind of a War Refugee Committee..." Later in the meeting, he asked his aides, "I am just wondering who the crowd is that got the thing that far," to which War Refugee Board director John Pehle replied: "That is the emergency committee, Peter Bergson and his group."[12]

At a March 16 Treasury staff meeting, Morgenthau referred to "the Resolution in the House and in the Senate by which we forced the President to appoint a Committee [the War Refugee Board]" and "not to have him forced by Congress to do this."[13] Likewise, at a May 24 staff meeting, Board director Pehle noted that the Bergson Group "brought considerable pressure on Congress to pass a resolution which called for the setting up of an agency such as the War Refugee Board, which was ultimately set up."[14]

---

[11] David S. Wyman and Rafael Medoff, *A Race Against Death: Peter Bergson, America, and the Holocaust* (New York, 2002), 49.
[12] MD 707, 220-221.

[13] MD 710, 194.
[14] MD 735, 224-226.

Although professor Friedman could not know it when he was writing his essay on Jewish power and powerlessness in 1983, the soon-to-be-uncovered full story of the Bergson-Morgenthau episode further confirmed the accuracy of his thesis. Jewish activists, operating outside—and sometimes in defiance—of the Jewish establishment created the political pressure that made it possible for a cabinet member to persuade President Roosevelt to change his refugee policy. The administration, which had adamantly claimed rescue was impossible, reversed itself and created a new government agency whose sole purpose was to bring about rescue; its very creation was an acknowledgement that rescue was possible. These developments demonstrated, exactly as Friedman argued, that American Jews were far from powerless during the Holocaust. The mainstream Jewish leaders who achieved so little during that era were hampered not by a lack of power, but by a lack of will to exercise the power they possessed.

"The Chairman"

Helene Sinnreich
Youngstown State University

One of the most controversial figures of the Holocaust was the leader of the Łódź Ghetto, Mordechai Chaim Rumkowski. Rumkowski led the Łódź Jewish community throughout the German occupation, from the time of his appointment as head of the Jewish council in October 1939 until August 1944, when during the liquidation of the Łódź Ghetto, he boarded an Auschwitz-bound train together with his family. The controversy over Rumkowski's role during the Holocaust and his role as leader of the Lodz Ghetto began during the early days of the war and continued to develop, particularly in the immediate post-war years. He has been characterized by some as a despotic, self-obsessed monster who had his own face printed on the ghetto currency, and who callously sent Jews, particularly children and the elderly, to their deaths in the gas vans of Chelmno. To others, especially the Jews who survived the war as a result of Rumkowski's benevolence or intervention, he was a hero whose attempt to sacrifice a portion of the ghetto in order to save the rest was nearly successful. Rumkowski was aware of the debates surrounding his actions even during the war period and claimed at the time a willingness to stand before a post-war tribunal to justify his actions.

I would contend that assessment of Rumkowski's actions during the war were heavily shaped by the immediate post-war period particularly the writing of immediate post-war historians and survivors. The result of these early writings has been a permeation into the larger body of Holocaust scholarship and general culture about Rumkowski's role which has resisted the evaluations of his role presented by more recent scholarship.[1]

---

[1] For more recent scholarship on Mordechai Chaim Rumkowski see: Michal Unger, *Lodz: The Last Ghetto in Poland* (Hebrew) (Jerusalem, 2005); and Andrea Löw, *Juden im Getto Litzmannstadt* (Göttingen, 2006)

Controversy surrounding Rumkowski began with his ascension to power. Rumors circulated over whether Rumkowski sought his position of power or whether it was foisted upon him. Stories even during the war period abounded over how he obtained his leadership position. The majority of immediate post-war Yiddish authors claimed that Rumkowski campaigned for the leadership of the Jews of Łódź.[2] Later historians, such as Michal Unger, noted: "Some said he finagled the appointment though this was apparently a groundless charge."[3] There are a variety of stories which purport to show that Rumkowski acquired his position unintentionally. Some are flattering, such as the story claiming that the Germans were impressed with Rumkowski's appearance — "erect, clean-shaven, with piercing blue eyes and a silvery head of hair" — and thus appointed him head of the Jewish council.[4] One early postwar testimony reflected this rumor, reporting that "the elder of the Jews was Mordechai Chaim Rumkowski....At the time the Germans marched in, he was one of the Jewish civic leaders, and because of his patriarchal appearance [the Germans] made him remain."[5]

Others are less kind and play on Rumkowski's lack of facility in the German language. One story of his rise to power claims that the Germans, upon entering a meeting of the remaining members of the Jewish community, asked who the Eldest (*Älteste*) was, meaning the elder statesman or highest-ranking person of those assembled. According to rumor, Rumkowski mistakenly thought they were inquiring which among them was the oldest and indicated that he was the "*Älteste.*" Others still claim that the Nazis recognized in him a man who lusted for power and thus gave it to him.

The events of the early days of the war make it clear that whether he campaigned for the position or not, he was a logical choice for leadership of the community. The prewar leader of the Łódź Jewish community, Leon Minzberg (Jacob Leib Mincberg), fled

---

[2] Philip Friedman, "Pseudo-Saviors in the Polish Ghettos: Mordechai Chaim Rumkowski of Lodz" in *Roads to Extinction: Essays on the Holocaust* (New York, 1980), 335.

[3] Michal Unger, *Reassessment of the Image of Mordechai Chaim Rumkowski.* (Jerusalem, 2004), ix.

[4] Leonard Tushnet, *The Pavement of Hell* (New York, 1972), 23.

[5] Testimony of Pinkus R., *Fresh Wounds: Early Narratives of Holocaust Survival*, ed. Donald L. Niewyk (Chapel Hill, North Carolina, 1998), 197–198.

Łódź before the arrival of the Germans. Under orders from the German authorities, the remaining Kehillah members held an election for new leadership. Abram Lejzor Pływacki was elected as leader and Mordechai Chaim Rumkowski as his deputy. Thus, Rumkowski was elected to a position of power by the remnant Łódź Jewish leadership. He was not an unknown entity, as has been argued in some works, in which Rumkowski has been depicted as one "who had not previously been a part of the leadership or who were not even respected members of the community."[6] On the contrary, he had served as a Zionist representative in the Łódź Jewish community and was chairman of a Zionist faction in the Łódź Kehillah.[7] He had broken ranks with the Zionists by refusing to join his fellow party members in their protest resignation from the Jewish Community Council. For this, he was ultimately expelled from the party.[8] He retained his seat on the council, however, and at the outbreak of war, Rumkowski was still a part of the Jewish community leadership, with a record of having led one of the major political factions.

Shortly after being elected chairman of the Jewish council, Pływacki fled Łódź, leaving Rumkowski the highest-ranking elected official in the remnant Jewish community. Rumkowski, next-in-line in leadership, and one of the few high-ranking officials who did not flee the city — a point he frequently raised — was the obvious successor. It is therefore not surprising that in October 1939, the German authorities designated Rumkowski Eldest of the Jews of Łódź.

Upon his appointment, the German authorities granted Rumkowski far-reaching powers over the Jewish community, which appeared to expand with the sealing of the ghetto. Throughout the war period, however, the German authorities were ultimately firmly in control. The *Judenräte* (Jewish Councils) appointed by the Nazis to lead the Jewish population had — from the German perspective — the transmission of German orders as its primary function. When on 21 September 1939, the Chief of the Security Police Reinhard

---

[6] Eve Nussbaum Soumerai and Carol D. Schulz, *Daily Life during the Holocaust* (Westport, Connecticut, 1998), 90.

[7] Robert Moses Shapiro, *Jewish Self-government in Poland: Lodz, 1914–1939* (Unpublished Ph.D. diss., Columbia University, 1987), 217.

[8] Shapiro, *Jewish Self-government,* 216–217.

Heydrich ordered the creation of Jewish Councils, the first responsibility he noted was that, "[t]he council is to be made fully responsible, in the literal sense of the word, for the exact punctual execution of all directives issued or yet to be issued."[9]

After he was made Eldest of the Jews, one of the first orders Rumkowski received was to assemble a council of leaders to assist him in overseeing the Jewish community. The first *Judenrat* (or *Beirat*) that Rumkowski led comprised thirty-one men who received letters informing them of their obligation to accept this appointment on 16 October 1939.[10] The group assembled did not have much opportunity to organize and rule. The original council members (save a few survivors) were tortured and killed in November 1939, after only one month of service.[11] Leon Szykier, a member of the second Jewish Council appointed by Rumkowski after the murder of the first council, contended that "[i]t was said that Rumkowski ordered to kill these people because they were dissidents."[12] Philip Friedman notes that the evidence at hand makes it impossible to know Rumkowski's role in their deaths.[13] He notes however that "The members of the [first] council…often disagreed with Rumkowski's policies…The second council was one after Rumkowski's own heart...After Rumkowski had removed his first obstacle, opposition within the Judenrat, he began to rule arbitrarily."[14] Rumkowski may have disagreed with his first *Beirat*, but he did not ask the Germans to kill them. On the contrary, Rumkowski attempted to defend the

---

[9] Yitzhak Arad, Israel Gutman, and Abraham Margaliot, eds., *Documents on the Holocaust: Selected Sources on the Destruction of the Jews of Germany and Austria, Poland and the Soviet Union* (Jerusalem, 1999), 173–178.

[10] Friedman, p. 336. Arthur Eisenbach, *Dokumenty i materiały do dziejow okupacji niemieckiej w Polsce* vol. 3, *Getto Łódzkie* (Warsaw, 1946), 20.

[11] According to the Testimony of Leon Szykier, ZIH 301/699, there were three survivors of the torture. According to Julian Baranowski in his work *The Lodz Ghetto, 1940–1944*, six of the thirty [sic] council members survived. See p. 28. According to Isaiah Trunk, "some were murdered through shooting and torture and five members were deported to Krakow in December." See his *Lodz Ghetto: A History,* trans. Robert Moses Shapiro (Bloomington, Indiana, 2006), 34.

[12] Testimony of Leon Szykier, ZIH 301/699.

[13] Friedman, 336.

[14] Friedman, 336.

members of his first council and was severely beaten for it.[15] Following the death of this first *Beirat*, Rumkowski appointed a second group of council members to assist him in his duties as leader in February 1940. Isaiah Trunk argues that Rumkowski effectively ruled the ghetto with the second *Beirat* merely serving as a rubber stamp. He states, "[i]n those fields of ghetto life where the German authorities left the Jews free hands, Rumkowski was the sole and final arbiter."[16] Trunk dismissed the power of Rumkowski's subsequent deputies, calling Leon Szykier too strong willed and Aaron Jakubowicz and Leon Rozenblat Rumkowski's pawns.[17]

It is not clear why Szykier left his position as Rumkowski's deputy. Szykier claims he stepped down because he did not have any power to effect positive change in the lives of ghetto dwellers, whereas Trunk cites a document stating that by order of Rumkowski, "Dr. Leon Szykier was removed from his office as the Chairman's deputy."[18] Szykier's removal from office may have played a role in the scathing testimony he gave against Rumkowski, in which Szykier accused the ghetto leader not only of playing a role in the end of the first council but of other reprehensible actions. As his deputy, Szykier would presumably have been in a position to know which orders came from the Germans and which were from the ghetto leadership.

In the immediate post-war period, Rumkowski attained a reputation as the ultimate collaborator with the Germans. His name became synonymous with egoism and dictatorship. Many early testimonies laid blame for Nazi actions and orders on Rumkowski. Some claimed that he was the source of a number of unsavory orders including sealing of the ghetto, deporting those from the surrounding area into the Łódź Ghetto, and confiscation of Jewish property. The reality is that these orders originated with the German authorities.

Such perceptions of Rumkowski were reinforced by articles in media such as *Commentary Magazine* and even fictional portrayals like that in Leslie Epstein's *King of the Jews*. The novel's character Isaiah C.

---

15 Dawid Sierakowiak, *The Diary of Dawid Sierakowiak: Five Notebooks from the Lodz Ghetto* (Oxford, 1998), 61.
16 Trunk, *Lodz Ghetto,* 36
17 Trunk, *Lodz Ghetto,* 35–36.
18 ZIH 301/699, Testimony of Leon Szykier; Trunk, *Lodz Ghetto,* 65.

Trumpelman, who was based upon an exaggeration and fictionalization of the character of Rumkowski, became confused in some circles with an accurate depiction of the Łódź Ghetto leader. These manifestations of Rumkowski's legend have reinforced perceptions of the historical figure.

Rumkowski's leadership of wartime Jewish Łódź can be divided into three periods. In the beginning, Rumkowski's fulfillment of directives from the German authorities lent the perception that he was helping his fellow Jews. During this stage, from his appointment in October 1939 until the establishment of the ghetto, Rumkowski was given control over Jewish communal organizations and served as the liaison between the Jews of Łódź and the German occupiers. Through management of the welfare services of the Jewish community, he was able to provide orphanages, medical care, and food to the poor Jews of the city. This was funded through a combination of taxation and fundraising, by cajoling better-off Łódź Jews to contribute to the support of those less fortunate, a talent Rumkowski had honed during the pre-war period when he raised funds for the orphanage he had established. Through operating the labor board which supplied Jewish labor to the Germans, Rumkowski sought to spare Jews from being seized in the streets for forced labor. It was during this period that Rumkowski recognized that he could help the Jewish community of Łódź and serve as a buffer between them and the German authorities.

The second stage of his leadership began with the sealing of the ghetto, when the Jewish community was cut off from the non-Jewish population of the city. It was at that point that Rumkowski gained far-reaching control over the Jews of Łódź and early in this period, he began to feel as though he had been granted vast power. He created an extensive bureaucracy with which to rule the internal life of the ghetto. It was during the first two years after the ghetto was sealed that the majority of the accolades in his honor were created including albums, portraits, and other items such as calendars bearing his image and birthday. In this period, he took to referring to "his" Jews and factories and began using other possessive references to people and things within the ghetto. It was also during this period that he developed the conception that the Jews of the ghetto must be employed and useful to the German authorities. In the words of Philip Friedman, "The madness of the Nazi policy regarding the Jews was still not clear to him…Rumkowski naïvely believed that he would be the redeemer of his fellow Jews."[19]

In the period before mass deportations to death camps began, Rumkowski's speeches indicate that he saw Jewish employment as a necessary means of bringing in funds to support the vast welfare programs in operation in the ghetto and then, once registration of ghetto inhabitants began in the fall of 1941, that increasing employment would spare families from having their loved ones sent to forced labor.[20] This is supported by one ghetto writer, who claimed that during 1941, Rumkowski had adopted a policy of trying to save the whole of the ghetto population at the expense of the health of the workers.[21] Rumkowski's bravado and bluster at this time was connected to his conception of himself as a dictator charged with keeping peace and order in the ghetto. He repeatedly said that he sought to create a sense of normalcy for the Jews of Łódź despite the ghetto conditions.

Rumkowski's sense of his own power waned during the third period. From the beginning of the deportations onward, Rumkowski began to see that he wouldn't be able to save all of the ghetto population. And the directives handed down from the German authorities became increasingly difficult to carry out. There are hints in his speeches that he might have been aware of the destination of the first deportation trains to Chelmno. In any case, by May 1942, enough evidence had reached the ghetto to indicate that the deportees had been sent to their death. In September 1942, Rumkowski as much as confessed that those being deported from the ghetto were being killed when he delivered his "Give me Your Children" speech, in which he beseeched ghetto residents to hand over their children and elderly to the Germans in order to save the lives of the remnant working population. From September 1942 onward, Rumkowski was described by others within the ghetto as a "broken man." His power within the ghetto at that point was openly

---

[19] Friedman, 336

[20] Adelson, 106, 147, 174, 189-190, 198–203.

[21] Zelkowicz, 225.

stripped away. He retained his title and some small amount of control but was left essentially powerless until his own deportation to Auschwitz in August 1944. Nevertheless, wielding what little power he retained, he sought ways to avoid the German death sentences through creating full employment within the ghetto. These efforts included labeling the ghetto orphanage the "Young Workers Home" and creating apprenticeships for the young still left in the ghetto. He additionally came up with the notion of "strengthening" meals, in which weak workers were given nourishing food for two weeks in an effort to rebuild their strength and save them from exhaustion from starvation. Even as his power was stripped away, Rumkowski did not let go of the notion of his importance to the Jews of Łódź nor did he back down from fighting with the German authorities in an effort to save more lives. In the end, over sixty thousand Jews survived in the Łódź Ghetto until the summer of 1944, when in the wake of the halted Russian advance from the east, they were mostly deported to their deaths.

This longevity of the ghetto has been interpreted as evidence of the success of Rumkowski's strategy to make the Jews of Łódź useful to the Germans and thus prolong their existence, and has been used to argue that Rumkowski was a savior of the Jews of Łódź. Rumkowski's signature on German-instigated orders, perceived self promotion, and uncouth manner, however, have all served to create a perception of Rumkowski as a power-hungry tyrant. This latter perception especially dominated early assessments of Rumkowski.

Early judgment of Rumkowski's leadership of the ghetto was molded by the tales and opinions of survivors of the ghetto who either benefited from his benevolence, or who observed him from afar and judged him based on their perception that he held far more power than he did, as well as by the accounts of a number of historians who recorded the history of the Łódź Ghetto. In particular, Rumkowski's negative reputation was largely formed as the result of early published memoirs which attributed great power to the ghetto leader. Rumkowski certainly had power but it was power limited by the German authorities' needs and dictates and orders flowed from the German authorities to Rumkowski. The perception that many of the orders originated with Rumkowski himself, however, is reflected in survivor testimonies.

One survivor who judged Rumkowski very harshly was Leon Szykier who, in his testimony of 30 August 1945, accused Rumkowski of closing the ghetto, banning smuggling and food packages, expropriating goods and money from the ghetto inhabitants, and deporting the Jews from the towns near Łódź into the ghetto.[22] While it is true that orders for many of these deportations went out with Rumkowski's name on them, the orders originated with the German authorities. And while Rumkowski battled smuggling more aggressively than his counterpart in the Warsaw Ghetto, it was ultimately the German administration which played the central role in combating smuggling in the Łódź Ghetto. Thus, Rumkowski was instructed by the German authorities to issue orders against ghetto residents talking to individuals outside it, over the fence.[23] Apparently, this order was not effective enough and had to be repeated.[24] Ultimately however, it was the German police, specifically the Schupo, who were in charge of patrolling the outer border of the ghetto and who were most effective in combating smuggling. They began to shoot anyone who came near the ghetto wall.[25] The Kripo, the German police section which was initially in charge of combating smuggling, was also very effective in finally eradicating smuggling in the ghetto. They even began operating inside the ghetto, relying on paid informants and information obtained in torture sessions.[26] Thus Rumkowski's image as a crusader against smuggling was partially formed by the anti-smuggling orders issued in his name (which however had really come from the German authorities), but also from the German police's deadly methods of

---

[22] ZIH 301/699 Testimony of Leon Szykier. Dr. Szykier was the head of the Department of Health in the ghetto until 6 May 1941. He also served as Rumkowski's deputy in beginning in January 1941, a position he held until June 12, 1941. On 8 March 1941, the *Chronicle* reported that Leon Szykier was also the lead medical commissioner in determining if Jews were healthy enough for deportation to forced labor outside the ghetto. It is unclear why someone so high up in the ghetto administration would be under the impression that Rumkowski was the originator of orders related to expropriation and deportation.

[23] Zon. 202; Order of July 9, 1940.

[24] Zon. 216; Order of July 30, 1940.

[25] Rubin, 220.

[26] Rubin, 221.

combating smuggling. Similarly, the orders to close the ghetto, stop food packages, deport Jews from surrounding areas to the ghetto, and expropriate valuables from the ghetto dwellers also all originated with the German authorities.

Such negative survivor impressions were canonized by early historians like Solomon Bloom and Isaiah Trunk, whose early histories of the Łódź Ghetto were heavily influenced by victim testimony. The accusations which laid the blame for German orders with Rumkowski frequently appeared in some of the early articles on Rumkowski and the Łódź Ghetto. One of the earliest evaluations of Rumkowski by a historian was Bloom's 1949 article "Dictator of the Łódź Ghetto."[27] Bloom, a history professor at Brooklyn College, condemned Rumkowski, claiming that the Łódź Ghetto "had the special misfortune to be ruled, from beginning to annihilation, by Mordechai Chaim Rumkowski."[28] Echoing the perception of some ghetto survivors, Bloom held Rumkowski responsible for the confiscation of Jewish wealth in the ghetto, writing that Rumkowski "...decreed the sale of jewels, furs, and other valuables."[29] While Rumkowski's signature was on the posters requesting Jews to hand such items over, it was in fact the German authorities who demanded the goods.[30] Similarly, Bloom blamed Rumkowski for the high price of food in the ghetto, though he did concede that "...this was not entirely his [Rumkowski's] fault, since the German paid him little for finished goods and charged him exorbitantly for imports."[31] The Germans did underpay for ghetto-produced materials, as well as charge a premium for the substandard provisions delivered to the ghetto. However, more significant than the high prices of food in the

---

[27] Solomon Bloom, "Dictator of the Łódź Ghetto," *Commentary,* vol. 7, 1949: 111–122.
[28] Bloom, "Dictator," 111.
[29] Bloom, "Dictator," 113.
[30] For the German discussion of the order to confiscate valuables from the ghetto, see protocols of the 18 October 1940 meeting in Eisenbach, *Dokumenty i Materiały,* vol. 3, 102–104.
[31] Bloom, "Dictator," 114.

ghetto were the deportations, a program instituted by the German authorities.[32]

Although Bloom sometimes acknowledged the control that the Nazis had over the ghetto, his reliance on survivor testimony and internal ghetto documents as the source base for his article limited his perception of how much power Rumkowski actually had as opposed to how much control was being exerted by the German authorities. Moreover, the early state of research in the field limited Bloom's ability to adequately assess Rumkowski. Nevertheless, his perception, expressed in a magazine with a wide readership — coupled with numerous published survivor accounts that condemned Rumkowski — contributed to the formation of the negative reputation of the so-called "Dictator of the Łódź Ghetto."

Five years later, another New York City-based scholar, Philip Friedman wrote about Rumkowski's role in his article, "Pseudo-saviors in the Polish ghettos: Mordechai Chaim Rumkowski of Łódź."[33] The article, which originally appeared in Hebrew in 1954, suggested that Rumkowski was somehow involved in the closing of the ghetto as a means of increasing his own power: "…as long as the Jews lived scattered about the city, his sovereignty was not complete. The reins of his government were strengthened when all the Jews of Łódź were enclosed within the ghetto."[34] Friedman also echoed Szykier's accusation that Rumkowski was responsible for the deportation of the Jews from the surrounding towns into the Łódź Ghetto, hinting that the deportation of these Jews into the ghetto increased Rumkowski's power. While Rumkowski may have been a difficult and even pompous man, and he certainly became intoxicated with the power he was granted, he did not have the authority to close the ghetto nor to determine which Jews would be deported to the ghetto. Similarly, although seizure of Jewish valuables and mail

---

[32] For more on the correlation between food prices in the Lodz Ghetto and deportations, see Helene Sinnreich, *The Supply and Distribution of Food to the Lodz Ghetto: A Case Study in Nazi Jewish Policy, 1939–1945* (Unpublished Ph.D. diss., Brandeis University, 2004), 152–155.

[33] Thank you to Benton Arnowitz of the United States Holocaust Memorial Museum for assisting me in locating information on Dr. Friedman's early days in the United States. Thank you to Dr. Raul Hilberg for providing the references for the biographical information on his dissertation committee member, Dr. Friedman.

[34] Friedman, 336.

censorship were ordered by the Nazis, Friedman places the blame and even the initiative for these activities on Rumkowski.[35]

Later historians with access to a larger document base and comparative studies revised these early histories. For example, Isaiah Trunk revised his negative opinion of Rumkowski while writing his book *Judenrat.* Later historians, such as Michal Unger and Andrea Loew, similarly demonstrated that many of the orders which survivors attributed to Rumkowski actually originated with the German authorities. Despite this, Rumkowski's name remains synonymous with morally-questionable Jewish leadership. Accusations against Rumkowski have been so oft repeated that a revision or reassessment of his role remains difficult to disseminate.

These perceptions had their origins in the war period and solidified in the post-war period. Early post-war testimony and histories written in the first quarter decade after the war uncritically adopted the negative view of Rumkowski. This first narrative has come to dominate subsequent popular discussions to the point that revisions by later historians go unnoticed. The persistence of early narratives in popular memory is not unique to reputation of a Łódź Ghetto leader. Many historical myths persist in popular discourse, including Sir Isaac Newton being hit on the head by an apple, and Marie Antoinette saying, "Let them eat cake."

The evaluation of Rumkowski's role as a leader and his decision making during the war is complicated by discussions of Rumkowski's character. In his "Pseudo-Savoir" article, Friedman focused on Rumkowski as an example of a ghetto dictator par excellence.[36] Of ghetto dictators, Friedman claimed, "They were ruthless men who ruled, like their Nazi masters, by coercion…they had little support in the Jewish community, which regarded them with fear and hatred (or, occasionally, with indifference), though it sometimes fixed its hopes upon them."[37] Many post-war evaluations of Rumkowski, particularly by survivors, were negative. For example, although she and her family were largely saved by Rumkowski, Felicia Karo Weingarten supports Friedman's claim when she reported that Rumkowski was

---

[35] Friedman, 338.

[36] Friedman, 333, 348.

[37] Friedman, 334.

"feared by all, hated by many."[38] Łódź ghetto historian Isaiah Trunk, who like Friedman was affiliated with YIVO Institute of Jewish Research in New York, similarly commented in his 1962 work on Łódź that:

> [t]here is surprising unanimity among the authors of the diaries, the later memoirists and eyewitnesses concerning several basic phenomena in the Łódź Ghetto, namely the Rumkowski regime and its negative influence on life in the ghetto....The fact that these data derive from persons of diverse social background and diverse communal position in the ghetto — an engineer, a writer, a laborer, a trained business employee, a ghetto policeman — makes this unanimity even more striking.[39]

Isaiah Trunk based his evaluation on a relative small group of diaries, memoirs, and testimonies. New material continues to be uncovered, however. More wartime diaries have been discovered since the time of his writing and survivors continue to produce testimonies on their experiences of the Łódź Ghetto and their assessment of its leader. In addition to the increase in the number of testimonies available, critical readings have become possible as other materials, such as photographs, artwork, and albums (some of which praise Rumkowski, while others deride him) have come to light.[40] Scholars have begun to examine the motivations and perspectives of both diarists and memoirists.[41] For example, the post-war work of Jacob Nirnberg, which claims that Rumkowski was told of the destination of the deportations in the spring of 1942 and which had

---

[38] Felicia Karo Weingarten, *Ave Maria in Auschwitz: The True Story of a Jewish Girl from Poland* (Rogers, Minnesota, 2005), 128.

[39] Isaiah Trunk, *Lodz Ghetto: A History,* 5.

[40] See Irena Kohn, "The Book of Laughter and Unforgetting: Countersigning the Sperre of September 1942" in *The Legend* of the Lodz Ghetto Children; *Partial Answers: The Journal of Literature and the History of Ideas,* Vol 4, Number 1, January 2006.

[41] A classic example in Jewish history of a memoir with which scholars were familiar, but which was reassessed in later years, is the diary of Leon de Modena, a seventeenth-century scholar. This diarist's work was, until the late twentieth century, regarded as a testament of antisemitism in the Italian states. It was later reassessed as depicting a vibrant relationship between Jews and non-Jews. See Leon Modena, *The Autobiography of a Seventeenth-Century Venetian Rabbi: Leon Modena's Life of Judah* (Princeton, 1988), as well as Howard E. Adelman's *Success and Failure in the Seventeenth-Century Ghetto of Venice, The Life and Thought of Leon Modena 1571–1648 (*Unpublished Ph.D. diss., Brandeis University, 1985.)

been used in Isaiah Trunk and other scholars' early assessments of Rumkowski's leadership, has been called into question.[42]

Among the materials that have come to light are some which judged Rumkowski less harshly during the ghetto period. One survivor noted of Rumkowski, "…he never lost sight of the main goal: the welfare of the Jews at large. The craving for authority was not yet the main motive in his activity…."[43] Another noted, "They [the Jews] didn't hate him. He provided food, everything. Every month everybody got cards and every month they got food. For every person, they get so much bread a week, so much sugar, so much potatoes, so much everything."[44] This testimony echoes the claims of Jozef Zelkowicz who, writing in the ghetto, noted that the population blessed Rumkowski as a result of the potato distribution. He notes, "When all hope was lost, God made Rumkowski to distribute the potatoes….and their hearts are now joyfully anticipating the real thing — the potatoes themselves. 'Rumkowski, may he live one hundred years; when he has, he gives.'"[45] In a sentiment that has perhaps been too sweeping, many of the artifacts praising Rumkowski created during the war (albums, poems, letters, paintings, sculptures, songs, and other items) have been dismissed as inauthentic, created merely in the hope of gaining favor from the leader of the ghetto. Given the vast numbers of these items, and some survivor testimonies which express support for Rumkowski, a portion of these may have been sincere praise, particularly if written by those who were beneficiaries of Rumkowski's sporadic benevolence.

Many, however, who received support from Rumkowski were still among his critics. For example in his immediate post-war testimony, Israel U. noted of Rumkowski, "One can say that 95 percent of the ghetto hated him terribly. A few times attempts on his

---

[42] See editorial footnote 73 by Robert Moses Shapiro in Trunk, *Lodz Ghetto: A History*, 423.
[43] Yani Shulman as cited in Unger, *Reassessment of the Image of Mordechai Chaim Rumkowski*, 17.
[44] Lillian Kranitz-Sanders, *Twelve Who Survived: An Oral History of the Jews of Lodz, Poland 1930–1954* (New York, 1984), 83.
[45] Adelson, 122.

life were made. They wanted to kill him."[46] Some are ambivalent. Michael Etkind said:

> ...indirectly, because of him, more people survived in the Łódź ghetto than in any other...He did collaborate, but would you accuse the British soldiers who were building the bridge over the River Kwai of collaboration? Those he put on the deportations list, because they were not working, hated and resented him; but the people who because of him survived, were very grateful to him. Czerniakow in the Warsaw Ghetto was in the same position...he committed suicide, took poison and killed himself. What do you think of a captain who, when the ship is about to sink, takes poison or jumps overboard? It is *impossible* to judge.[47]

Hence, due to conflicting testimonies, it is difficult to judge how Rumkowski was perceived by the ghetto population.

Behind the perceptions of the man lay the real individual. Rumkowski was noted for his sincere love of orphans, and he had worked diligently to raise the funds to establish the orphanage in Helenowek.[48] One early survivor account called him, "A man who was childless, who had done much for orphans."[49] Some admired his energy and ability to accomplish tasks. Others, however, expressed distaste at his pushy nature in soliciting funds and focused on negative aspects such as his lack of education and domineering personality, describing him as "an impetuous, energetic man of autocratic character."[50] Historian Michal Unger characterized him as, "...domineering, centralist, and intolerant."[51] His self-obsessed personality led to his portrait hanging on the walls of all offices in the ghetto. His face and birthday were on the ghetto calendar. His

---

[46] Testimony of Israel U., *Fresh Wounds,* 174.

[47] Lyn Smith, *Remembering: Voices of the Holocaust: A New History in the Words of the Men and Women who Survived* (New York, 2006), 125.

[48] The building, which went back into operation after the war to house war orphans, was featured along with its inmates in "*Undzere Kinder*" [Our Children], the last post-war Yiddish-language feature film made in Poland. After the orphanage ceased operations, the building slowly crumbled to the ground. Today it stands as an unmarked ruin on the outskirts of the city of Lodz.

[49] Testimony of Pinkus R, in *Fresh Wounds: Early Narratives of Holocaust Survival,* 197–198.

[50] Friedman, 335.

[51] Unger, x

egotism was so extolled that it led to the erroneous accusation that his face appeared on the ghetto currency. Perhaps the most difficult of his character flaws to grapple with in the present day and which complicates evaluations of his leadership, however, was his penchant for physical and even sexual abuse.

Rumkowski employed corporal punishment as a means of reprimand. He not only hit people as a disciplinary measure but apparently also to vent his own anger.[52] Department heads, ghetto police, and others followed the example of the ghetto leader.[53] One case of a department head utilizing physical punishment was when Maksymilian Seligman, commissioner of the Leather and Saddlery Workshop, hit a female worker for insubordination. The result was that several of the male workers attacked Seligman and beat him. Rumkowski settled the matter by telling Seligman "that if any workers needed hitting, it would be done by him [Rumkowski] personally and no one else."[54] It is not clear if physical discipline was a tactic used by Rumkowski before the war or if he adopted it from the German authorities who beat him as a measure of discipline or as a means of venting anger.

There were a number of accusations that Rumkowski engaged in inappropriate sexual activities with women in the ghetto. For example, Ann M., in an oral testimony given to the Shoah Foundation, reported that there were rumors in the ghetto that Rumkowski took beautiful girls and slept with them.[55] Philip Friedman noted that despite the rumors, "no sexual offenses or licentious acts like those identified with Jacob Frank, the eighteenth century mystic, and his sect are known to have occurred in Rumkowski's circle"[56] Jacob Frank was associated with orgies and Friedman was discounting rumors that Rumkowski and his circle engaged in orgies with the approximately seventy women employed by the ghetto leader who were referred to as "Rumkowski's harem."[57]

---

[52] *Chronicle*, 7 September 1943.
[53] *Chronicle*, 7 September 1943.
[54] *Chronicle*, 30 January 1944.
[55] Ann M. (42256), USC Shoah Institute Testimonies Archive.
[56] Friedman, 338.
[57] Friedman, 338.

Rumors that Rumkowski was engaged in sexual improprieties in the ghetto, however, were substantiated by post-war testimonies. In 2000, Łódź Ghetto survivor Lucielle Eichengreen revealed in her memoir that Rumkowski had engaged in sexual molestation in the ghetto.[58] She named herself and others as victims. Related to this, historian Michal Unger identified two post-war testimonies dealing with Rumkowski's indiscretions— those of Leon Hurowitz and Yitzhchak Russ.[59] Similiarly, Warsaw Uprising fighter Yitzhak Zuckerman claimed that Rumkowski's first secretary, Rivka Glanz, who ran away from Łódź in spring 1940, did so to get away from Rumkowski's unwelcome advances. Zuckerman, from his discussions with Glanz concluded, "the man was obviously sick or a pervert. And that was known even before the war."[60]

Accusations about Rumkowski's predilection for young women were not only noted during the war period; there were several accusations before the war that Rumkowski had been guilty of sexually inappropriate behavior with his wards. In the 1930s, a physician accused Rumkowski of being overly familiar with his female employees and the young girls in the orphanage of which he was director.[61] Additionally, a teacher who Rumkowski fired from his orphanage accused him of "committing immoral acts with female orphans."[62] Rumkowski's sexual abuse was mentioned in the earliest of the written histories about the ghetto, as early as Solomon Bloom's 1949 article. He wrote, "It was whispered that he was guilty of familiarities with grown girls and women employed in the institution [the orphanage he ran before the war]."[63] Nevertheless, Eichengreen's revelation about the abuse she suffered at Rumkowski's hands was doubted, as it was perceived as too shocking an accusation.

---

[58] Lucielle Eichengreen, *Rumkowski and the Orphans of Lodz* (San Francisco, 2000.)
[59] Unger, 13.
[60] Yitzhak Zuckerman, *A Surplus of Memory: Chronicle of the Warsaw Ghetto Uprising* (Berkeley, 1993), 108.
[61] Friedman, 335, 335ff.
[62] Tushnet, *The Pavement of Hell,* 21. Tushnet notes that the charges were never proved but neither were they investigated.
[63] Bloom, "Dictator of the Łódź Ghetto," 112.

In the ghetto, one of the ways in which Rumkowski lured women into sexual liaisons with him was through bestowing favors in the form of food or desirable work details. It was not only young women who Rumkowski favored. Like many dictators who in reality have very little real control, Rumkowski was able to bestow favors on a small group of individuals. The occasional lucky individual who found favor with the Jewish ghetto leader could be benefited. For example, upon seeing a woman hard at work removing ice, Rumkowski promised food, money, and to place one of her children at the Marysin camp.[64] Thus, even a common person could have the benefits of the ghetto elite.

This granting of gifts led to ghetto inmates attempting to petition Rumkowski for benefits. It was not only the hard working who might catch his attention and thus receive benefits. Those associated with his pre-war life — his orphans, his patrons, and others — were able to gain favors from the Jewish ghetto leader. Bloom pointed out that Rumkowski as an insurance agent and as the manager of an orphanage was constantly soliciting funds — donations or insurance payments — "from the same wealthy citizens of Łódź."[65] Some of Rumkowski's pre-war wealthy acquaintances were able to benefit from their relationship with him. Blanka R.'s grandmother, who was a pre-war donor to Rumkowski's orphanage, was rewarded with special ration cards and a job at a bakery for her granddaughter.[66] The bestowing of several weeks of work at a bakery was one of the most common ways in which Rumkowski favored individuals. This work allowed the person to engage in light labor and receive adequate food for a couple of weeks during which he or she could regain strength.

Rumkowski also dispensed benefits to newlyweds. Friedman noted, "He schemed to monopolize the function of arranging and performing marriages...Glorying in this role, he would deliver a sermon at the wedding and present the bride and groom with a special gift of food."[67] Rumkowski gave three kilograms of flour and

---

[64] Adelson, 111.
[65] Bloom, "Dictator of the Łódź Ghetto," 111.
[66] Blanka R. (2273), USC Shoah Institute, Testimony Archives.
[67] Friedman, 338.

half a kilogram of honey as gifts to newlywed couples.[68] He performed marriage ceremonies on Sundays, twenty to thirty in a single day.[69] One couple received an extra-special wedding gift from Rumkowski. A man whose name was on a deportation list was granted a reprieve from deportation so that he could marry his bride. Rumkowski performed the wedding ceremony and gifted the couple with food.[70] This exemption contained a slight irony in that deportation summonses were referred to in ghetto lingo as "wedding invitations."

In addition to granting favors of extra food or easier work, Rumkowski's ability to determine who would live and who would die lay in his ability to deny someone the right to work, which effectively stripped them of the ability to obtain food. Although obvious items such as criminal activity could bar someone from employment, smearing Rumkowski's reputation could have dire consequences as well. As one survivor recalled,

> Szaja looked at me aghast. "You'd be playing with fire. Rumkowski is a pig. I don't even consider him a human being. Two years ago, before you arrived in the ghetto, I wrote a song about a small infant in a crib, the father scrounging for food to feed his family and not succeeding. Rumkowski heard about it and thought it was an insult. He threatened me and created a ruling that outlawed my writing. It was only with the intervention of Henryk Neftalin that he agreed to leave me alone. I in turn promised to ignore him in my poetry and prose.[71]

Rumkowski's ruthlessness towards those who crossed him was in fact his deadliest trait. It was in his withholding of work and consequently access to food that Rumkowski most effectively issued

---

[68] Zelkowicz, 190 (writing on 6 May1942.)

[69] The ceremonies were simple, without the accoutrements of a normal Jewish wedding, such as a marriage canopy (*Huppah*) or a marriage contract (*Kettubah.*) Rather, the couple would stand before two witnesses as the man gave his bride a ring and stated the Jewish wedding betrothal formula. A question arose after the war as to whether or not this was adequate. It was held that it satisfied the requirements of Jewish law. See Robert Kirschner, trans, *Rabbinic Responsa of the Holocaust Era* (New York, 1985), 131, 132, 138.

[70] *Chronicle*, 17 August 1943.

[71] Lucille Eichengreen, *From Ashes to Life: My Memories of the Holocaust* (San Francisco, 1994), 72.

death sentences in the ghetto. The unemployed were also the most vulnerable to deportation out of the ghetto. It is for these activities that Rumkowski should be most harshly judged.

Rumkowski, however, as former head of an orphanage, is also most known for particularly favoring children and ultimately for deporting the children of the Łódź Ghetto. In the early days of the ghetto, he set up schools and orphanages for the care of children. Individuals making requests for food or other items often sent children to make their requests, knowing the ghetto leader would be more inclined to accept their petitions. For example, one such petition was issued by nine-year-old Sarenka Lewi requesting assistance for her family:

> Good Mr. Chairman,
>
> My name is Sarenka Lewi. I am 9 years old. My daddy works very hard, but he cannot feed our family. Aside from dried bread and soup from the soup kitchen, we do not have anything else. Dear Mr. Chairman, please put in a good word at the hat-making workshop to give my Mommy a job. Good Grandpa, have mercy on hungry Sarenka and write such a letter. I am very tired now.... I would like so much to survive the war.
>
> Sarenka Lewi
> 8 June 1941[72]

In this early period, Rumkowski tried to distribute food evenly to all the ghetto residents.[73] The increase for the general population came at the expense of the laborers, who saw a thirty-three percent decrease in their bread ration.[74] Rumkowski used his access to extra food to channel supplemental nourishment and other benefits towards children and occasionally to the infirm. Those engaged in hard labor, however, soon rose up in violent protest, striking and

[72] Transcript of United States Holocaust Memorial Museum Temporary Exhibition "*Give Me Your Children: Voices from the Lodz Ghetto.*" [http://www.ushmm.org/wlc/article.php?lang=en&ModuleId=10007282] Accessed on 27 April 2007.

[73] *Chronicle*, 12 January 1941. In January 1941, Rumkowski reorganized the food distribution system and raised the daily bread ration from 300 grams to 400 grams per ghetto resident.

[74] *Chronicle*, 21 January 1941.

demanding food supplements to allow them to continue to work, as the reduced food allocations were insufficient to meet the caloric demands of heavy labor.[75] Although he did not raise the bread ration of workers, Rumkowski was forced to grant supplemental food to workers at the expense of the non-working population.[76] Speaking to a carpentry workshop a month after the strike, Rumkowski stated that he was unable to fulfill all their requests because, "In order to save the ghetto, I am forced to act decisively, like a surgeon who cuts a limb so the heart won't stop beating."[77] Throughout 1941, Rumkowski persisted in trying to distribute food evenly to the ghetto population, granting food privileges to the weak, particularly children.[78] For example, in September 1941:

> ...the Chairman delivered a short speech in which he indicated that concern for children would remain at the forefront of his activities. There is no sacrifice too great when it is a question of helping the ghetto's youngest inhabitants. After the Chariman's speech, the little children made a ring around him on the stage and dance joyously accompanied by the sound of music and cheers for the ghetto's first citizen. The Chairman gave a present of bread and candy to each of the show's young performers.[79]

A year later, Rumkowski was asked by the German authorities to turn over the children to the deportation trains. The September 1942 deportations, known as the *Szpera*, were the impetus for Rumkowski's most infamous speech, "Give me Your Children," in which he beseeched ghetto residents to hand over the children,

---

[75] See section on resistance in the ghetto in chapter five.

[76] Zelkowicz, 226. He distributed meat and sausage, which he could obtain only in small quantities, to workers.

[77] Adelson, 116. From the personal notes of Szmul Rozensztajn, Rumkowski's personal secretary. The words he employed are similar to those he would use a year and a half later during his infamous "Give me Your Children" speech.

[78] Zelkowicz, 222, 225. Rumkowski's argument for not giving supplemental rations was that he had argued to the German authorities that the entire ghetto was a giant labor camp and that by giving supplemental rations to one group, he might set a precedent by which the German authorities might deny bread to the non-working population of the ghetto. This excuse might very well have been based on a real exchange in which the German authorities stated that only those working were entitled to food.

[79] *Chronicle*, September 1941.

elderly, and sick for deportation noting, "I must carry out this difficult and bloody operation, I must cut off limbs in order to save the body! I must take away children, and if I do not, others too will be taken."[80] Rumkowski claimed that only a sacrifice of the children and elderly could save the rest of the ghetto population as a whole. Some have compared Rumkowski's decision to ask the ghetto inhabitants to give up children and elderly as a "sacrifice to the altar" compared with the actions of his counterpart in the Warsaw Ghetto, Adam Czernokiow, who committed suicide rather than fulfill the order.[81] However, Czernokiow — whose suicide well preceded Rumkowski's speech — did not stop the deportations. Nor did the leaders of the Krakow Ghetto who refused to hand over Jews for deportation; rather, they were themselves deported with their families. Nevertheless survivor Roman Halter critiqued Rumkowski on his delivery of the "Give me Your Children" speech stating, "He stood there and uttered those words. I found that speech of Rumkowski's *terrible*. At a certain point you have to say, 'No, I will not do this, I will not say this.'"[82]

After the deportations of the children, Rumkowski marked children for benefits. In a speech delivered on 17 October 1943, Rumkowski informed the workers that 4,000 children were being taken care of in special hostels where they were given two good soups a day.[83] Of course, as this was after the mass deportation of children in September 1942, the children being well cared for could only be those who survived, including the children of the ghetto police and others involved in the deportations, as well as the few children who managed to hide.

After the deportations of the children, Rumkowski was broken and uncommunicative.[84] From September 1942 onward, Rumkowski's power was severely diminished. Although orders on a variety of issues had long come from the German authorities to

---

80 Arad, 283.

81 Trunk, *The Łódź Ghetto*, 311, 312.

82 Lyn Smith, *Remembering: Voices of the Holocaust*, 124.

83 Adelson, 391.

84 Adelson, 366. Oskar Rosenfeld records this on 27 October 1942. Isaiah Trunk speculated that in mid-October, Rumkowski was beaten severely by Biebow (see *Judenrat,* p. 302.)

Rumkowski, including demands for individuals to be deported, instructions related to food supply, demands for valuables from the ghetto, and other items, after the September deportation, Biebow rapidly took over the daily administration of the ghetto. Trunk identifies the collapse of Rumkowski's "monocracy" in 1943.[85] It is clear, however, that Rumkowski was already losing power in 1942, immediately following the deportations of the children and elderly in September 1942. It was Biebow who announced that the Jews of the ghetto must return to work (on 14 September 1942) following the deportations.[86] Biebow stripped Rumkowski of his power over the two most important responsibilities in the ghetto: factory production, which was placed in the hands of Aron Jakubowicz, and control of the food supply, which was given to Dawid Gertler.[87] It is unclear how Biebow enforced this change of command, because Rumkowski's title was not changed. Trunk speculates that Biebow administered a severe beating to Rumkowski in mid-October 1942 for continuing to meddle in food distribution issues.[88] Under Gertler (and Biebow's) control, food distribution policy in the ghetto was transformed to favor workers. In December of 1942, meal cards were withheld from those who did not show up for work.[89] Gertler's

---

85 Trunk, 510.

86 Zon. 113

87 Isaiah Trunk gives the date of 9 October 1942 for Gertler taking over food distribution and reporting on it directly to Biebow. See Trunk, *Lodz Ghetto*, 43.

88 Trunk, *Judenrat*, 302. Trunk notes that he dates the beating to mid-October based on the cryptic notation that after fourteen days, the chairman is recovered and back at work (See Trunk, *Judenrat*, 302ff.) A similar notation on 12 April 1943 that "The Chairman has more or less recovered and has resumed his normal duties at Bałut Market" was made in the *Chronicle of the Lodz Ghetto*, and this may indicate another beating. However, on 16 June 1944, the *Chronicle* reported that Biebow attacked Rumkowski but that this was the first time the Amtsleiter had ever laid hands on the chairman. The *Chronicle* speculated that the beating was in connection with Rumkowski's meeting with the Mayor of Litzmannstadt and the Chief of the Gestapo, Dr. Bradfisch. It also noted that "Anyone who knows the Amtsleiter knows that this was one of his fits of rage." Rumkowski remained hospitalized for a lengthy period following this beating. It is not clear whether Biebow was beating Rumkowski for a long period of time and his violence escalated, particularly in 1944, or if the June 1944 beating was the beginning of his severe violent streak which culminated in extreme violence, including raping women and torturing men during the liquidation of the ghetto, and continuing after he fled along with Lodz Ghetto inmates into Germany. (See Trunk, *Judenrat*, 285.)

89 YIVO RG 241, doc. 1002.

control, however, was short lived, as he was arrested by the Gestapo in July 1943.[90] *The Chronicle* reported a month later that the ghetto community attributed the lack of food available in the ghetto to the fact that Dawid Gertler was no longer in charge of the food distribution.[91] It is more likely, however, that Biebow slowed food delivery in light of his August 1943 inspections of internal food distribution.[92] In October 1943, Biebow announced that he would personally take over the distribution of food due to corruption.[93] Immediately following this declaration, in November 1943, numerous supplemental foods were cancelled, including supplemental soups and "B" food cards.[94] Supplemental foods were instead offered as a reward for workers. The top ten percent of workers were offered supplemental soups.[95]

Although his actual power was largely stripped, Rumkowski retained his title of Eldest of the Jews of the Litzmannstadt Ghetto even when, in February 1944, he was kicked out of his offices in Baluty Market and those were made available to the German Ghetto Administration.[96] Rumkowski's signature continued to appear on orders which flowed from the German ghetto administration to him including, for example, notices to show up for the deportation trains to Auschwitz.[97] Ultimately, however, Rumkowski himself boarded a train to Auschwitz with his family.

---

[90] *Chronicle*, 21 July 1943. Strangely enough, a week after her husband's arrest, the *Chronicle* reported that Mrs. Gertler dispensed hundreds of apples baked with sugar from her personal store to the patients in the hospital. (See *Chronicle*, July 1943.) It is possible she was trying to unload her private stores in the face of accusations from the Germans that Gertler had been hoarding food. Her vast personal store of apples seems like a strong indication that the Gertlers had been hoarding food.

[91] *Chronicle*, 28 August 1943.

[92] *Chronicle*, 8 August 1943.

[93] Zon. 117.

[94] Zon. 526; Zon. 528. The "B" rations had provided extra food for 800 families, including the higher-ups in the Jewish ghetto administration, police, factory directors and managers, doctors and pharmacists. Rumkowski retained control of enough food to supplement only forty families. For more on this see Sinnreich, The Supply and Distribution of Food to the Łódź Ghetto, 136.

[95] Zon. 529.

[96] *Chronicle*, 5 February 1944.

[97] Wiener Library Archives 500 series/559 at Leo Baeck Institute.

Rumkowski was a deeply flawed individual with reprehensible personality traits. He was an egotist who shamelessly promoted himself to the point that he was perceived as the source of the orders he gave. At the same time, he was a man who genuinely tried to help his fellow Jews in a hopeless struggle against Nazi designs for their extermination. Behind his bravado and posturing, however, lay the reality that while Rumkowski could bestow assistance on a small number of ghetto inmates, overall, he had limited control of the ghetto. In the beginning, he was granted wide ranging powers over the internal life of the ghetto but Rumkowski's control in the ghetto rapidly decreased to the point where he was completely removed from any real power and only left with the inflated title of "Eldest of the Jews." Whether his self-absorption blinded him or he made morally questionable decisions to "cut off limbs in order to save the body itself," ultimately it was the Nazis and not Rumkowski who were responsible for the deaths of the majority of Jews in the Łódź Ghetto. Rumkowski himself was a victim of their murderous policy. Along with his wife, adopted child and other family members, Rumkowski was placed on a train car to Auschwitz.

"Betrayal: Recognition and Non-Recognition in the Traumatic Encounter"

Dennis B. Klein
Kean University

Saul Friedman's 1993 *Holocaust Literature*,[1] like all his work, was a statement about a subject that he believed demanded hyper-critical attention. Recognizing that the Holocaust tended to become a pretext for ulterior agendas—a convenient metaphor for and warning against selective contemporary behavior—he set out with this work to assemble research that instead deferred to the event's intrinsic significance. For him, it was the event's specificity that deserved scrutiny: the Church's unholy alliance with Nazi Germany, the development of killing centers, national paths to mass murder, and survivors' accounts of serial brutality. As I wrote in my foreword, Friedman's timely commitment to scholarly integrity "came at a time when the subject [was] victim to ideological warfare." As Professor Friedman's students, we labor in this field grateful for the high standards he asserted.

In his essay "Torture," Holocaust survivor Jean Améry's flashback to "Reception Camp Breendonk," where he was held captive for several days by the SS after his arrest in 1943 by the Gestapo for his activities within the Belgium resistance movement, Améry recalled a rupture, or "threshold," that was infernal: "This physical overwhelming by the other then becomes an existential consummation of destruction altogether."[2] Throughout this and his other essays that he collected for his significant account *At the Mind's Limits*, Améry's assertions of resentment were unrelenting. He wrote about the immutability of the victim's condition with an obsession designed to "return the blow." It is an account that seeks to hold all

1 Saul Friedman, ed., *Holocaust Literature: A Handbook of Critical, Historical, and Literary Writings* (Westport, Connecticut, 1993).
2 Jean Améry, *At the Mind's Limits: Contemplations by a Survivor on Auschwitz and Its Realities*, trans. Sidney Rosenfeld and Stella P. Rosenfeld (Bloomington, Indiana, 1980), 26, 28.

Germans accountable, then and in his time, in the mid-1960s, when he wrote these essays. He was determined to keep the "moral chasm 'wide open'" between the Nazis' victims and their assailants, to whom he believed contemporary Germans were linked as their descendants.[3] As he observed, he harbored a "retrospective grudge," which, he wrote, "I neither can nor want to get rid of."[4]

Though more conscious than most other survivors of their right to resentment, Améry's account exemplifies survivors' determination to distance themselves from their criminals. The classic reading of survivors' accounts have come to see genocidal assailants as the estranged "other." I believe we have not read survivors' testimonies correctly. In this article I will argue that memoirists' intentions represent only part of their expression. Using Jean Améry's *At the Mind's Limits* as a case study, I assert a significant range of expression and will develop an argument to illuminate counter-narratives of recognition and dispositions of forgiveness. To characterize Améry's memoir-cum-meditation as an expression of forgiveness might seem an article of overreaching, since he explicitly rejected forgiveness as an option. Indeed, critics regard Améry as a champion of resentment. In a close reading of his essays, I will show that *At the Mind's Limits* is a meditation not only on resentment's virtues but also on its limits. If he repudiated forgiveness as lazy and cheap,[5] he also reworked his relationships with his enemies that presented them as something other than hopeless, even though he remained adamant about the depravity of their crimes. In so doing, Améry alerts us to alternative ways of regarding forgiveness.

It is important to observe the assertion of intimacy in many memoirists' reflections on their experiences with radical crimes. The significance of "intimate killing," or "micro-annihilation," is now a staple of current scholarship in genocide studies.[6] It is based on

---

[3] Améry, *At the Mind's Limits,* 76-79.

[4] Améry, *At the Mind's Limits,* 63-67.

[5] Améry, *At the Mind's Limits,* 72.

[6] Derrida's conception of forgiveness was extreme, asserting "forgive both the fault and the guilty *as such*, where the one and the other remain as irreversible as the evil, as evil itself, and being capable of repeating itself, unforgivably, without transformation, without amelioration,

research since the late 1980s on local destruction—episodes of mass assault on neighbors—in eastern Europe (Bartov, 2008), Rwanda (Fujii, 2009), Herzegovina (Becirevic, 2009), Cambodia (Hinton, 2004), and China during the cultural revolution (Su, 2011).[7] The study that has set the stage for this subfield is Jan T. Gross's *Neighbors: The Destruction of the Jewish Community in Jedwabne, Poland* (2002).

Améry's elaborate meditations on torture and its implications for a moral society are not philosophical ruminations but a conversation with his compatriots. The fact that he addressed himself personally to them is key to understanding these essays as a struggle to work through agony. Witness accounts are often better understood as memories on many levels. They not only seek to report on extreme crimes and appeal to the conscience of world opinion. They also refer to the contexts of crime, to brutality that was embodied by assailants who had inhabited the same space as their victims and whose descendants continue to do so. Améry surely insisted on the distance he felt from his contemporaries, but, in fact, it is his sense of kinship with them that is the remarkable and elucidating discourse framing his diatribe.

Even if he did not directly know his assailants, he claimed to know them as his compatriots. They comprised both his torturers and the German people, his contemporaries, who, he believed, were complicit in the crimes and, possessing the Nazi regime in their "pedigree," "must continue to bear the responsibility for those twelve years that it certainly did not terminate itself."[8] Indeed, he asserted that they knew each other. After all, on the one hand, "We [victims] lived in the midst of the German people."[9] On the other, the German

without repentance or promise." Jacques Derrida, "On Forgiveness," in *On Cosmopolitanism and Forgiveness*, trans. Mark Dooley and Michael Hughes (London, 2001), 27-60.

7 Omer Bartov, "Testimonies As Historical Evidence: Reconstructing the Holocaust from Below" unpublished manuscript, 2008; Lee Ann Fujii, *Killing Neighbors: Webs of Violence in Rwanda* (Ithaca, New York, 2009); Alexander Laban Hinton, *Why Did They Kill?: Cambodia in the Shadow of Genocide* (Berkeley, California, 2004); Yang Su, *Collective Killings in Rural China During the Cultural Revolution* (Cambridge, 2011).

8 Améry, *At the Mind's Limits,* 76.

9 Améry, *At the Mind's Limits,* 73.

people—everyday "laborers, file clerks, technicians, typists"—"knew exactly...what was taking place around them and with us."[10]

Améry's essays originated in a series of invited radio broadcasts for the South German Broadcasting Corporation beginning in 1964 after 26 years in exile—all but two, 1943-45, voluntary—from his Austrian homeland. Austria, for centuries an integral part of German culture, rejoined Germany, after some 70 years of political independence, when the Nazis annexed it in 1938. Though it was the event that led Améry to flee, many Austrians welcomed the *Anschluss* and their renewed identification with German destiny. He spoke personally, noting in the preface to his essays' first edition, published in 1966, that it was "To the Germans [that]...I would like to relate a few things here."[11] Even his assailants, far from the intimacy and immediacy that characterized communal relationships in Eastern Europe, struck a chord that was "familiar;" he affirmed a proximity by referring to them by name and by rehearsing the scrutiny of their faces.[12]

Narratives of recognition, which philosopher Paul Ricoeur maintained was implicated in every act of memory, deepen descriptions of crimes into expressions of betrayal.[13] In her 1937 essay, "Love, Guilt, and Reparation," Melanie Klein suggestively illustrated the psychodynamics of betrayal, arguing that the impulses to hate an intimate for violating a sacred bond (the infant's hatred toward his mother for failing to satisfy his insatiable needs) hasten a counter-urge to repair and preserve the relationship.[14] As John Steiner commented in his psychoanalytic study of resentment, only when the child feels an impulse to attack "good objects" that have injured and betrayed him "can he face the task of reconstructing his world and setting in motion the long and painful task of finding

---

[10] Améry, *At the Mind's Limits,* 74.

[11] Améry, *At the Mind's Limits,* xiv.

[12] Améry, *At the Mind's Limits*, 32, 70-71; 35.

[13] Paul Ricoeur, *Memory, History, Forgetting*, trans. Kathleen Blamey and David Pellauer (Chicago, 2006).

[14] Melanie Klein, "Love, Guilt, and Reparation," in *Love, Guilt, and Reparation and Other Works, 1921-1945* (London, 1981).

forgiveness and of making reparation."[15] Though Améry was not dependent on Germans or anyone else for his survival, these studies alert us to the dialectics of resentment and its potential for precipitating a different course of action. Moreover, even if he were not interested in merely reconstructing his broken relationships, the original relationships, as Klein observed, must have been sufficiently strong for him to seek some sort of reworking. His frequent references to his "fellow man," and the betrayal he expressed, certainly suggest this.

They demand a re-reading of survivors' memoirs as expressions on at least two levels: the level of intention, or denotation, that bears witness to the crimes that were committed, and the level of allusion, or connotation, that expresses a violation of trust and a search for a renewed orientation to the world. Améry's references to his experiences of torture captured the time when he was a victim of unbearable torture. It represents his destruction, "his helplessness and all-encompassing weakness."[16]

Perhaps Améry's main theme in these essays is his loss of trust in the world—the betrayal of his "fellow man" who became "the counter man."[17] Time and again he insisted that his experience with assault "blocks the view into the world in which the principle of hope rules."[18] The "social contract" that regulated parity among citizens vanished with "the first blow," and trust in the world completely broke down. These are signature observations, but their implications are not as fatalistic as his critics assert. His requiem to trust in the world is an expression not of despair but of radical revision, for he confessed that his trust in the world before he encountered the threshold of ruthless assault was groundless and naïve. He had believed that his underground resistance activities would have brought German soldiers back to their senses. He even once clung to

---

[15] John Steiner, "Revenge and Resentment in the 'Oedipus Situation.'" *International Journal of Psychoanalysis*, Vol. 77 (1996): 433-43.

[16] Améry, *At the Mind's Limits,* 68.

[17] Améry, *At the Mind's Limits,* 28.

[18] Améry, *At the Mind's Limits,* 40.

the social contract which included the "expectation" or "certainty" of help for anyone in distress. That expectation, he noted, is "one of the fundamental experiences of human beings," but even that could not survive the brutality—he called it "evil"—he had come to know.[19]

But it is clear that he also sought to find his way back to a world that had abandoned him. It wouldn't be easy. He wrote that the "foreignness" he felt "cannot be compensated by any sort of subsequent communication."[20] Torture, it seems, eviscerated human transaction as well as the victim's soul. It compelled a "withdrawal" into the damaged self.[21] But despair was a price too high to pay for resentment and crippling helplessness—the reality of having "succumbed to torture" that compelled his alienation from humanity.[22] He exalted his release from abandonment, observing "There are even euphoric moments in which the return of weak powers of reason is felt as an extraordinary happiness. The bundle of limbs that is slowly recovering human semblance feels the urge to articulate the experience intellectually."[23] Albert Camus made the point in *The Rebel*: "To talk of despair is to conquer it. Despairing literature is a contradiction in terms."[24] Even though communication, as he observed, could not erase his sense of alienation, the very fact of writing his memoirs manifested an underlying wish to reconnect with the world and to parry his devastating sense of loneliness. It was a desire built on the basis of an "enormous perception at a later stage" that would begin by jettisoning a bankrupt social contract with its postulates of implicit mutual trust and the certainty of help.

The real work of Améry's accounts is apparent in his articulation of desires to renegotiate his fraternal bonds with those who sought and seek to diminish or destroy him. If he resented Germans for their betrayal, he also regarded resentment as a spur to renewal. As he

---

19 Améry, *At the Mind's Limits,* 25, 28, 70, 81.

20 Améry, *At the Mind's Limits,* 39.

21 Améry, *At the Mind's Limits,* 68.

22 Améry, *At the Mind's Limits,* 40.

23 Améry, *At the Mind's Limits,* 39.

24 Albert Camus, *The Rebel: An Essay on Man in Revolt*, trans. Anthony Bower (New York, 1991).

saw it resentment would compel the criminal to "integrate" Nazi crimes and their legacies into a chastened, new world. That, he said, would be the criminal's "redeeming act."[25]

Freud's distinction between two types of reactions to historical trauma clarifies the narrative tension in Améry's reflections. In "Remembering, Repeating, and Working-Through," and in "Mourning and Melancholia," Freud characterized responses as a reproduction of traumatic loss or violence, or as a "working-through" or overcoming of the impasse.[26] This analytic framework has been useful for scholars concerned with the nature of survivors' difficult memories, pointing out that both reactions are normative and, indeed, are interrelated in the text. Evidence of grief in Améry's essay is surely ample and is especially apparent in his preoccupation with, indeed valorization of, the dark emotions of pain and resentment as well as in his sense of hopelessness reflected in what he believed was the collapse of the social contract and in his final resignation. Dominick LaCapra observed that this kind of memory represented a possession by the past and an identification with loss.[27] Some survivors, he wrote, return "to the position of helpless victim. Sidra Dekoven Ezrahi observed that such an approach is static and non-negotiable.[28] But just as deep memory is revisionary, an alternative reaction to loss—what Susan Rubin Suleiman called "narrative" as opposed to "traumatic memory"—reverses the severity of a non-negotiable approach.[29] It is dynamic and affirmative. As LaCapra noted, it "allows one to begin again." This perspective, especially as it applies to Améry's reputation, is significant and draws attention to his counter-narratives of worldly reengagement. Suleiman illustrated this

---

25 Améry, *At the Mind's Limits,* 78, 79.

26 Sigmund Freud, "Remembering, Repeating and Working-Through (Further Recommendations on the Technique of Psycho-Analysis II)," *Standard Edition,* 12 (London, 1914), 145-56 and Sigmund Freud, "Mourning and Melancholia," *Standard Edition*, 14 (London, 1917), 237-60.

27 Dominick LaCapra, *Writing History, Writing Trauma* (Baltimore, 2001).

28 Sidra DeKoven Ezrahi, "Representing Auschwitz," *History and Memory,* Vol. 7, No. 2 (1996): 121-56.

29 Susan Rubin Suleiman, *Crises of Memory and the Second World War* (Cambridge, 2006).

"ongoing renegotiation of that historical reality" in her discussion of survivor Jorge Semprun's reworked accounts. In a late account, Semprun, himself a member of the resistance (the French resistance, in his case) modified the story of his arrival in Buchenwald. He wrote that a German scribe noted his occupation as "*Stukkateur*," a skilled craftsman in stucco, instead of "*Student*." Noting that Semprun believed that this intervention probably saved him from a fatal selection, Suleiman observed Semprun's late discovery of a gesture embodying "a generous idea of humanity," or what Suleiman termed "human solidarity."[30]

Améry's allusions to his "fellow man" represent a reworking, and indeed, he observed the shape of a new reality even if he were never sure it would materialize. At the end of his original preface, he permitted himself to imagine a renewed community of "all those who wish to live together as fellow human beings."[31] The German revolution, indeed, seemed remote, but there were enough good Germans to set the stage: "There were those who, in the Third Reich, broke out of the Third Reich….I have forgotten nothing, including the few brave people I encountered."[32] What counted were these reminders of his compatriots' "better origins" as well as the recognition of their kinship. His desire to reconsider Germans besides their crimes expanded his field of vision, paving the way for a new orientation that could permit the criminal—in his prelapsarian, morally affirmative state—to "join his victim as a fellow human being."[33]

An assertion of kinship with "the other"—the enemy—invites us to inspect survivors' memoirs for expressions of forgiveness. Certainly, Améry's belief in moral, if not redemptive, possibilities suggests a desire to bridge the chasm to his enemies and expunge their abject other-ness. Yet he refused to forgive the German past and the present indifference to it. His wholesale refusal, however,

---

[30] Susan Rubin Suleiman, *Crises of Memory and the Second World War.*

[31] Améry, *At the Mind's Limits,* xiv.
[32] Améry, *At the Mind's Limits,* 73.

[3333] Améry, *At the Mind's Limits,* 72.

was—like his exposure to criminality—an assertion in reaction to outrageous circumstances and does not represent deeper considerations.

His rejection of forgiveness as an option is set against the background of what he simply referred to as "social pressure" In fact, the pressure Germans exerted on him and other survivors to "forgive and forget" was considerable.[34] When he began to collect his thoughts for the 1964 radio broadcasts, West Germany was in the midst of what scholars agree was one of the largest and most closely observed West German trials dealing with National Socialist crimes following World War II.[35] According to polling data at the time, a substantial minority expressed hostility toward the Auschwitz Trial in Frankfurt am Main, which had begun on 20 December 1963 and would end in a judgment more than a year later on 20 August 1965. Many German citizens were concerned that they and others might be implicated in the trial of 20 defendants for abetting crimes or at least for their unwillingness to oppose their commission. As theologian Helmut Gollwitzer commented at the time, Germans wanted the trial to end "for the sake of a quiet conscience."[36]

Indeed, pressure was mounting throughout Europe to exercise nations' Statutes of Limitations, now that 20 years since the war had elapsed, and it was certainly no coincidence that the year 1965 represented the pinnacle of Nazi trials' unpopularity. As historian Devin Pendas observed, "A substantial portion of the German public, and a number of high-ranking public officials as well, in fact used the trial to argue against holding further trials like it."[37] The Federal government in Bonn explicitly opposed extending the prescribed period of statutory limitations, asserting that to do so would constitute a "Lex Auschwitz."

---

[34] Améry, *At the Mind's Limits,*72.
[35]Adalbert Rückerl, *NS-Verbrechen vor Gericht:Versuch einer Vergangenheitsbewältigung.* Heidelberg, 1984; Devin O. Pendas, *The Frankfurt Auschwitz Trial, 1963-1965: Genocide, History, and the Limits of the Law* (Cambridge, 2006).
[36] Helmut Gollwitzer, in *Zeugen im Aushwitz-Prozess: Begegnungen und Gedanken,* ed. Emmi Bonhoeffer (Wuppertal-Barmen, 1965), 7.
[37] Pendas, *The Frankfurt Auschwitz Trial.*

Holocaust survivors, including Améry, spoke up against what they heard was a demand to forgive Nazi criminals still at large and to forget their massive crimes. Several participated in what became a growing international public debate over the applicability or non-applicability (also referred to as the imprescriptibility) of the statutes to radical crimes, such as crimes against humanity.[38] Améry signed petitions opposing enforcement of statutory limitations in these cases. Vladimir Jankélévitch, a prolific French philosopher and musicologist who was also active in the French resistance during the war, wrote polemical texts on the question. Survivor Simon Wiesenthal, like Améry from Vienna, mobilized a substantial postcard campaign in the 1970s addressed to the West German chancellor, stating that "justice for crimes against humanity must have no limitations."

This debate represented the first time many survivors elected to comment publicly about their experiences under Nazi rule. In fact, it is entirely plausible that the phenomenon of witnesses' testimonies as a cottage industry is rooted in their determination to defeat Europe's impatience with legal proceedings that disturbed its social peace. Reflections by Jankélévitch, Wiesenthal (, and Améry all date from this period.[39] Améry, himself, commenced the preface to his memoir, "When the Auschwitz trial began in Frankfurt in 1964, I wrote the first essay on my experiences in the Third Reich, after twenty years of silence." Writing this essay on Auschwitz, he recalled, appeared to break a "gloomy spell." "Suddenly," he added, "everything demanded telling."[40] Reinforcing the urge to communicate—to reenter into the "realm of German history"—was the confirmed sense that, for once, they were on the history's right side.[41] In 1964 France and East Germany declared that crimes against humanity (France) and Nazi

---

[38] Peter Banki,. "The Forgiveness to Come: Dreams and Aporias." Ph.D. diss., New York University, 2009.

[39] Vladimir Jankélévitch, "*Pardonner?*' ["Should We Pardon Them?], in *L'Imprescriptible* (Paris, 1965); Jankélévitch, *Le Pardon* (Paris, 1967); Jankélévitch, "Should We Pardon Them?," trans. Ann Hobart, *Critical Inquiry,* Vol. 22, No. 3 (1996): 552-72; Simon Wiesenthal, *Die Sonnenblume: Von Schuld und Vergebung* (Paris, 1966); and Améry, *Jenseits von Schuld und Sühne: Bewältigungsversuche eine Überwältigten* (Munich, 1966).

[40] Améry, *At the Mind's Limits,* xiii.

[41] Améry, *At the Mind's Limits,* 77.

and war crimes (East Germany) were imprescriptible. In 1965 Austria declared the imprescriptibility of war crimes and crimes again humanity. Also that year the West German Bundestag voted to extend its statutes of limitations for another four years, to 1969, starting the clock not with the period of offenses but with the constitution of the Federal Republic. When the extension expired it voted to lengthen the prescribed period for adjudicating "crimes of genocide" for ten more years, and then, in 1979, abolished statutory limitations altogether.

Améry regarded the Statute of Limitations for radical crimes as an exoneration of criminals removed in time from their commission that invited his contemporaries to "lose the memory of the crime." "Not backward let us look," he heard, "but forward, to a better, common future!"[42] The subtext of his reflections was a fear of a broader evasion—the public's complacent dispossession of its own errant behavior. That, even more than bringing fugitive criminals to justice, concerned him and motivated him to impose the burden of "disquiet" so that his contemporaries could join him in at least one respect: an inability to forget.[43] In all these formulations, it is clear that Améry heard in the campaign to exempt Nazi-era criminals from conviction not only the demand "to forget" but also the urge "to forgive." Other survivors twinned the terms as well: Forgiving, like forgetting, implies "closure," asserted Ruth Kluger.[44] Primo Levi wrote, "I am not inclined to forgive...because I know of no act that can erase a crime."[45] Wiesenthal considered forgiveness weak because it would "finish with [that is, dispose of] the painful business."[46] Like Améry, Jankélévitch refused to "forgive and forget."

The debate over statutory limitations gave rise to yet another development—a reevaluation of the conception of forgiveness itself. The term, so strongly derided, seemed like an anachronism. Jankélévitch wrote that Nazi crimes—"out of all proportion to

---

[42] Améry, *At the Mind's Limits,* 69.
[43] Améry, *At the Mind's Limits,* 71.
[44] Ruth Kluger, Forgiving and Remembering." *PMLA*, Vol. 117, No. 2 (2002): 311-313.
[45] Primo Levi, *The Drowned and the Saved*, trans. Raymond Rosenthal (New York, 1986).
[46]Simon Wiesenthal, *The Sunflower: On the Possibilities and Limits of Forgiveness* (New York, 1998)."

everyday wrongdoing"—were too extreme for conventional forgiveness. "The crimes of the Germans are exceptional from every point of view....They are *crimes against humanity*...an assault against the human being as *human being*."[47]

In a three-year seminar spanning the years 1997-2000 Jacques Derrida revisited the debate over statutory limitations. Elaborating on *"Pardonner?"* he recognized an underlying tendency to forgive Germans in Jankélévitch's observation, "We could have conceived granting it to them."[48] Indeed, elsewhere in "*Pardonner?*" Jankélévitch imagined a "sensible" forgiveness for Germans were they to assert "a single word of understanding and sympathy. We have wished for it, this fraternal word."[49] Although he regarded Jankélévitch's struggle but failure to forgive as nascent thinking about forgiveness that is commensurate with radical crimes—a radical forgiveness that exceeded Judeo-Christian conventions—Derrida asserted that he boxed himself in by expecting repentance as a precondition. Against radical crimes' excesses, Peter Banki observed, forgiveness, too, must exceed reconciliation, reparation, healing, and apology. Derrida's interrogation of Jankélévitch's essay "*Pardonner?*" expanded on possibilities to forgive extreme evil.

Derrida contended that radical forgiveness required a conception of the term that would grant victims the prerogative of setting something in motion. Instead of expecting criminals to repent, victims could forgive unconditionally. Moreover, by allowing criminals to remain unrepentant, an act of unconditional forgiveness required a willingness to forgive the unforgiveable; that is, the crimes and criminals regardless of any conceivable redemptive gesture toward sincere contrition. Unconditional forgiveness must be "gracious, infinite, aneconomic [asymmetical], forgiveness granted *to*

---

[47] Jankélévitch, "Should We Pardon Them?,"

[48] Derrida,"On Forgiveness."

[49] Jankélévitch, "Should We Pardon Them?,"

the guilty as guilty...even to those who do not repent or ask forgiveness."[50]

Unconditional forgiveness was purer than its conditional opposite, which, rendered only after the guilty repents and "mends its ways," was meaningless and, in fact, logically impossible. By affirming the imprescriptibility of extraordinary crimes, he opened a space between punishment, which survivors from the 1960s regarded as nonnegotiable, and forgiveness, which he asserted was "heterogeneous [i.e., alien] to the order of politics or the juridical as they are ordinarily understood." Indeed, he detected in Jankélévitch an inclination to forgive extreme crimes, even though Jankélévitch ruled out that possibility since in theory radical crimes were "exorbitant" and in practice "Germans are an unrepentant people" anyway.[51] In other words, by seeing in the debate over statutory limitations the outlines of an alternative conception of forgiveness—forgiveness as unconditional—he exposed a narrative in witness accounts that competed with intentional narratives that summarily rejected forgiveness as an option.

Améry's desire to abandon his tenacious resentment and set in motion a new course of action anticipating a connection with his fellow man expresses an unconditional disposition, though not the words, to forgive. But Améry diverged from Derrida by drawing a line that separated criminals from their crimes. He and other survivors remained adamant about the crimes' malevolence. Significantly, however, but on the basis of recognizing Germans who tortured him and who, after the war, conspired in tacit consent, he recalled their "better origins" that permitted him to dream about their moral renewal and about a reconfigured fellowship of man. This distinction between the offense and the offenders—what Ricoeur called a "radical uncoupling"[52]—made it possible for Améry to forgive without forgetting; that is, to forgive the criminals, whom he claimed he knew in counter-narratives of recognition, without ever forgetting their unforgivable crimes.

---

[50] Derrida,"On Forgiveness."

[51] Jankélévitch, "Should We Pardon Them?,"

[52] Ricoeur, *Memory, History, Forgetting.*

Améry's narratives of recognition, and the crime-criminal uncoupling implicated in them, advance our understanding of the possibilities of forgiveness in other survivors' deep memory accounts as well. Noteworthy are Jankélévitch's reflections on Germans who "are beginning to realize what it was that they had diverted their thoughts from"[53] and Wiesenthal's attenuated estimation of the murderers. By insisting on several occasions that they ended up but did not start that way, he concentrated his concerns strictly on their crimes. These, not the criminals, were "unspeakable" and "monstrous." As Ricoeur remarked, "Separating the guilty person from his act, in other words, forgiving the guilty person while condemning his action, would be to forgive a subject other than the one who committed the act."[54] Améry's inclination to see the criminal beyond—indeed, before—the crime complicated his bitter accusations of German betrayal with revealing expressions of deep forgiveness. It served to diminish the other-ness in his estimation of the "counter-man."

---

[53] Jankélévitch, "Should We Pardon Them?,"
[54] Ricoeur, *Memory, History, Forgetting.*

"The *Jewishness* of Raphael Lemkin"

Steven Leonard Jacobs
University of Alabama

In Chapter One—"Lemkin, Culture, and the Concept of Genocide"—in his *Empire, Colony, Genocide: Conquest, Occupation and Subaltern Resistance in World History*, A. Dirk Moses makes the following comment:

> It goes without saying that Lemkin's upbringing as a religiously conversant Jew flowed into his thinking. But how exactly? Did common Yiddish phrases form his social imaginary? 'May his name be blotted out' was the standard saying about an enemy, itself derived from the Biblical verse, 'I will utterly blot out the remembrance of Amalek (Exodus 17:14; cf. Deuteronomy 25:19), the Amalek[ites] being the congenital enemy of ancient Jews.[1] The Jewish festivals of Passover and Purim commemorate escapes from slavery and genocide, respectively; during the latter the name of the Persian king Haman[2] a descendant of the Amalek[ites][3] is met with booing and other noise in order to 'blot' it out. We can only speculate exactly how these rituals impacted on Lemkin, but this background cannot be ignored in accounting for his worldview. The survival of the Jews over the millennia, the maintenance of their traditions, their cultural flourishing in the lands of the former Polish-Lithuanian Commonwealth, where the vast majority of world Jewry lived, and, equally, the intense consciousness that peoples and their

[1] See, for example, Louis H. Feldman, *"Remember Amalek!" Vengeance, Zealotry, and Group Destruction in the Bible according to Philo, Pseudo-Philo, and Josephus* (Cincinnati, 2004).

[2] Haman was *not* the king of Persia; rather he was its Prime Minister. Such an error points towards the contention of this author that only one reasonably well-versed in the sources of the Jewish religious tradition is in a better position to examine them and their applicability to the subject at hand. It is, however, like any other academic discipline, one which requires intensive study and mastery.

[3] Not literally so, but at least according to Jewish tradition religiously interpreted, *all* enemies of the Jewish people—from Haman to Hitler—*Y'mach sh'mo*/May his name be blotted out!—trace their ultimate lineage back to Amalek and the Amalekites.

> memories could be entirely erased—these were the cultural milieu and drama in which Lemkin was steeped.[4]

Unfortunately, but perhaps understandably, Moses did not follow upon this tantalizing thought—that Lemkin's Jewish identity was a *primary* and perhaps central motivating and influencing factor in his ultimate drive and determination to securing the passage of the 1948 Genocide Convention. This essay, therefore, is a re-examination and re-reading of Lemkin's "story" by one well-versed in the sources of the Jewish religious tradition, and how these core-values are reflected in both the man and his life's work.

Thus, it seems to this author, we may Jewishly frame Lemkin's story under seven primary core-values within the Jewish religious tradition: (1) *mishpakha*/family, (2) *hinukh*/education, (3) *hayyim v'mavet*/life and death, (4) *halakha*/law, (5) *tzedek*/justice/righteousness, (6) *k'lal Yisrael*/Jewish community, and (7) *shalom*/peace.[5] Therefore, discussion of each of these categories with reference to Lemkin will consist of two parts: Firstly, a summary of the Judaic understanding of these values, and secondly, how Lemkin's tale, in specific, relates directly to these values. Primary among the summary sources consulted are the original 1901-1906 *Jewish Encyclopedia* now available online as of 2002 (www.jewishencyclopedia.com) [JE]; the revised and updated electronic edition of the twenty-two volume 2007 *Encyclopedia Judaica*, edited by Michael Berenbaum and Fred Skolnik [EJ]; and the 2003 CD-Rom Edition of *The Encyclopedia of Judaism*, edited by Jacob Neusner, Alan J. Avery-Peck, and William Scott Green [TEJ]. (With the addition of well-respected editor and translator Fred Skolnik, all of these scholars are themselves well-known and well-respected in the field of Judaic Studies.)

Mishpakha/Family

---

[4] A. Dirk Moses, *Empire, Colony, Genocide: Conquest, Occupation and Subaltern Resistance in World History* (New York and Oxford, 2008), 23, 24.

[5] Though universally understood as "peace," the Hebrew word contextually also means "wholeness" and/or "wellbeing" and can refer equally to one's physicality or mental state.

Predominant among Jewish core-values is that of *mishpakha*/family which, historically understood, is inextricably intertwined with that of the Jewish religious tradition itself; indeed, "the main reason for the solidarity of the family may be found in its religion" [JE]. Statements such as "God dwells in a pure and loving home" (Babylonian Talmud, *Kiddushin* 71a[6]), and "Marriages are made in heaven" (Babylonian Talmud, *Shabbat* 22a & b) attest to this intertwining. As Kaufmann Kohler (1843-1925), German-born American Reform Rabbi, theologian and later President of the Hebrew Union College, Cincinnati, OH (1903-1921), and Rabbi Adolph Guttmacher (d. 1915) attest in their article "Family and Family Life" in the *Jewish Encyclopedia*:

> The observances of the faith are so entwined with the every-day customs of the home as to make the Jewish religion and the family life one, a bond in sanctity. Most of the religious ceremonies are to be celebrated in the bosom of the family; the observance of the dietary laws is an especially prominent nature in the daily routine.[7]

The family unit, Jewishly understood, was not only husband and wife but children as well, for according to Psalm 127, children were a blessing from God, and assured the continuity of the family name (Numbers 27:4 & 8, and 36:8). The relationship is one of mutual respect and responsibility: Children are to honor their parents as God's representatives here on earth (Exodus 20:12; Leviticus 19:3; Proverbs 1:8 & 30:17), and parents are obligated to instruct their children and "to lead them in ways of virtue and righteousness" [JE] according to Hebrew Scriptures, for example, Deuteronomy 6:6-7;

---

[6] When referencing the Babylonian (and Palestinian) Talmuds, the tradition has been that the initial page is "a" and its obverse "b." Thus BT *Kiddushin* 71 a and *Shabbat* 22a. Individual volumes—*Kiddushin* and *Shabbat*—are referred to as "Tractates." As Judaism has evolved religiously, the Babylonian much more so than the Palestinian Talmud has become the authoritative source for the Jewish past and present. It is fuller, more complete, and its commentaries far more extensive than the Palestinian Talmud. The BT remains today the primary source for much of traditional Jewish education.

[7] Kaufmann Kohler and Adolph Guttmacher, "Family and Family Life," *Jewish Encyclopedia*, www.jewishencyclopedia.com.

Exodus 13:14-15 & 26.[8] As Orthodox rabbi, historian, and philologist Louis Isaac Rabinowitz (1906-1984) summed it up:

> This constant insistence upon the value of family as a social unit for the propagation of domestic and religious virtues and the significant fact that the accepted Hebrew word for marriage is *kiddushin*, "sanctification," had the result of making the Jewish home the most vital factor in the survival of Judaism and the preservation of the Jewish way of life, much more than the synagogue or school. It was also a major factor for moral purity...The traditional Jewish home exemplified the maxim 'where there is peace and harmony between husband and wife the *Shekhinah* [God's Indwelling Presence] dwells between them.' A religious spirit of practical observance pervades it, from the *mezuzah*[9] on the doorpost to the strict observance of the dietary laws in the kitchen. The home was the center of religious practice and ceremonial.[10]

Living far from the major city-centers of Jewish religious life in pre-World War I and II Poland-Lithuania, Lemkin's was a close-knit family of father Joseph, mother Bella, and sons Samuel,[11] Elias, and Raphael. (Only brothers Elias, the oldest son, and Raphael, the middle son, would survive the Second World War; Raphael escaping to the United States, and Elias and his family to Canada.) As was normative Jewish tradition, among the mother's primary responsibilities was the raising of her children until they were old enough to attend traditional religious schools; that his mother Bella

---

[8] Jews do not refer to their sacred scriptures by the Christian designation "Old Testament," but, religiously, use the term Torah (literally "path," "way" or "guide." Academically, these same set of texts—Genesis through Chronicles II are referred to as the Hebrew Bible.

[9] A *mezuzah* (Hebrew, literally "doorpost") is a piece of parchment contained within a decorative case and inscribed with specific verses from the Hebrew Bible (Deuteronomy 6:4-19 and 11:13-21). These verses include the central affirmation of Jewish faith, "Sh'ma [Listen] Israel: the LORD is our God, the Lord alone."

[10] Louis Isaac Rabinowitz, "Family," *Encyclopedia Judaica*, Second Edition, Volume 6 (Detroit, 2007), 695.

[11] William Korey (1922-2009) states that "The youngest Samuel died, probably of tuberculosis, during World War I," but does not indicate the source of this information. See William Korey, *An Epitaph for Raphael Lemkin* (New York, 2001), 5.

did so brilliantly, imbuing her three sons with a love of learning and intellectual curiosity would sustain Lemkin all his life, as he records in his still-unpublished full autobiography *Unofficial Man*.[12] Though the family appears to have lived too far to practice regular synagogue Sabbath attendance, there is no reason whatsoever to suggest that their home rituals did not include the *major* observances of the Sabbath, Rosh Ha-Shana (New Year), Yom Kippur (Fast of Atonement), Sukkot (Festival of Booths), Chanukah (Festival of Dedication), Purim (Festival of Esther), Pesach (Festival of Passover), and Shavuot (Festival of Weeks).[13] In all likelihood, such observances were shared with his father's brother's family who also lived, worked, and jointly-owned the family farm. Reading the aforementioned *Unofficial Man*, especially Chapter 2 entitled "Early Childhood," Cooper notes:

> ...the fact that these teachers [both itinerant and resident in a nearby unspecified village, and possibly the location of the synagogue] had eaten chicken in Lemkin's home seems to suggest that the family kept a kosher[14] kitchen. A number of boys from the village came to Bella's house to join the teacher's classes. Lessons started at six o'clock in the winter mornings, the only warmth in the room coming from a kerosene lamp, and the teacher taught the [Hebrew] Bible with such reverence and love that some of this feeling was imparted to his pupils and Lemkin made rapid progress.[15]

[12] For a lengthy excerpt, see Raphael Lemkin, "Totally Unofficial Man," in Samuel Totten and Steven Leonard Jacobs, eds., *Pioneers of Genocide Studies* (New Brunswick, 2002), 365-399.

[13] John Cooper, however, notes that "Saul Lemkin [Elias' son, interviewed by J. C. 12 August 2004] recalled that his grandfather, Joseph, the father of Raphael, went to synagogue on every Sabbath. [He does not say where or whether his sons accompanied him, put on *tefillin* (phylacteries) every day, and celebrated all the festivals.] He was a gentle and hardworking man." John Cooper, *Raphael Lemkin and the Struggle for the Genocide Convention* (London and New York, 2008), 8. This assessment is somewhat at odds with William Korey's undocumented comment, "Lemkin, like his parents, was indifferent to Orthodox Judaism and was not attracted to Zionism." William Korey, *An Epitaph for Raphael Lemkin*, 6.

[14] While usually associated with the dietary system (i.e. no pork, shellfish or mixing milk and meat and all eatable animals slaughtered according to religiously-specified standards), the actual Hebrew word *kasher* means "fit," that is, properly prepared according to the Jewish religious tradition. For example, the prayer shawl worn at worship, *tallit*, when made properly, is "kosher."

[15] John Cooper, *Raphael Lemkin and the Struggle for the Genocide Convention*, 8.

Thus, we see early on, the centrality of the Jewish family reflected not only in their love of learning but intertwined as well with the Jewish religious tradition, whether or not strictly or liberally observed.[16]

Hinukh/Education

Among the primary values of Jewish family life was that of *hinukh* or education, initially that of traditional Jewish education—defined as the knowledge of the textual sources of Judaism: Torah/Hebrew Bible, Talmud, Midrash, and Law Codes; *Siddur, Makhzor,* and *Hagaddah* (prayer books), and *Musar* (ethics)—with the stated goal of Jewish religious observance. However, beginning at the end of the 18th and start of the 19th centuries and continuing, university education was included as well as Jews more and more were admitted to and hungered for secular education and the economic and political opportunities presented by them as well. Lemkin's life was reflected of both. Again, John Cooper:

> As was customary for children between the ages of three and five years, one winter he was enrolled in a *heder*, the Jewish elementary school. His teacher lived in a nearby [unspecified] village, in the house of Bella, a playmate of Lemkin's, to whom he was attracted. Because in previous years itinerant teachers had taught Lemkin to read Hebrew in a competent fashion, he and his brother [Elias] joined a higher education class to study the [Hebrew] Bible...The following winter the teacher taught Lemkin about the Prophets. Phrases such as the following melted into the boy's memory: 'Cease to do evil; learn to do well; relieve the oppressed; judge the fatherless; plead for the widow.' These words stirred the imagination of the young Lemkin, and he was equally moved by Isaiah's message for nations to beat swords into plowshares.[17]

Thus, as Cooper notes and correctly so, Jewish religious education, is, ultimately, composed of two parts: the ritual-ceremonial

---

[16] It should be noted, perhaps, that Lemkin's family was what we today call Jewishly traditionally observant rather than *strictly* "Orthodox," and decidedly *not* Hasidic. Liberal or Reform Judaism, birthed in 1810 in Session, Germany, was confined to the larger cities such as Warsaw.

[17] John Cooper, *Raphael Lemkin and the Struggle for the Genocide Convention*, 8-9.

and the moral-ethical, both having equal weight in Judaism. "The moral and religious training of the people from childhood up was regarded by the Jews from the very beginning of their history as one of the principal objects of life...All the festivals and ceremonies have for their object the inculcation of religious and moral lessons in the children...Many rabbinical sayings indicate the extraordinary value placed by the Rabbis on education, on the school, and on the teachers" [JE] Indeed, as William W. Brickman (1913-1986), Founder and President (1956-1959 and 1967-1968) of the Comparative and International Education Society, wrote:

> The Jewish people has an educational tradition as old as history...From the very beginning of their identification as a distinct entity, Jews have contributed not only to the advancement of their own education, but to that of the world at large...ancient Jewish education anticipated, and not doubt indirectly and remotely influenced, modern education...For most of their history, Jews educated their children in their own institutions and expressed their educational ideas in their own languages, until the late 18th century.[18]

Strongly influenced by a mother who was herself both a student and teacher of her own children of philosophy, literature, and languages, in a home filled with books, Lemkin would master Polish, German, Hebrew, Russian, Yiddish, and, later, French and Spanish, and other languages as well, attending Jewish parochial schools, the town's/village's public schools, and, later, the University of Lvov in Poland, and the University of Heidelberg in Germany, seeking a career in law, a profession already well-valued within his own Jewish community. That his childhood extensive reading of what we today may call genocide—a term he himself coined—led him, ultimately to purse international law is self-evident.[19] In addition, because the

---

[18] William W. Brickman, "Education, *Encyclopedia Judaica*, Second Edition, Volume 6: 159. See also the lengthier article "Education, Jewish," *Encyclopedia Judaica*, Second Edition, Volume 6 (Detroit, 2007), 162-214.

[19] For Lemkin's coinage of the term genocide and his early reading, see Steven Leonard Jacobs, "Genesis of the Concept of Genocide According to Its Author from the Original Sources," *Human Rights Review*, Vol. 3, No. 2 (2002): 98-103.

profession of teacher, and, ultimately, rabbi remains so revered among the Jewish people, Lemkin saw himself very much the scholar, though his published oeuvre was somewhat mixed.[20]

Hayyim v'Mavet/Life and Death

The boldest affirmation of Judaism's commitment to life as a supreme value and gift of God is that said out loud on the eve of the Sabbath after consecrating the sweet sacramental wine (Hebrew, *Kiddush*/Sanctification: "*Barukh Ata Adonai Elohenu Melekh haolam, Borai p're hagafen.*'Praised are You, our God, Ruler of the universe, Creator of the fruit of the vine."), "*L'hayyim*/To Life!" "Life is sacred, and it should accordingly be guarded and treated with due regard and tenderness in every being, man or beast." [JE] Two biblical statements, among many, many others, attest to this overriding value:

(1) "I have set before you life and death, blessing and curse; therefore *choose life*. (Deuteronomy 30:19; emphasis added.)

(2) "You shall keep my statutes and my ordinances, which if a man do he shall *live* by them." (Leviticus 18:4; emphasis added.)

Post-biblically, rabbinically, such statements as the following are further examples and affirmations of this primary value:

(1) "Whoever destroys a soul, it is considered as if he destroyed an entire world. And whoever saves a life, it is considered as if he saved an entire world. (Babylonian Talmud, *Sanhedrin,* 4:8a & 37a)

(2) *Pikuakh nefesh dokheh et haShabbat*/The saving of a life overrides (even the strictest laws of) the Sabbath. [Appears in numerous places in the Babylonian Talmud in a variety of phrasings.]

Such an affirmatively-positive value is part and parcel of normative Jewish religious education, and there is no reason whatsoever to

---

20 Steven Leonard Jacobs, "The papers of Raphael Lemkin: A first look," *Journal of Genocide Research,* Vol. 1, No. 1 (1999): 105-114.

suggest that Lemkin's own religious education fell short in this department. Thus, if anything, his commitment to punishing those guilty of the crime of genocide and preventing it from happening are testaments to and evidences of that commitment. What must be noted is that all four of the representative statements quoted above—two from the Torah/Hebrew Bible and two from the Babylonian Talmud—do *not* single out Israelites/Jews only as worthy; such values were understood by both their biblical predecessors and the rabbis later on as applicable to *all* humanity. Thus, Lemkin's work as a lawyer in Poland, as a teacher of law in the United States, as a legal and genocide scholar, as a member of the United States legal delegation to the International Military Tribunal at Nuremberg, Germany, at the end of World War II (20 November 1945 to1 October 1946), and his subsequent singular and obsessive devotion to the passage of the Genocide Convention are all evidences of his personal commitment to life in the aftermath of the Holocaust/Shoah[21] for *all* humanity.

Additionally, religious Judaism itself, over the long course of its history, has worked out a system of mourning procedures designed to bring the mourner back from the "valley of death" (Psalm 23) into the light of day. That system may be outlined as follows:

(1) *Aninut*: the period from the moment/announcement of death until the funeral when the family remains secluded and helped by extended family members and the closest of friends.

(2) *Shivah*: the period from the funeral for seven days (from the Hebrew word for the number seven) when the family's grief is at its most intense.

(3) *Sh'loshim*: the first thirty day period (from the Hebrew word for the number thirty) when, slowly, the mourner

---

21 While the English word "Holocaust" (said to be coined by Elie Wiesel [b. 1928] and its various permutations in other languages is universally recognized, more and more because of its origins within religion (Hebrew *'olah* translated as the Greek *holocaustos*—a totally consumable sacrifice to God), the Hebrew term *Shoah* ("Destruction" or "Devastation") is fast becoming its replacement. (Though the Hebrew language has no capitalizations as such, it is proper to do so in English when referring specifically to the wanton murders of the Jews between 1939 and 1945.)

attempts to reintegrate himself/herself back into normative life, and which, ultimately continues for eleven months.

(4) *Yahrtzeit*: the annual anniversary of the death of a beloved family member when the name is offered aloud in the synagogue at the end of the Sabbath worship service and associated with the traditional mourner's prayer, the *Kaddish* [Hebrew, Sanctification of God]. Traditionally, by the eleventh month after the death, the *matzevah* or monument/marker/gravestone has been placed in a Jewishly-consecrated cemetery at the head or foot of the grave.[22]

Among the traditions associated with honoring the memory of the deceased are visits to the cemetery on periodic and regular occasions (but *not* on the Sabbath and festivals), gifts directly to the synagogue and/or other communal institutions, and the like. Also, on the anniversary of the death of a loved one, it is Jewishly religiously traditional to light a twenty-four hour candle in memory (*Yahrtzeit* [German, "year-time"] anniversary).

For Lemkin, however, such normative Jewish religious practices appear not to have been the case with regard to his own family. He makes no references to such anywhere in his autobiography. Additionally, during his post-World War II life in New York prior to his death (1945-1959), there is no evidence of his active or inactive involvement in or participation in Jewish synagogue life, though Jews were themselves actively involved with him in urging passage of the Genocide Convention by the United Nations. For example, the U.S. Committee for a Genocide Convention was headed by James N. Rosenberg (1874-1970) of New York, a distinguished jurist and philanthropist and active in Jewish communal affairs.

---

[22] For a brief discussion of these practices, see Steven Leonard Jacobs, "Death, Burial, and Mourning" in *The Jewish Experience: An Introduction to Jewish History and Jewish Life* (Minneapolis, 2010), 161-164. In its evolution, Judaism has acknowledged two "circles" of mourners while not assessing the intensity of the grieving experience: those who take upon themselves the primary obligations—husband, wife, father, mother, brother, sister, son, and/or daughter. All others—family members and friends—may choose to do so but are not obligated to do so.

That having been said, we may further understand Lemkin's work as a fitting memorial tribute to his own mother Bella murdered by the Nazis. In an interview after the Genocide Convention was passed in December of 1948, he told a reporter that it would serve as a "fitting epitaph on my mother's grave."[23] Thus, the Genocide Convention—Lemkin's fitting and proper legacy—remains a "living memorial" not only to this mother but to the forty-nine members of his own family murdered by the Nazis, all Jewish and other victims of National Socialism, and, by extension, all previous and subsequent victims of genocidal barbarity.

Halakha/Law and *Tzedek*/Justice/Righteousness

The distinctive and singularly unique contribution of Judaism to any extended conversation regarding human behavior and that of the Divine-human encounter is contained within the Hebrew word *halakha*. Usually translated as "law," it is more properly understood as "path," "guide," or "way" (paralleling our understanding of the Hebrew word for the biblical corpus Torah), that is, concretely spelling out in behavioral terms how human beings should act in the two realms which comprise the Jewish religious tradition: ritual-ceremonial and moral-ethical. As leading Judaic scholar Jacob Neusner writes: "the Halakah then serves as the means for the translation of theological conviction into social policy."[24] Both their biblical forbearers and the rabbis themselves fully well realized that we human being function best individually, familially, and societally where behavioral boundaries are set and rewards and punishments are in place.[25] Thus, it is not surprising that in organized Jewish communal life, after the rabbi—who was himself historically expected to be a master of Jewish legal materials—the two most

---

[23] Gavriel Horan, "Call It Genocide: the man who coined the term 'genocide' also fought to make it an international crime." www.aish.com.

[24] Jacob Neusner, "Halakhah, Religious Meaning of," *The Encyclopedia of Judaism* (Leiden, 2003), CD-Rom Edition.

[25] The author's own *smikha*/rabbinical certificate of ordination, for example, has at its heart the Hebrew phrase *Yoreh yoreh. Yadin yadin*: "May he teach (Judaism)? Yes, he may teach (Judaism). May he adjudicate (Jewish) law? Yes, he may adjudicate (Jewish) law."

revered professions were and are the medical doctor and the lawyer. The university professor, initially denied to the Jews of Europe as non-Christians, now ranks a relatively close fourth, and, in the eyes of some, akin to a rabbinical parallel.[26]

It must also be pointed out that, after the codification of the Hebrew Bible in the year 90 CE, the next significant text was the *Mishnah* (Hebrew, "Second Teaching"), the operative laws of the Jewish community of Palestine assembled by its leader Rabbi Yehuda ha-Nasi in the year 220 CE, and which, in turn, gave rise to the expanded Palestinian and Babylonian Talmuds which are, at their center, extended commentaries and discussions of these laws. Later scholars such as Moses Maimonides (1135-1204) and Yosef Karo (1488-1575) would abstract out and restructure from these discussions the essences of these laws, Maimonides text being entitled *Mishneh Torah* ("Second Torah") and Karo's *Shulkhan Arukh* ("Set" or "Prepared Table").[27]

Assessing the system of *halakha* devised by the rabbis and building upon the "thou shalts" and the "thou shalt nots" of the Hebrew Bible, Wilhelm Bacher (1850-1913), Hungarian Jewish scholar and rabbi, and Ludwig Blau (1861-1936), Hungarian scholar, wrote that "these [rabbinic] scholars, all working without compensation, evolved a legal system which in scope and excellence stands far above the period of civilization for which and in which it was created."[28]

Regarding the aforementioned interface between Jewish legal traditions and its moral obligations:

> Many significant principles inform and direct Jewish law in the ethical arena. Primary among these is the mandate to imitate the

---

[26] Interestingly enough, in both nineteenth century and later academic writing on the Pharisees and their rabbinic successors, both groups were sometimes referred to as "Doctors of the Law (of Judaism)."

[27] Karo, like Maimonides was a Sephardic or Spanish/Mediterranean Jew (versus an Ashkenazic or Germanic Jew). Moses Isserles (1520-1572) wrote his own Germanic commentary on Karo's work and emphasized the different religious practices between the two communities. He called his work *Mapakh* ("Tablecloth").

[28] Wilhelm Bacher and Ludwig Blau, "Talmudic Law," www.jewishencyclopedia.com, 2002.

> divine (*imitatio dei*), which provides the adherents of Jewish law to seek to function in an ethical and just manner, aspiring to do as the divine would...Second, Jewish tradition recognizes the related mandate of *tikkun olam*, "fixing the world," which imposes a duty on members of society to seek to improve the daily life of God's creatures through a variety of socially constructive projects.[29]

Indeed, Lemkin himself addressed this very interface in a two-part piece entitled "The Legal Case Against Hitler" in the American left-of-center publication *The Nation* on 24 January and 10 March 1945. There he wrote:

> The interpretation of the law *must* have a social meaning; otherwise it overrules itself intellectually...it destroys the very foundations of its own existence...Legal technicalities and niceties have been and must continue to be *subordinate to the basic principles of human conscience and responsibility*. International law should be an instrument for human progress and justice, not an obstacle to them.[30]

Such understandings are framed, however and always, by a biblical underpinning with which Lemkin most certainly would have been familiar, and about which Saul Berman, leading Orthodox rabbi and scholar wrote:

> First, the very unity of morality and law in the Pentateuch [Five Books of Moses] created a new basis of authority for the behavioral precepts of Hebrew civilization. Secondly, in the Torah individualistic morality gave way to national morality which was addressed to the people of Israel as a corporate moral entity...Thirdly, despite the exclusivity of the covenantal relationship between God and the Jewish people, God's role in

---

[29] Emanuel Rackman (1919-2008), Michael Broyde, and Amy Fishkin, "Halakhah, Law in Judaism," *The Encyclopedia of Judaism* (Leiden, 2003), CD-Rom Edition.

[30] Raphael Lemkin, "The Case Against Hitler," *The Nation*, 24 February 1945, 205. Emphases added.

> the enforcement of legal-moral behavioral norms is clearly pictured as universal.[31]

Finally, the biblical concept of *tzedek*—justice or righteousness—may be best understood as "righteous obligation," and demands of the Jewish person that he or she function as such at all times. Hence, *Tzedek, tzedek tirdof*/"Justice, justice shall you pursue" (Deuteronomy 16:18) remains a moral mandate throughout all Jewish history, as well as its variant *Ashrei shomrei mishpat oseh tzedek b'khol ate*/"Happy are they that keep justice and do righteousness at all times" (Psalm 106:3).

Summarizing these understandings on the issue of justice, Rabbi Gilbert S. Rosenthal, Executive Director of the National Council of Synagogues in the United States, has it: "Judaism is a faith that eschews quietism and indifference to the sufferings of others, that decries and denounces injustices perpetrated against all peoples—not just Jews—and that calls upon its adherents to work tirelessly and passionately for the establishment of God's kingdom of justice and righteousness here on earth."[32]

Thus, Lemkins' own choice of profession—law—was in accord with the Jewish religious tradition's understanding of one's responsibility to work towards a better world as well as the principle of *tikkun olam*, fixing a world which was broken as it most assuredly was in the aftermath of the Second World War. His childhood reading of *Quo Vadis* predisposed him towards that sense of obligation; and the fact that the focus of this text was the non-Jewish/Christian victims of Roman Emperor Nero' s (37-68 CE) genocidal practices furthered that sense of universal obligation to all humanity with which the Jewish religious tradition has been concerned as well. Lemkin, as has been previously stated, was a product of a solid Jewish religious education in which he would have studied Torah/Hebrew Bible and Babylonian Talmud (in which was embedded the *Mishnah*). In all likelihood he would have also studied

---

[31] Saul Berman, "Law and Morality," *Encyclopedia Judaica,* Second Edition, Volume 12 (Detroit, 2007), 535.

[32] Gilbert S. Rosenthal, "Judaism's Pursuit of Justice," *Midstream,* Summer 2010, 30.

the *Shulkhan Arukh*/Code of Jewish Law, and, possibly, but not necessarily Maimonides' *Mishneh Torah*. Given his own psychological orientation to the pain of others, these texts could not but have influenced him in preparation for his life's work.

K'lal Yisrael/Jewish Community

Equally a part of Lemkin's training, embedded into those educational texts and religious practices, would have been his teachers' obligation to remind their charges that *Kol Yisrael areivim zeh l'zeh*/"All Israel are responsible one for another." (Babylonian Talmud *Shavuot*, 39a) Even while universalizing his quest for international anti-genocidal legislation, his magnum opus *Axis Rule in Occupied Europe: Laws of Occupation, Analysis of Government, Proposals for Redress* lists twenty-three sub-entries in its Index for "Jews," and includes such topics as "anti-Jewish legislation," "denial of wages" to," "deportation," "exclusion from professions," "forced labor," and "genocide," among others. His sense of obligation to his fellow Jews, especially his own family murdered by the Nazis during World War II (though he genuinely did not know their fate at the time of the book's publication, but could only surmise their tragic end), and, by extension, the other victims as well, is further related in his comment taken from that unpublished autobiography:

> Soon I transferred my personal disaster into a moral striking force. Was I not under a moral duty to repay my Mother for having stimulated in me the interest in Genocide? Was it not the best form of gratitude to make a "Genocide pact" as an epitaph on her symbolic grave and as a common recognition that she and many millions of others did not die in vain? I redoubled my efforts and found temporary relief from my grief in that work.[33]

In a lecture entitled "The Legacy of Raphael Lemkin," delivered by then-Professor Michael Ignatieff of Harvard University

---

[33] Steven Leonard Jacobs (2010), "The Human, the Humane, and the Humanitarian: Their Implications and Consequences in Raphael Lemkin's Work on Genocide," in *Rafal Lemkin: A Hero of Humankind,* ed. Agnieszka Bieńcyk-Missala and SŁawomir Dębski (Warsaw, 2010), 154.

and now leader of the Liberal Party of Canada and leader of the Official Opposition in Canada, at the United States Holocaust Memorial Museum in Washington, DC, said of Lemkin: "Lemkin remained trapped by the hopeful optimism of a civilization in twilight, just as he was trapped, I think, by another illusion, which is that Western Civilization is universal."[34] A Judaic reading of both his "hopeful optimism" and his "delusion" would find Lemkin thoroughly ensconced in a religious tradition which, despite the seemingly overwhelming odds against success, continues to strive for it, despite its setbacks (including the Holocaust/Shoah), and understands its followers fully committed to realizing both the visions and the goals enumerated above.

Shalom/Peace

Finally, or perhaps firstly, there is no more important ideal in the whole of religious Judaism than that of *shalom*/peace. There are so very many statements throughout the whole of religious Judaism and its texts—which Lemkin would have undoubtedly studied and with which he would have been familiar—that the following are only representative examples:

(1) "Love truth and peace." (Zechariah 8:19)
(2) "For the sake of peace, truth may be sacrificed." (Babylonian Talmud, *Yevamot,* 65b)
(3) "The whole Torah exists only for the sake of peace." (Babylonian Talmud, *Gittin*, 59b)
(4) "By three things is the world preserved: by truth, judgment, and peace." (*Pirkei Avo*t/Sayings of the Fathers,[35] 1:18)
(5) "Love peace and pursue peace." (*Pirkei Avot*/Sayings of the Fathers, 1:12)
(6) "Great is peace, for the priestly benediction [Hebrew, *Birkat Cohahim*, Numbers 6:24-26) closes with peace." (*Sifrei*/Commentary to Numbers, 6:26)[36]

[34] Michael Ignatieff, "The Legacy of Raphael Lemkin," www.ushmm.org, 2005.

[35] "Fathers" = the earliest rabbinic scholars.

[36] *Yisa Adonai panav alekha, v'yasem l'kha shalom.*/"May God lift up your face to His and give you peace."

Thus, given the realities of Jewish history, both that about which Lemkin would have surely read and been taught by his teachers and his mother Bella, and that which he would have experienced in the antisemitic world of pre-World War I Poland-Lithuania and the outbreak of the Second World War, and his flight ultimately to the United States in 1941, the Jewish dream of *shalom*/peace is very much a part of his story and his determination to secure the passage of the 1948 United Nations Convention on the Punishment and Prevention of the Crime of Genocide. In the aftermath of the Holocaust/Shoah and the growing realization that not only his own immediately family were its victims but millions of his fellow Jews and others as well, and that his reading of history saw episode after episode of the victims of genocide paraded before his memory, one cannot help but conclude that the ages-old dream of *shalom*/peace for Jews as well as for all humanity framed everything that was precious to him both as a Jew and as a human being. To divorce Raphael Lemkin the universal legal fighter for all humanity, especially its victims of genocide, from Raphael Lemkin the Jew is to tell an incomplete story. Ideally, this contribution further completes that telling.

"American Religious Voices and the Holocaust: *Mizrahi* and *Agudat Yisrael* Responses"

Gershon Greenberg
American University

Mizrachi—The Religious Nationalists

Representative *Mizrahi* perspectives have included different views about the role of America. Aharon Halevi Petshenik, who situated the Holocaust between exile and redemption, held that redemption was imminent, its vessel was the Land of Israel, and that American Jewry must dedicate itself to restoring the Land towards that end. During World War II, Gedaliah Bublick blamed America for failing to stand up for the people of Israel in the great struggle between the forces of Jacob and the forces of Esau. After the war, he hoped that American Jewry, as the new center of world Judaism, would serve as the impetus for universal democratic civilization and become a partner with the *Yishuv* in developing Judaism's future.

Petshenik

Petshenik (born in Ostra, Volyn in 1940), the son of Rabbi Nahum Yehoshua Petshenik of Dombrovitch, a brother in law of Yissakhar Dov, *Admo"r* of Belz, studied at Meir Balaban's Tahkemoni Rabbinical Seminary in Warsaw and came to New York in the 1920s.[1] Beginning with *Kristallnacht*, he formulated a correlation between persecution and redemption. Israel was not frightened by the "midget" Hitler, the people having endured so much in the past and knowing that persecution implied redemption. After he attended the

[1] Petshenik returned *via* Vladivostok and Tokyo. Petshenik, "Raban shel yisrael [Aharon Rokeah]," in *Ha'rav ha'kadosh mi'belza*, ed. Betsalel Landau and Natan Ortner (Jerusalem, 1967): 258-260; Petshenik, *Tsiyonim un idishkayt in sovet-rusland. Ah rayze ibern sovetn-farband in 1940*, forward by Meir Berlin (New York, 1943); Petshenik, "Khronikah shel shoshelet hasidit ahat," in *Shanah be'shanah* (1966/67): 379-396; and "Avi mori ha'rav hashem yinkom damo," in *Shanah be'shanah* (1967/68): 497-50). Petshenik served as editor of *Shanah be'shanah* through 1974.

August 1939 Zionist Congress in Geneva, he traveled in western Poland and Russia, and Hasidim in Siberia told him how they were motivated to survive because the Radzhiner Rav Shemuel Shelomoh Layner identified the era as the *Hevlei mashiah* and predicted that the messiah would first appear in Russia. Petshenik believed that the metahistorical process would be channeled through the Land of Israel, and it was imperative for Jews of the *Yishuv* to return to *Torah* as they restored the Land itself.[2] When Hitler's forces stopped before invading Palestine in May 1941, Petshenik took this as a sign of imminent redemption.[3]

The correlative process required a new mindset. Abraham ibn Ezra observed (*ad Exodus* 14:13) that the camp of 600,000 people were so afraid of the Egyptian pursuers that they would not go to war against them. Having internalized their lowly status as slaves, they resorted to prayer instead. The generation of the exodus had to die out, so a new one could begin, one capable of taking the land. Twentieth century Jews corrupted by the "flesh pots" of exile (See *Deuteronomy* 32:5) resisted return. The interwar generation had to die away, to make room for a new generation, with the ability to take the land. Petshenik spoke of a forty year period—alluding to the year when World *Mizrahi* was founded.[4] As ancient Jews, intimidated by *Amalek,* suffered the death of the males so that a new, unfettered generation could arise, the interwar generation which failed to fight its "*Amalek*" suffered the death of men, women and children so that a fresh generation could arise. Petshenik cited Halevi: "The trials which meet us are meant to prove our faith, to cleanse us completely

---

[2] Petshenik, "In den pamlia shel ma'alah," *DMV*, Vol. 3, No. 1 (September 1938): 4; Petshenik, "Al ha'nisim ve'al ha'gevurot," *DMV*, Vol. 3, No.. 2 (December 1938): 2; Petshenik, *Tsiyonizm*; Petshenik, "Unzer vafen," *DMV*, Vol. 3, No.. 4 (March 1939): 3; Petshenik, "Tsadikei rizhin ve'tshernobol le'erets yisrael," in *Hasidut ve'tsiyon*, ed. Simon Federbush (New York, 1963).

[3] Petshenik, "Al ha'nisim ve'al ha'niflaot," *DMV*, Vol. 6, No. 1 (September 1941): 6, 15.

[4] Petshenik, "Al ha'nism ve'al ha'niflaot;" Petshenik, "Der mizrahi oyf sheydeveg," *DMV*, Vol. 8, No. 3 (November 1943): 7, 13; Petshenik, "Galut un geulah," *DMV*, Vol. 8, No. 6 (March 1944): 5, 13; Petshenik, "Oyfn erets yisrael front," *DMV*, Vol. 5, No. 4 (March 1941): 3.

and to remove all taint from us. If we are good, the divine influence is with us in this world" (*Kuzari* 2:44) (See *Ezekiel* 20:37-38, 22:22).[5]

Following the war, Petshenik addressed memorializing the six million holy ones as a *Tikkun* for their tragic deaths. While the Blozhover Rav Yisrael Shapira (a concentration camp survivor who was now in New York, 1891-1989) suggested the composition of a new *Sefer Torah* in eternal memory to their souls, and the Radzhiner Rav Avraham Yissakhar Anglard sought to have their ashes gathered for reburial in the Land of Israel, Petshenik thought in terms of creating independent life for Jews in a land of their own, where they would defend themselves.[6] American Jewry should both help the victims of the *Hurban* and restore the Land. During Petshenik's sojourn in Eastern Europe, Aharon Levin of Reysha, Mosheh Friedman of Bayon and Zusha Tversky of Rave-Ruska (brother in law of the *Admo"r* of Belz) prevailed upon him to appeal to American Jews, who surely would help.[7] During the war, he called upon American Jewry, which was now flourishing, to serve as an older brother to the orphan in Europe, and dedicate itself to the Land of Israel—whose agricultural development was itself a sign of redemption. Appropriately, he observed, the March 1943 assembly of American *Mizrahi* convened with *Psalms* 140 ("Deliver me, O Lord, from the evil men"), the *Star Spangled Banner* and *Ha'tikvah*.[8]

---

[5] See also Petshenik, "Di shturm fun blut;" Petshenik, "A bashuldigung un a varnung," Vol. 2, No. 4 (January 1938): 9.

[6] Petshenik, "Vi tsu fareybigen andenk fun zekhs million idishe kadoshim," *DMZ*, Vol. 45, No. 13, 593 (20 June 1946): 4, 6. On gathering the ashes see Gershon Greenberg, "To Stay or To Go? Orthodox Considerations," *Polish Historical Review* (2013, forthcoming).

[7] Petshenik, "Ven der shturm hot hat oysgebrokhen," *DMV*, Vol. 7, No. 3 (December 1942): 6, 10 Petshenik, "Mizrahi konvenshen [14-16 March 1943]," *DMV*, Vol. 7, No. 5 (March-April 1943): 6-17; Petshenik, "Va'ad hatsalah," in *Di oyftun fun amerikaner mizrahi far hizuk ha'torah veha'yahadut* (New York, 1943): 8. See also Petshenik, "An ernst vort vegen dem angevegten inyan: Diskriminatsies fun va'ad hatsalah," *DMV*, Vol. 11, No. 5 (February 1947): 8-9; Petshenik, "Derklerung fun mizrahi vegen der frage fun di plitim kinder in erets yisrael," *DMV*, Vol. 4, No. 5 (February 1945): 1, 5; Petsheni, Retungs konferents in bazel hot klagen gegen va'ad hatsalah," *DMV*, Vol. 11, No. 4 (January 1947): 2, 13.

[8] Petshenik, "An entfer tsum artikel von dr. vays rosmarin, 'Di durkhfalen fun der ortodoksie,'" *DMV*, Vol. 5, No. 1 (September 1944): 2-3; Petshenik, "Di amerikaner stsene," *DMV*, Vol. 4, No. 6 (March 1945): 6, 14; Petshenik, "Mizrahi konvenshon eyngehilt in tsar un troyer oyf dem shreklikhen hurbn fun di milyonen iden. Fordern ah idishe medinah [14-

Using classical sources, Petshenik verified his correlation between suffering and redemption, as effectuated through the restoration of the Land of Israel (with the support of American Jewry). While he recoiled from probing the secrets behind the catastrophe, or trying to justify the deaths, he was certain that the murder of 1,200,000 children and the destruction of *Torah* was tied to God's loving intervention: "Chastisements come to Israel only out of God's love for her" (*Tanna de'be eliyahu zuta*, ch. 11). The suffering was tied to Israel's mission in the world to inherit the land to send forth the *Torah* from it (*Deuteronomy* 4:20, 26:17-18) ("It is the eternally inescapable duty ... of everyone belonging to the stock of Jacob to abide by the law." Rambam, *Igeret teman*), as it cleansed Israel from any sinful failure to do so: "Just as the olive produces its oil only after pounding, so Israel returns to the right way only after suffering" (*Menahot* 53^{b}). Redemption would come once purification was complete. It was also inevitable: The same God who poured out his anger over Israel (*Isaiah* 29:13-14, *Ezekiel* 19:20) was endlessly merciful. Exile, repentance, ingathering and redemption implied one another (Nahmanides *ad Leviticus* 26:16).[9] Yehudah Halevi admonished Israel not to emulate their predecessors in Babylon, who preferred dependence and slavery and thereby obstructed God's restoration of the Temple: "Divine Providence was ready to restore everything as it had been at first, if they had all willingly consented to return." Hayim ibn Attar (1696-1743) held that: "Redemption will awaken the hearts of men saying, Is it good for you to sit outside, exiled from the table of your fathers? And what guarantees your life

---

16 March 1943]," *DMV*, Vol. 7, No. 5 (March-April 1943): 6-17; Petshenik, "Problemen fun tsiyonistishen kongres," *DMV*, Vol. 10, No. 8 (June 1946): 3, 23; Petshenik, "Shver tsu zayn an amerikaner gast: Eyndrukn fun mayn erets yisrael rayze," *DMV*, Vol. 11, No. 7 (April 1947): 2, 10. See also Petshenik, "Fun torah-dikn erets yisrael," *YS*, Vol. 1, No.. 22 (9 May 1947): 5-6; Petshenik "Di nisim fun undzere teg," *YS*, Vol. 2, No. 44 (September 1948): 5; Petshenik, "Di shturm fun blut," *DMV*, Vol. 12, No. 2 (October 1947): 3; Petshenik, "Dos groyse tsoybervort," *DMV*, Vol. 10, No. 5 (February 1946): 6; Petshenik, "Torat hayim un teokratie," *DMV*, Vol. 10, No.. 6 (March 1946): 7, 14; Petshenik, "Medinat ivrit be'erets ha'ivrim lifnei avraham," in *Shanah be'shanah* (1970/71): 237-247; and "Ha'hinukh ha'dati be'artsot ha'berit," in *Shanah be'shanah* (1962/63): 476-488.

[9] See also Petshenik, "Der hekherer zin fun teshuvah," *DMV*, Vol. 12, No. 5 (September 1947): 3, 15.

in the [exiled] world *vis a vis* the higher fellowship?" Ya'akov Emden (1697-1776) called upon Jews to leave the false Jerusalems in exilic *Tumah*, where they suffered at the hands of their enemies without respite (see *Leviticus* 26:38), for the true Jerusalem. The Hofets Hayim (1838-1933) observed that while justice prevailed in God's judgment (*Psalms* 19:9), man had to have long-term experience to comprehend it. For example, upon seeing the ruins of the Temple, Rabbi Akiva knew that restoration was imminent—for once the prophecy during the days of Uriah were fulfilled (*Micah* 3:12), that of Zechariah would be fulfilled as well (*Zechariah* 8:4) [*Makkot* 24^{b}]. Ya'akov Mosheh Harlap (1883-1951) wrote that darkness and oblivion implied divine redemption, but the metahistorical passage from catastrophe to redemption required Israel's initiative.[10]

In sum, Petshenik understood the Holocaust as an act of divine love intended to align Israel with the metahistorical passage from exile to redemption. Insofar as suffering was inherent to Israel's metahistory, catastrophe was inevitable. Nevertheless, the Holocaust could have been avoided had the people taken the initiative and gone to the Land of Israel in time. God let the hesitant and resistant generation of the interwar period be destroyed so that an assertive generation would take hold. Now the people of Israel, led by religious nationalists, had to go to the Land, and participate there in the redemptive process. Petshenik called upon American Jewry to commit itself to supporting the process.

Bublick

Gedaliah Bublick (1875 Grodno – 1948 New York), who grew up in Bialystok and studied in Lomza and Mir yeshivas, arrived in New York in 1902. A Yiddish and Hebrew journalist, he served as

---

[10] Yehudah Halevi, *Kuzari* 2:24; Ya'akov Mosheh Harlap, "*Tehillim* 13:2" and "*Tehillim* 18:1," in Y. Gerstenkorn, *Na'im zemirot yisrael*, vol. 1 (Benei Berak, 1955): 390, 408; Ya'akov Emden, "Hakdamah," in *Siddur amudei shamayim* (Tel Aviv, 1966): 31; Hayim ibn Attar, "Va'yikra…," in *Or ha'hayim* (Warsaw 1862 [1742]): 20b; Petshenik, "Onesh, segulah, ve'yiud: Be'shulay ha'poraniut veha'nehamot shel dorenu," *Or ha'mizrah* 3 nos. 3-4 (August-September 1957): 61-66.

Vice President of American Mizrahi.[11] In his writings in the 1920s he described antisemitism as a conflict between the forces of Jacob and those of Esau, which were separated by an abyss, which would last forever. The economic discrimination and scapegoating, antagonism towards Jewish law, Christian and Muslim triumphalism, were all too deeply rooted—not even a Jewish polity would bring respect for Israel. At the same time, it was not antisemitism which threatened Israel's existence, nor racial distinction—whether used positively (Aha'd Ha'am) or negatively (De Gobineau, Wagner, Houston Stewart Chamberlain). Israel's existence was based upon *Torah*, and the threat to its existence came from the sort of materialism and unrestrained assimilation represented by America—i.e., Reform and Conservative Judaism.[12]

Following *Kristallnacht*, he condemned modern civilization for its absence of religious culture and its obliviousness to ultimate questions about human identity. Fascism and Nazism replaced it.[13] As Christopher Dawson concluded, "Modern civilization not only ceased being Christian; it set itself up as an anti-religion which claimed sole mastery of the world."[14] Carl Schmitt spoke of blanket recognition of "might as right," of the human being, entirely free to indulge in natural wickedness.[15] Nietzsche's anti-moral, instinct-

---

[11] See Gershon Greenberg, "Jerusalem, Vilna and Chicago: Gedaliah Bublick's Wartime Dilemma," in *America and Zion: Essays in Honor of Mosheh Davis*, ed. Jonathan Sarna (Detroit, 2002): 255-276. Petshenik, "Der zibetsig-yeriger yubileum fun gedalyah bublik," *DMZ,* Vol. 10, No. 1 (October-November 1945): 3; Y. Bistritzer, "R. gedalyah bublik z"l," YS 25 (9 April 1948): 2; Petshenik and A. Gelman, "Mi'toldotav," in *Gedalyah bublik z"l: Ketavim nivharim*, Vol. 1 (Jerusalem 1962): 7-9; Editor, "R. gedalyah bublik z"l," *YS,* Vol. 2, No. 28 (May 1948): 4.

[12] Bublick, *Min ha'metsar* (New York, 1923); Bublick, "Ha'rav kook—rav, dikhter un filosof" and "Di kraft fun aybikayt," in *Mayn rayze in erets yisrael* (New York, 1921): 331-338, 379; Bublick, "Di ziben zaylen fun antisemitizmus," and "Antisemitizmus an aybige zakh," and "Di reform in amerika," in *Min ha'metsar*, pp. 345-350, 357-362, 381-386; Bublick, "Kamf fun reform un idishkayt," "Konservatives yudentum," "Di rasen-teorie," and "Dos yudentum un di rasen-teorie," in *Der sakh ha'kal in amerikanem yudentum* (New York, 1927): 15-19, 40-44, 140-149.

[13] Bublick, "Hatsalat ha'enoshut," *Ha'yesod*, Vol. 8, No. 261 (29 March 1939): 1, 8.

[14] Christopher Dawson, *Religion and the Modern State* (London, 1935): 151.

[15] Carl Schmitt, *Der Begriff des Politischen* (Munich, 1932).

oriented, dismissive of right and wrong was revived by Hitler.[16] Life-blood was regarded as sacred, such as to devalue the pursuit of truth; in the new godless and blood-national (Nazi Germany) culture, Judaism's *Uebermensch*, the humble *Tsadik* (*Isaiah* 2:11, 17) who respected law and who opposed violence (*Psalms*18:48) and power of the sword (*Exodus* 15:9) became Nietzsche's *Untermensch*. For their part, German-Jewish thinkers dissolved Judaism's absolute *Torah* principles into general philosophy (Moses Mendelssohn, Solomon Formstecher, Samuel Hirsch and Solomon Ludwig Steinheim), while American Jews undermined their religion with secularism and assimilation.[17]

Bublick: Wartime

The dualism was radicalized during World War II. On one side there was the *Sitra ahra* (anti-being), evil and satanic idolatry: Tribal Teutonic barbarism, Germanity (of Johann Gottfried Fichte), egoism (of Max Stirner), the blond beast (of Chamberlain) and the Nazi bible *Mein Kampf* which was to be implemented by sword, whip and concentration camp. The attacks on *Kristallnacht* ("Juda verrecke")

---

[16] On Nietzsche and Hitler see also Yehudah Layb Gerst, *Peletat ben yehudah: Pirkei hagut u'mehkar* (Jerusalem, 1971); Y. Gan-Tsevi, "Hatsi nehamah," *Ha'tsofeh,* Vol. 4, No. 1139 (25 September 1941): 2; D. Yisrael, "Kelapei sanigoriyah al nietzshe," *Ha'tsofeh,* Vol. 5, No. 1342 (29 May 1942): 6; Mosheh Avigdor Amiel, "Hirhurei teshuvah," *Ba'mishor: Shevuon mizrahi be'sifrut ule'she'elot ha'zeman*, Vol. 3, No. 124 (14 August 1942): 2-3 through 4 no. 36 (13 November 1942): 2-3.

[17] Bublick, "Ken man di velt besser um shehner makhen?" *IV,* Vol. 1, No. 4 (30 October 1936): 2; Bublick, "Di volfishe filosofie vos farfihrt masen menshen," *IV*, Vol. 2, No. 69 (21 May 1937): 3; *IV*, Vol. 2, No. 70 (28 May 1937); Lev Shestov, *Dostoevski I Nitshe* (1922). "Mensh, 'oybermensh' un untermensh," *IV*, Vol. 2, No. 72 (11 June 1937): 2; *IV*, Vol. 2, No. 73 (18 June 1937): 2; Bublick, "Kamf fun avodah zarah gegen di nevi'im," *IV*, Vol. 2, No. 83 (27 August 1937): 3; 2 no. 84 (3 September 1937): 3; Bublick, "Unzer aybigen kamf gegen der 'avodah zarah'," *IV*, Vol. 2, No. 85 (10 September 1937): 2; 2 no. 85 (17 September 1937): 2; Bublick, "Der kval fun dos gute und nabele baym menshen," *IV*, Vol. 2, No. 76 (9 July 1937): 2; 2 no. 77 (16 July 1937): 3; Bublick, "Di iden zaynen an originale natsion," *IV*, Vol. 2, No. 51 (15 January 1937): 2; Bublick, "Der kamf for freyhaupt fun der menshlikher neshamah," *IV*, Vol. 2, No. 62 (2 April 1937): 2; *IV*, Vol. 2, No. 63 (9 April 1937): 2; Bublick, "Unzer shtelung tsum tsiyon kongress," *DMV*, Vol. 1, No. 8 (June-July 1937): 8; Bublick, "Di shtadt fun kedushah un aybikayt," *IV*, Vol. 2, No. 95 (19 November 1937): 2; Bublick, "Yerushalayim: Der zimbol fun yudentum," *IV*, Vol. 2, No. 97 (3 December 1937): 2.

and ultimately on the God of Israel, began a campaign against all civilized human beings; on morality and justice *per se.* As articulated by John MacMurray:

> [Fascism] succeeded in making the world of spirit—the world of freedom, equality and humanity, of ideals and religion and culture—another world; and *this* world has become, in consequence, a world of dark unconscious forces of destruction. It has insisted that the realization of humanity shall be postponed to another life, and so has made inhumanity the automatic law of this life. It has decided that the kingdom of God shall be a kingdom in heaven, and delivered this world over to the powers of darkness.[18]

On the other side stood civilization, centered around Judaism and (non-racist) Christianity, committed to morality and holiness in emulation of God (*Isaiah* 56:1).[19]

It was an either/or struggle. he Nazi assertion that man was the highest being and was to rule by physical force, constituted a denial of God and that God created the world for righteousness (*Micah* 6:8; *Midrash bereshit rabbah*, *Parashah* 26, *Siman* 6). The heroes of the lower world were now the *Uebermenschen* (Nietzsche), and animals of prey were regarded as noble (Oswald Spengler). According to Hitler, if a nation had the power to enslave, it had a natural and racial duty to do so—and was not accountable. Instead of perfecting the world in the name of God, he sought to perfect it in terms of power and impurity. Against this stood Judaism, England and America, which were rooted in Hebrew scripture; the England of the *Magna Carta* and Churchill,

---

[18] John MacMurray, *The Clue to History* (London 1938): 236.

[19] Bublick, "Tsvay generishe veltn," *Beit ya'akov literarishe shrift for shul un haym*, Vol. 16, No. 152 (November-December 1938): 7-8; Bublick, "Di zind vos die menshhayt iz bagangn tsu tsivilizatsie," *IV*, Vol. 5, No. 241 (6 September 1940): 2, 3; Bublick, "Bay vemn hitler hot gelerent zayn rasen teorie," *IV*, Vol. 5, No. 254 (20 December 1940): 2; Bublick, "F. Nitch'h-rabo shel hitler be'torat ha'sinah," *Ha'yesod*, Vol. 10, No. 352 (30 April 1942): 2; Bublick, "Der tamtsit fun gedalyah bublik's … referat iber itstiger politischer lage … problemen fun Mizrahi velt-konferenz," *DMV*, Vol. 3, No. 6 (June 1939): 12; Bublick, "Unzer politisher matsav [19 May 1940]," *DMV*, Vol. 4, No. 6 (June 1940): 10; Bublick, "Di vos farmesten zikh gegen iden gehen alayn unter," *IV*, No. 249 (6 December 1940): 2; Bublick, "Tsvay 'bibel-lender' vos kemfen for der menshhayt," *IV*, Vol. 6, No. 256 (24 January 1941): 2; Bublick, "Vos vet itst zany mit der velt un mit di iden?" *IV*, Vol. 6, No. 276 (11 July 1941): 2; Bublick, "Di rol fun di iden in dem itstigen velt-krizis," *IV*, Vol. 6, No. 253 (3 January 1941): 2.

the America of the *Constitution* and Roosevelt,[20] Bublick assured that Israel, having survived 4,000 years without political or physical power, would last—for it was tied to eternity.[21] As rooted in Israel's principles, the Allied nations would as well. Moreover, the current struggle was that of Gog and Magog, the pre-messianic war. At the end, Nazism would disappear from history—just as Babylon, Assyria, Greece and Rome.[22]

Israel's response was to be rooted in freedom: "'And the writing was the writing of God, graven upon the tables' [*Exodus* 32:15]…. Read not *Harut* (graven), but *Herut* (free) from captivity" (*Midrash shemot rabbah, Parashah* 41, *Siman* 7). Freedom required adhering to *Torah*, and adherence had to be active, with *Torah* renewed daily (*Joshua* 1:8), and with each generation adding to the ancient source. With the spiritual center in Europe destroyed, Jews in the rest of the diaspora and in the Land of Israel were obliged to build anew. It also required *Teshuvah*, turning to the God who awaited the return—as the Jews who once placed their faith in socialism or *Wissenschaft* performed *Teshuvah*, after they were forced to wear yellow patches and into concentration camps.[23] It also meant restoration of the Land of Israel—finally heeding the warnings of Leon Pinsker and Theodor Herzl that safety for the Jews of Warsaw, Cracow and

---

20 Bublick, "Milhemet ha'ruah veha'tsedek," *Ha'yesod*, Vol. 11, No. 368 (30 October 1942): 21; Bublick, "Tsvay bible-lender;" Bublick, "Tshoyrtshil un rozvelt bashitser fun tsivilizatsie," *IV*, Vol. 6, No. 257 (31 January 1941): 2-3; Bublick, "Amerika hat dem shlisel tsu ale fier problemen," *DMV*, Vol. 5, No. 6 (June 1941): 11; Bublick, "Di tsukunft iz unzere," *DMV*, Vol. 8, No. 8 (June 1944): 7.

21 Bublick, "Ma tsafui lanu le'maharat ha'nitsahon?" *Ha'yesod*, Vol. 12, No. 392 (25 May 1943): 2.

22 Bublick, "Shuvi enoshiut shuvi," *Ha'yesod*, Vol. 12, No. 397 (27 August 1943): 2; Bublick, "Unzer shtelung;" Bublick, "Oyf di vegen fun roym," *DMV*, Vol. 8, No. 6 (March 1944): 5.

23 Bublick, "Frayhayt in kayten iz nit kayn fantazie," *IV*, Vol. 6, No. 26 (26 February 1941): 2; Bublick, "Iden vos hoben zikh entoysht in der menshhayt," *IV*, Vol. 5, No. 238 (12 July 1940): 2; Bublick, "Farvos gloybige menshen tragen durkh laykhter perzenlikhe un velt krizisen?" *IV*, Vol. 7 no. 279 (1 August 1941): 2; Bublick, "Haziat yehudit ruhanit le'aharei ha'milhamah," *Ha'yesod*, Vol. 13, No. 413 (11 February 1944): 2.

Vienna lay in a Jewish state. The removal of the threat to the land by Hitler in summer 1942 offered a positive sign.[24]

Finally, the Jewish community in America had to be developed. When the nation was endangered in the past, it re-located to Babylon, Greece or Rome ("If Esau came to the one company and smite it, then the other company which is left, shall escape." *Genesis* 32:8). With the destruction in Europe, to the extent they preserved the roots of Eastern Europe, major cities of America (Chicago, Boston, Cleveland and New York), could and should become new centers of Judaism, the new Warsaw, Vilna and Cracow.[25] "The *Keneset yisrael* of America must become the bridge over which a great portion of Judaism is carried to our children's children, to Jewish eternity."[26]

Bublick: Postwar

Bublick's optimism about the Allies following Biblical precepts was finally shaken. In May 1943 he had observed that Britain and America did not perceive the bond between antisemitism and anti-democracy, and that opposing Nazism required defending Judaism. Otherwise they would have opened their doors for Jews.[27] Indeed, Allied leaders were oblivious to the nineteenth century theoretical grounding for Nazism and to the centrality of Jew-hatred to the Nazi campaign.[28] Oswald Mosley in England and Charles Caughlin in America spouted hatred of the Jews without restraint, even in 1944. Should the principles of truth and righteousness underlying Anglo-Saxon civilization continue to be threatened and antisemitism

---

[24] Bublick, "Politishe redes fun dr. hayim vaytsman, gedalyah bublik und ha'rav ze'ev gold: Gedalyah bublik's referat iber der politisher lage in tsiyonizm," *DMV*, Vol. 7, No. 5 (March-April 1943): 2-3.

[25] Bublick, "Dos yohr 5705," *DMV*, Vol. 9, No. 1 (September 1944): 5; Bublick, "Tshoyrtshil;" Bublick, "Amerika hot dem shlisel tsu ale fier problemen;" Bublick, "Der goral fun idisher folk iz itst oyfun vagshal," *IV*, Vol. 4, No. 275 (4 July 1941): 2-3.

[26] Bublick, "Di greste gefahr for iden yetst iz fartsvayflung," *IV*, Vol. 5, No. 231 (28 June 1948): 2.

[27] Bublick, "Ma tsafui lanu le'maharat ha'nitsahon?"

[28] Bublick, "Al ha'antishemiut lo hukhrazah milhamah," *Ha'yesod*, Vol. 13, No. 403 (29 October 1943): 2.

continued, Nazism would not end with the war.[29] In November 1947, Bublick concluded that the Allies indeed separated antisemitism from the defeat of Nazism: "They raised not the slightest objection—after all, the subject was only the Jews—as the neck [of Israel] was twisted by the demons until she choked to death." Jews were abandoned, to be hated forever.[30] His optimism about American Jewry was shaken as well. It cut itself off from Eastern European roots, its source of vitality. The one center left was the Land of Israel—which itself was a focus of antisemitism—thus the beating of Jews in D.P. camps who sought *Aliyah*.[31]

Still, Bublick kept hoping that the Biblical civilizations would join the people of Israel. The concentric relationship, Israel at the center and encircled by the civilized (Biblical) world, was an objective reality. The eternal Israel-of-*Torah* was always spread between the Land of Israel and diaspora centers (Babylon, Spain-Southern France, Poland or Lithuania) and this would continue. American Biblical civilization remained a positive environment for American Jews to become the focal point of the diaspora: "Will not a new Jewish people rise here to replace those lost in Europe?... What America is for the world, Judaism in America should be for the Judaism of the world, only to a far greater extent." That is, if American Jewry would "lift up the banner torn from the hands of dying Eastern European Jewry." This was not to say, Bublick added, that American Jewry was more important than the Jewry of the *Yishuv*: "Around these two [points] the Jewish communities of the world would find their points

---

29 Bublick, "Sha'atam shel ha'anglo sakhsim," *Ha'yesod*, Vol. 13, No. 425 (16 June 1944): 2; Bublick, "Haba'ayah ha'yehudit," *Ha'yesod*, Vol. 15, No. 436 (13 October 1944): 2; Bublick, "Torat ha'kezav ha'natsit she'nitbadah," *Ha'yesod*, Vol. 15, No. 439 (10 November 1944): 2.

30 Bublick, "Ha'amnam rak tehiyah leumit," *Ha'yesod*, Vol. 16, No. 554 (7 November 1947): 3.

31 Bublick, "Tsvay masen: Mir un di goy'she velt," *DMV*, Vol. 10, No. 3 (December 1945): 5; Bublick, "The New Season for Jews," *DMV*, Vol. 10, No. 5 (February 1946): 2, 4; Bublick, "Di velt gayt unter," *Basha'ar*, Vol. 23 (20 March 1947): 2; Bublick, "Di sprakh fun milhamah," *YS*, No. 26 (23 April 1948): 4.

of origin, and cooperate to the extent they could, to rescue the people from their greatest crisis."[32]

Da'at torah

Agudat yisrael thinkers emphasized that their reflections did not affect their faith, which remained intact. Eliyahu Meir Blokh (1894-1955) came to America *via* Siberia and Japan to fundraise for the Telshe yeshiva. He was unable to return and turned to establishing the Telshe yeshiva in Cleveland in 1941. Questioning God about the Holocaust was out of place, because questions tied to time did not apply to the God of eternity.[33] Yisrael Halevi Rosenberg (1875-1958), who studied in Slobodka and was ordained in Novaredok by Yehiel Mikhel Epstein, came to America in 1902 and served as president of *Agudat ha'rabanim*, and (with Eliezer Silver) as co-founder of Ezrat torah. He held that not even relentless persecution or the nation's failure to acknowledge sin affected Israel's faith. Faith was between Israel and God; not a function of the nations' treatment of the people of Israel over the course of history. The basis for reflection on the part of *Agudah* leaders was *Da'at torah*. It was the foundation of the world (metaphysical), present deeply within each Jew (personal), and the source of creative existence (metahistorical). *Torah* and Israel related reciprocally, giving life to one another, such that abandoning *Torah* removed Israel from the life of empirical history—although without affecting its trans-historical, ontic reality.[34]

---

[32] Bublick, "Di naye role fun amerika in idishen leben," *DMV*, Vol. 10, No. 2 (November 1945): 5; Bublick, "The New Season for Jews," *DMV*, Vol. 10, No. 5 (February 1946): 5; Bublick. "Hasel seder ayrope," *DMV*, Vol. 10, No. 6 (March 1946): 3; Bublick, "Der mizrahi oyf kumendigen kongres," *DMV*, No. 8 (June 1946): 5; Bublick, "Ortodoksen vos haben lib dem galut," *DMV*, Vol. 12, No. 1 (September 1947): 5.

[33] See Tamar Ross, "Ha'mahshavah ha'iyunit be'kitvei mamshikhov shel r. yisrael salanter bi'tenuat ha'musar" (Hebrew University dissertation 1986); and Gershon Greenberg, "Holocaust and Musar for the Telsiai Yeshiva," in *The Vanished Jews of Lithuania*, ed. Alvydas Nikzentaitis, Stefan Schreiner and Darius Staliunas (Amsterdam, 2004); Blokh, "Der zin fun unzere tsarot," *OY* (April 1943): 11, 12, 16.

[34] See Y. Eskolsky, *Sefer ha'zikaron mi'mosad ezrat torah* (New York, 1919); Rosenberg, "Have'idah ha'shenatit ha'shishah ve'sheloshim shel agudat ha'rabanim de'artsot ha'berit ve'kanada, 5707. Neum ha'petihah," *Ha'pardes*, Vol. 21, No. 9 (May-June 1947): 3-4.

Da'at torah provided a path for life and meaning through the Holocaust, and was the source for *Tikkun* (rectification, healing).[35] In the wake of the war, Yisrael Dushavitz, who arrived in America in 1927 and was a member of the *Va'ad ha'rabbanim* and a *Va'ad hatsalah* officer, observed that the *Hurban* was worse for the *Agudat yisrael* devotees of *Da'at torah*, as eighty percent of the six million were *Torah*-observant.[36] While the magnitude of the horror left Jews to silence—having no words to describe it, they could recite the *Kaddish* in memory of the millions, and study the *Mishnah* derived from Torah.[37] Mosheh Shatskes was a stepson of Yitshak Blazer, and studied at Slobodka and Telshe yeshivas. He fled from Lomza (where he served as community rabbi), reached America, via Vilna and Japan in 1941, and lectured at Rabbi Isaac Elhanan Theological Seminary. He recalled Hananiah ben Teradyon: "If I were burned by myself the judgment would be difficult for me. But I am burning with the *Torah*, so anyone who bemoans the *Torah* bemoans me as well" (*Avodah zarah* 18[a]). The fact that the persecution was aimed at *Torah*—its rabbis, students and synagogues—assured God's vengeance against the murderers and the bystanders. He called upon surviving Jews to establish yeshivas and to strengthen the light of *Torah*.[38]

Abandoning Torah

For Agudah thinkers, the internal spiritual reality coalesced with external, empirical reality. The recession of the *Torah* was responsible for the tragedy, for as a vessel of life, its absence meant chaos; In December 1940, Rosenberg explained that as long as Jews accepted suffering with love for God, they did not question His ways or His presence, and they responded with prayer, they could endure.

---

[35] Editor, "Konvenshon in tsintsineti: Retungs-asefah," *DIS*, Vol. 1, No. 1 (August 1940): 1.

[36] Dushavits, "Ve'idat agudat yisrael be'belmar [12 September 1946]," 13.

[37] Yisrael Dushavits, "Konferenz le'hizuk ha'dat fun va'ad ha'rabanim [10 September 1946]," *Ha'mesilah*, Vol. 11, Nos. 4-12 (May 1946 – January 1947): 15-16.

[38] Mosheh Shatzkes, "Have'idah hashre'natit ha'shishah ve'sheloshim shel agudat ha'rabanim [1947]," 7.

That faith became depleted in the twentieth century.[39] Pinhas Teitz, who studied in Slobodka and Telsiai yeshivas, and came to America in 1934, wrote in 1945 that Israel's failure in terms of *Torah* and to follow God's direction coincided with the onset of suffering. As long as Jewish life included faith in *Torah*, even to the point of being ready to sacrifice life for it, the enemy's war against that faith would be defeated. When it did not, such that the body swallowed the soul, the enemy declared war against the body.[40] Blokh wrote that *Torah*-observance was to co-create with God (*Mekhilta ad Exodus* 18:13). Assimilation and idolatry meant suffering (e.g. in Egypt), even death, while raising its banner above the flames and blood meant survival—as happened in ancient times with Mordekhai, when he responded to the decrees of Haman by leading discussions about the *Omer* offerings on the sixteenth day of the month of Nissan (*Midrash esther rabbah*, *Parashah* 10, *Siman* 4).[41] He assured, however, that God remained ever-present to be called upon (*Rashi ad Genesis* 2:5).[42] Contemporary Jews were using the "holy sparks" of the "altar" for idolatry, for false causes and immorality, when they should be turning to God. By spring 1944, he believed it was too late.[43] God could only murmur in the distance, leaving victims in the death chambers to cry out in pain (*Song of Songs* 2:6-8). The *Torah*, which awaited the people and could have rescued them, was abandoned by them.

Eliezer Silver, who studied with Meir Simhah of Dvinsk, Yosef Rozen of Dvinsk and Hayim Ozer Grodzensky in Vilnius, came to America in 1907 and served as president of *Agudat ha'rabanim*, American *Agudat yisrael*, and formed the *Va'ad hatsalah*. He spoke of

---

[39] Rosenberg, "Have'idah ha'shenati ha'shalosh ve'sheloshim: Petihat have'idah," *Ha'pardes*, Vol. 14, No. 9 (December 1940 – January 1941): 3-5; Rosenberg, "Neum ha'petihah shel ha'gaon ha'rav r. yisrael halevi rosenberg shlit"a," *Ha'pardes*, Vol. 23, No. 7 (March-April 1949): 2-9.

[40] Pinhas Teitz, "Kumt a gezerah oyf dir ah tsarah," *DIS*, Vol. 6, No. 5 (February 1945): 4.

[41] Blokh, "Ha'yeshivot be'galutan," *Ha'pardes*, Vol. 14, No. 11 (January-February 1941): 12-13. Blokh, "Di yeshivot unzere festung [Agudat yisrael third convention, Baltimore, 22 August 1941]," *OY* (December 1941 – January 1942): 11 and (January-February 1942): 6-7.

[42] Blokh, "Der zin fun unzere tsarot," *OY* (April 1943): 11, 12, 16.

[43] Blokh, "Ven s'klapt ah idish harts," *OY* (April 1944): 14.

Torah as a source of life, *Torah*-failure as a cause of death ("If a man sees that painful sufferings visit him, let him examine his conduct," *Berakhot* 5[a]), and he associated the destruction of Jewish communities and *Torah* centers (Warsaw, Vilna, Lublin, Cracow) with Israel's severing its bonds of *Torah* (*Jeremiah* 10:20). In 1939-194, he called for both the rescue of *Torah* Jews in Europe, and for *Torah* centers to be established in America and the Land of Israel.[44] It was imperative for Jews to do *Teshuvah* as a way to prevent further destruction, to look at their own actions as they pleaded to God to stop the annihilation. The fire burned, but it was not yet "midnight," and the "burst-off limbs" could still be returned to the "altar of sacrifice" (*Yoma* 20[a]).[45] Over the generations, *Torah* had protected Israel against persecution and the evil torrents of history, and united the people in their dispersion. Now, he called upon the "soldiers" of *Agudat yisrael* to be the "anti-aircarft cannons in defense of *Torah*."[46] The loss of *Torah* accounted as well for the disunity which was devouring Israel from within. While in ancient times the people called out together to God in times of danger (*Numbers* 10:35), the non-*Torah* movements of Reform Judaism and Zionism were splitting nation apart;[47] while Jews in Europe disappeared into their blood, heretics ripped apart the roots of *Torah*.[48] He was heartened to see the steadfast observance of *Torah* among survivors of the Holocaust, when he journeyed to the Land of Israel in 1946.[49]

---

44 See Gershon Greenberg, "Rabbi Eliezer Silver (1881-1968): Centerpoint of Torah and History," in *Burton D. Morris Jubilee Volume*, edited by Menahem Butler (New York, 2013, forthcoming); Silver, "Uru yeshenim mishe'natkhem...," *Ha'pardes*, Vol. 13, No. 6 (August-September 1939): 2-3; Silver, "Beza'akekha yatsilukh kibutsayikh," *DIS*, Vol. 2, No. 5 (August 1941): 1.

45 Silver, "Di derefenungs-rede," in *Derefenungs-rede fun nasi fun agudat yisrael in amerika ... gehalten bay der konferents lema'an hizuk ha'yahadut* [Belmar, New Jersey 20 August 1942]" (New York, 1942): 2, 23.

46 Silver, "Di torah-unzer festung," *DIS*, Vol. 4, No. 1 (November 1942): 1.

47 Silver, "Neum ha'petihah shel nasi agudat yisrael ha'gaon, r.e. silver shlita"h," *Ha'pardes*, Vol. 18, No. 4 (June-July 1944): 18-20.

48 Silver, "Vekt aykh oyf, iden," *DIS*, Vol. 5, No. 9 (June 1944): 1.

49 Silver, "Have'idah ha'shenatit ha'shishah ve'sheloshim shel agudat ha'rabanim be'artsot ha'berit ve'kanada," 5-6.

With their mindset grounded in metahistory (Objective *Torah* reality, God's covenantal presence) *Agudat yisrael* thinkers correlated *Torah*-failure in America itself with the catastrophe in Europe. American Jews, Silver declared in fall 1939, had to look to their own actions as they bemoaned the sufferings—and join the rest of world Jewry in *Teshuvah*.[50] Yisrael Gustman was dismayed at the silence of American Jewry as Jews in Poland were being murdered; how they attended parties while Jews in Europe were reciting the *Shema* as they entered the gas chambers, splitting the heavens with a last plea, and the earth convulsed with the bodies of holy ones who were buried alive. They could no longer claim they did not know (September 1946) what happened, and yet they remained silent.[51] In 1948, Avraham Shapiro, brother of Meir Shapiro of Lublin, described students of the Hakhmei Lublin yeshiva who studied *Torah* in bunkers and cellars until the moment came for them to ascend the flaming altar and die in sanctification of the name. He had looked to America to restore the yeshiva, convinced that providence had carried the *Torah* to its shores. Instead, along with the *Hurban* in Europe, Jews in America were carrying out a *Hurban* of religion.[52]

Assimilation

The primary form of *Torah* failure was assimilation. Elazar Simhah Wasserman, son of Elhanan Wasserman, Head of the Baranowicz (Poland) yeshiva, wrote in March 1942 that Jews endured only when their thoughts were lofty and the soul dominated; as the soul weakened, the body became sick. It was only when Moses lifted his hands to heaven, that Israel prevailed over *Amalek (Mishnah rosh ha'shanah* 3:8). Jews in modern times placed body above soul, and

---

50 Silver, "Uru yeshenim."

51 Yisrael Gustman, "Ve'idat agudat yisrael be'amerika be'belmar [12 September 1946]," 14-15.

52 Avraham Shapiro, "Yeshivat hakhmei lublin," *Or ha'meir*, Vol. 1, No. 1 (December 1947 – January 1948): 4-6; Shapiro, "Mador histadrut yaha"l," *Or ha'meir*, Vol. 1, No. 3 (March-April 1948): 30-31.

used their freedom and equality to assimilate.[53] Yosef Eliyahu Henkin, who studied in the Slobodka yeshiva under Isser Zalman Meltser, arrived in New York in 1922 and became executive director of Ezrat torah. The death of the pious, he wrote in 1940, should serve as an impetus for *Teshuvah* among the survivors, and thereby prevent further evil (*Sanhedrin* 37[a]).[54] *Teshuvah* required ending assimilation (Secular Zionism in the Land of Israel was a prime example). It was not Israel's separateness which caused trouble, but attempts at inroads into the Gentile world. Haman hated Jews when they became idolatrous and sought the luxuries of others, but he retreated when they turned to prayer (*Esther* 3:13, 4:16).[55] While it was true that Gentiles would have inevitably attacked Israel, assimilation aggravated the built-in antagonism and provided pretext. Gentiles saw it as an underhanded attempt to benefit materially from the church, while weakening Christianity. For example, assimilated Jews in Spain were accused of church desecration. During the Nazi period, the disciples of Heine, Marx and Freud were especially resented. Stephen S. Wise's activities in America incited jealousy[56] Gentiles accused Jewish leaders and intellectuals in America of stealing their jobs.[57] The people of Israel, Henkin stressed, could be either of Jacob or Esau. As long as Jacob's voice persisted in the synagogues and houses of study, Esau's hands would not touch him. If the voice left, they would (*Midrash ekhah rabbah, Pesikta, Parashah 2, Siman* 1).[58]

---

53 Elazar Simhah Wasserman, "Batsiungen tsvishen gaystige un material klal arbayt," *OY* (March 1942): 1, 7; See Gershon Greenberg, "The Religious Thought of Elhanan Wasserman, 1921-1940," in *The Gedolim: Festschrift for Menachem Friedman*, ed. Benny Brown (Jerusalem, 2013, forthcoming).

54 Henkin, "Silukan shel tsadikim ve'ezrat torah," *Ha'pardes,* Vol. 14, No. 8 (November 1941): 5-7.

55 Henkin, "Rikhtige un falshe refuot for iden," *DIS*, Vol. 5, No. 6 (March 1944): 6.

56 Henkin, "Sinat ha'umot le'yisrael u'mekoram," *Ha'mesilah*, Vol. 4, Nos. 11-12 (November 1939 – January 1940): 4-6.

57 Henkin, "Ten li yavneh ve'hakhmeha!" *DIS*, Vol. 1, No. 1 (August 1940): 15.

58 Henkin, "Ha'kol kol ya'akov veha'yadaim yedei esav," *DIS*, Vol. 6, No. 2 (November 1944): 2.

Hillel Zaydman, who received a doctorate in philosophy from the University of Warsaw, was political secretary of *Agudat yisrael* in Poland, and directed the Polish kehillah archives. After imprisonment in the Warsaw ghetto and internment in Vittel and German DP camps, he came to America in 1946. He believed that Israel could achieve a posthumous victory, by rejecting assimilation and returning to *Torah*: "This is the triumph from the grave, the posthumous victory of those Jews who sacrificed themselves for *Torah*, who became victims, the poorest of whom gave away their last penny so their children could learn *Torah*." He remained hopeful that Judaism would survive in America, even should the "branch" be severed from the "root" and "climate" of Poland, Lithuania and Hungary.[59] Zaydman was also convinced that assimilation could only backfire. Contrary to the view of philosopher Hermann Cohen, Jewish assimilation in nineteenth century Germany was less a matter of spreading ethics among the nations and more a matter of material comforts and the benefits of civil emancipation. Apologetic talk about ethical mission was solely to soothe the conscience about the underlying motives—and "We see indeed what came of that."[60]

The Land of Torah—and Sovereignty (Melukhah)

Agudat yisrael thinkers did not correlate failure to settle and restore the Land in the interwar period with the Holocaust. They focused rather on the Land as a refuge, and a vessel for Torah. They differed about the dialectical relationship between *Torah* and restoration—whether the establishment of *Torah* should be a precondition for development of the sovereign state, or the two could develop in tandem.

As to the former value of the Land, the editors of the *Agudat yisrael* journal *Di idishe shtime* (Yitshak Meir Firstenberg, Asher Zelka Rand and Zida Eichenstein), wrote in 1940 about its holiness as a gift

---

[59] See Zaydman, *Renesans Religijny Kobiety Zydowskiej* (Lodz, 1936) on the Beit ya'akov movement, and *Yoman ghetto varshah* (Tel Aviv, 1945); Zaydman, "Dos religieze identum in amerika for ah naye tekufah," *OY* (April 1947): 19-21.

[60] Zaydman, "In troyer nokh hurbn ligt kern fun geulah," *Kol yisrael ba'golah*, Vol. 2, No. 25 (15 August 1948): 4.

from God—not in its becoming a *Melukhah* (sovereign political entity).[61] Also in 1940, Henkin warned against any political initiative in establishing the Land before *Torah* was firmly established—lest long range problems result (*Baba batra* 73[a]).[62] Redemption was not a matter of political or military initiative, rather of divine authority and a united Israel laboring for salvation through *Torah* as it waited for God's initiative.[63] In November 1942, citing Yitshak Meir Levin and Jakob Rosenheim, Henkin said that Quixote-like declarations about raising an army would only provide Nazis with the pretext to attack for which they were looking.[64] In 1939, Rosenberg had described the *Melukhah* as incidental to the Land, which was primarily a means for *Torah*. By itself, the Land was meaningless, even doomed to failure. Israel existed ever since Sinai by virtue of its spiritual bond with *Torah*, and while the Land was a "limb" of the national body, it could be removed without affecting the soul.[65] At the end of 1948, with the state established, he reiterated that it could never flourish without *Torah*, while if the leadership was *Haredi* and *Torah* issued forth, redemption itself could be expected.[66]

Blokh, Silver and Zaydman spoke in terms of developing Land and *Torah* in tandem. Blokh rejected the accusation that *Agudat yisrael* leaders hated the Land; to the contrary, they were committed to building it, assuming that the *Torah* would flourish—albeit without denying the validity of diaspora Judaism, where millions of Jews

---

61 Editor, "Vos iz aygentlikh agudat yisrael," *DIS*, Vol. 1, No. 1 (August 1940): 17.

62 Henkin, "Hafganah lo tigore," *Ha'mesilah*, Vol. 5. Nos. 6-8 (July-October 1940): 3-5.

63 Henkin, "Atsumo ve'kiyumo shel yisrael be'amim," *Ha'mesilah,* Vol. 6, No. 2 (February-March 1940): 2-4; Henkin, "Vos mir darfen gedenken," *DIS*, Vol. 2, No. 2 (March 1941): 10.

64 On Jakob Rosenheim see Gershon Greenberg, "Sovereignty as Catastrophe: Jakob Rosenheim's *Hurban Weltanschauung," Holocaust and Genocide Studies*, Vol. 8, No. 2 (fall 1994): 20-225 and Greenberg, "Alienated forever: Neturei karta and Agudat yisrael in the Wake of the Holocaust," Van Leer Jerusalem Institute Conference on Ultra Orthodoxy Between Modernity and Post-Modernity (Jerusalem, 2014, forthcoming); Henkin, "Vi azoy optsuhalten di oysratung fun idishen folk," *DIS,* Vol. 4, No. 1 (November 1942): 5.

65 Rosenberg, "Neumo shel ha'gaon r. yisrael halevi rozenberg shlit"a bi'yeshiva rishonah shel ve'idat agudat yisrael," *Ha'pardes*, Vol. 13, No. 5 (July-August 1939): 10-12.

66 Rosenberg, "Neum ha'petihah shel ha'gaon ha'rav r. yisrael halevi rozenberg shlit"a," *Ha'pardes*, Vol. 23, No. 7.

would remain until redemption.[67] Silver attacked secular Zionists for believing that the sacrifices they made for the Land would be acceptable to God even though they desecrated the Sabbath.[68] He criticized their desire for a Jewish army and bitterly attacked them for obstructing immigration of pious Jews lest their large families create a majority and steering refugee orphan children away from *Torah.*[69] But he was firmly committed to settlement (stressing the spiritual, rather than physical dimension)[70]—and in 1946 rejoiced over the religious survivors who were "so inspired by the Land that they were like ladders standing on earth and reaching into heaven."[71] He also explicitly supported *Melukhah.* On 3 March 1944 he cabled Sol Bloom of the Foreign Affairs Committee, that reconstruction of Palestine as a Jewish commonwealth was accepted and supported by pious Jews, as a *Torah* precept,[72] and in 1947 he identified both settlement and *Torah*-based political sovereignty as *Mitsvot ase.*[73] Earlier, at the *Agudat ha'rabanim* convention in November 1933, he had proposed unifying *Mizrahi* and *Agudat yisrael* and his support for the *Mizrahi* eventually set off efforts to remove him from the presidency of *Agudat yisrael.*[74] Zaydman, for his part, wrote in October 1946 that given the removal of divine grace (*Hesed*) from the world, Jews had to provide a

---

67 Blokh, "Forshtayende idishe problemen," *OY* (September-October 1944): 26; Blokh, "Aharei Marienbad," *Kol yisrael,* Vol. 27, No. 5 (30 October 1947): 1.

68 Silver, "Kenisiyah ha'sheniyah shel agudat yisrael be'tsintsineti ohiyoh: Neum ha'petihah shel ha'gaon r. eliezer silver shlit"a,' *Ha'pardes,* Vol. 14, No. 6 (September-October 1940): 12-15; Silver, "Di derefenungs-rede."

69 Silver, "Unzere ta'anot tsu di tsionisten," *DIS*, No. 7 (April 1944): 2; Silver, "Tihle shanah ve'harbenotehah ve'tahel shanah ve'tanhumehah," *DIS*, Vol., No. 1 (October 1944): 1.

70 Silver, "Neum ha'petihah shel ha'gaon r. eliezer silver, nasi agudat yisrael be'amerika," *Ha'pardes,* Vol. 13, No. 5 (July-August 1939): 3-4, 7-10.

71 Silver, "Ha'rav silver's hatsalah-rayze ibn ayropah."

72 Silver[Cincinnati] to Sol Bloom [Foreign Affairs Committee]. Telegram (3 March 1944) cited in Aaron Rakeffetz Rothkoff, *The Silver Era in American Jewish Orthodoxy. Rabbi Eliezer Silver and His Generation* (New York, 1981): 275.

73 Silver, *Ah grus fun di she'erit ha'peletah fun idishn folk. Rayze barikht*, ed. Z. H. Wachsman (Toronto, 1947): 28.

74 Aaron Rakeffet-Rothkoff, *The Silver Era in American Jewish Orthodoxy,* 63, 156-157, 162-164, 169-172, 301-302.

Melukhah of their own, in their homeland—assuming that the *Torah* would be the constitution.[75] He called upon collective Jewry, in America, England and across the *She'erit ha'peleitah* to join in effort to build a strong Land of Israel, materially and spiritually, working actively for the historical act of *Shivat tsiyon* (the settlement of Zion).[76]

Redemption

Agudat yisrael thinkers correlated the Holocaust with redemption. They presumed a correspondence between metaphysical *Da'at torah* and time-space history, which reflected it. They were challenged by the fact that eighty percent of the victims were pious. In response, they projected the dilemma, with faith, into the future—where it would be resolved within redemption. In it, the human need for resolution coincided with the messianic premise of theology. Redemption (as objective reality and subjective experience together), which was something inevitable, would balance out a universe which had been captured by disaster.

Agudat yisrael leaders believed that redemption was implicit to the catastrophe. Shelomoh Kohen of Chicago, a grandson of the Hofets Hayim, certain that messianic light followed darkness (citing *Micah* 7:15), called for American Jews to leave for the Land of Israel and await redemption.[77] Teitz directed Jews to retreat to an inner world, to recite the *Shema* as the wild animals passed outside, in anticipation of salvation—citing the light within the houses of the Israelites amid Egypt's darkness and Akiva's *Shema* as his body burned (*Berakhot* 61[b]).[78] Rosenberg assured that current threats implied the imminence of Elijah (as per Pinhas *vis a vis* Balak, *Pirkei de'rabi eliezer ad Numbers* 22-25), and he cited Rabbi Abbuah's declaration that the messiah was to come "when darkness covers the

---

75 Zaydman, "Agudat yisrael muz anhoyben ah naye erets yisrael politik," *OY* (October 1946): 1-13.

76 Zaydman, "Dos religieze identum."

77 Kohen, "Hirhurim u'mahshavot le'sof ha'shanah ha'shevi'it le'histalkuto shel ziknei kadosh yisrael maran ha'hofets hayim zts"l," *Hapardes*, Vol. 4, No. 8 (November 1941): 6-7.

78 Teitz, "Geh mayn folk," *DIS*, Vol. 6, No. 5 (February 1945): 4.

land and shadows fall over the nations" (*Sanhedrin* 9a).[79] For his part, Blokh thought of new life emerging out of the destruction, as Israel once drew power out of the ruins of the Temple, and Jews of the Inquisition left a legacy for the future by continuing to celebrate the holidays.[80] In April 1941, Silver drew from the slavery in Egypt-liberation sequence to instill hope that the European valley of tears (Lublin, Buchenwald, Sachsenhausen) would be followed by redemption. In 1946, he cited the *Haggadah*'s assurance of Israel's continued salvation over the generations, as nations arose to destroy it, when he met Queen Wilhelmina of Holland. Conversely, he said in April 1947, the very hope in that salvation assured Israel's endurance. The current crisis climaxed the process—for it constituted *Hevlei mashiah*, to be followed by *Tikkun olam*.[81]

The anticipation of redemption, in turn, allowed *Agudat yisrael* thinkers to maintain *Da'at torah* at the center of their universe and consciousness. The Holocaust represented its absence, and redemption the restoration. The existence of *Da'at torah* provided grounding for the transition from *Hevlei mashiah* to *mashiah*; it was present at creation and would be there when creation turned into redemption.

Conclusion

Mizrahi and Agudat yisrael thinkers in America represented different views of the relationships between Holocaust, America, the Land of Israel and redemption. For Mizrahi, the Land was essential to the metahistorical process from destruction to salvation. Had the Jews grasped the opportunity for redemption which existed prior to the war, the *Hurban* would not have been necessary. Once it took

---

79 Rosenberg, "Neumo shel ha'gaon r. yisrael halevi rozenberg shlit"a bi'yeshivah rishonah shel ve'idat 'agudat yisael.'" Rosenberg, "Have'idah ha'shenatit ha'shishah ve'sheloshim shel agudat ha'rabanim," 3-4.

80 Blokh, "Evel yahid ase lekha," *DIS*, Vol. 4, No. 3 (January 1943): 3.

81 Silver, "Der yom tov fun yiddisher aybikayt," *DIS*, No. 3 (April 1941); Silver, "Rishmei masa'ai bikurai be'artsot ha'harevot be'ayropah ube'erets yisrael: Vaye'hi erev va'yehi voker," *Ha'pardes*, Vol. 20, No. 6 (August-September 1946): 4-5; Silver, *Ah grus*, 28; Silver, Lomir zikh grayten tsu der geulah," *DIS*, Vol. 8, No. 4 (April 1947): 1.

place, the Land was key to restoring balance in the universe. It was also the key to dealing with (albeit without resolving) the built in, ongoing antagonism between the forces of Esau and the forces of Jacob. *Agudat yisrael* thinkers did not look to the struggle between Esau and Jacob to explain the Holocaust; the disaster was a matter internal to Israel's positive or negative relation to *Torah*. *Da'at torah* made Israel safe; its loss, particularly in the form of assimilation, brought danger. Nor did restoration or non-restoration of the Land contribute to the calamity. When it came to the Land, their focus was on whether the establishment of *Torah* had to be a precondition for the advance of settlement, restoration and sovereignty, or could be pursued in tandem with that advance.

Nevertheless, the two movements were not mutually exclusive. Mizrahi thinkers were committed to *Torah*-observance, while those of *Agudat yisrael* did not demur from supporting the religious *Yishuv*. Both anticipated redemption—one within the framework of Land, the other within the framework of *Da'at torah*. They shared the view of Eastern European Judaism as paradigmatic, and the belief that America could and should be a means for its revival—although for *Mizrahi* America was peripheral to the Land-center; for *Agudat yisrael*, the center was *Torah* surrounded by the Land of Israel and then by America.

Notes

OY = *Ortodoksishe yugent. Ha'noar ha'haredi.* Or *Ortodoksisher_yugentblat.* Or *Di ortodoksishe tribune.*

DIS = *Di idishe shtime*

DMV = *Der mizrahi veg*

YS = *Yidishe shtime*

IV = *Idishe vokhntsaytung*

DMZ = *Der morgen zshurnal*

* The Hebraica staff of the Library of Congress provided extraordinary help in gathering sources, and the Finkler Institute for Holocaust Research at Bar Ilan University provided encouragement and financial help. Earlier versions of this study appeared as Gershon Greenberg, "Wartime American Orthodoxy and the Holocaust: Mizrahi and Agudat Yisrael Religious Responses," *Mikhael* 15 (2000): 59-94; and Greenberg, in "*Das Leben leise wieder lernen:" Jüdischer und christlicher Selbstverständniss nach der Shoah*, ed. Marcel Marcus and Ekkehard W. Stegemann (Stuttgart, 1997): 61-80.

"Irving Howe and Secular Jewishness: An Elegy"

Edward Alexander
Professor Emeritus
University of Washington

> It's as hard to return to old-fashioned words
> As to sad synagogues, those thresholds of faith.
> You know exactly where they are.
> Troubled, you can still hear their undertones.
> Sometimes you come close and look longingly
> At them through the windowpanes.
>
> You who still take your ease
> In the shadow of biblical trees,
> O sing me the cool solace
> Of all you remember, all that you know.
>
> *Jacob Glatstein. "Without Gifts"* [1]

The last letter Irving Howe wrote to me was dated April 30, 1993, five days before his death. He reported in it that 1992 had been "a dreadful year" for him, with three operations immediately after each other, but that he was "OK now." Nevertheless, what he mainly wanted to tell me was this: "I have 'lived' for the last 4 months with the group of young people who led the Warsaw Uprising—a wonderful bunch of kids."[2] Irving was referring to the then recently-published 700 page book of memoirs of Yitzhak Zuckerman, a leader of the Warsaw Ghetto uprising. At first sight it may appear unremarkable that Howe should have been, in his last days, imaginatively immersed in the heroic armed defense, mainly by Zionist socialists, of the ghetto. But one must remember that this is the same Irving Howe who had, at least as early as 1953, committed himself to the salvage of Yiddish literature partly because its great

[1] *The Selected Poems of Jacob Glatstein*, trans. Ruth Whitman (New York, 1972), 109.

[2] Letter to the author, 30 April 1993.

themes were "the virtue of powerlessness, the power of helplessness,"[3] and who had often commented acerbically on Zionist impatience with Yiddish literature precisely because of its anti-heroic bent. Howe's sympathetic involvement, during his last months, in the memoirs of a Zionist hero, was a sign not only of his intellectual flexibility but also a reminder of what he had once, ruefully, said to me about the values of the Yiddish tradition. They would, he thought, sustain him for the rest of his life, but they could not (and perhaps should not) be prolonged beyond that. "One of the arts of life," he used to say," is to know how to end. "[4]

This final letter from Irving prompted me to go back to the first one he sent me, in 1972, an unsolicited response to the first piece I ever wrote on a Jewish subject, an essay on Chaim Grade in *Judaism* magazine. "That's a very fine essay on Grade's story; I always wondered why ["My Quarrel with Hersh Rasseyner"] didn't attract more attention; but then I wondered why the anthology in which it appears never got reviewed in any American literary magazine. As a friend once said to me, 'In the warmest of hearts there's always a cold spot for the Jews.' Perhaps."[5] The parochialism and unearned condescension toward Yiddish literature (especially among Jewish critics) was among the few literary offenses that could ruffle Irving's temper. "You are right," he told me in 1983, "in thinking [Lionel] Trilling spoke differently about Jews depending on whether he spoke to Jews or gentiles. Once, hearing I was working on Yiddish literature, he told me, 'I suspect Yiddish literature.' This hurt and angered me deeply, and I never forgave him for it, since he didn't know a damned thing about it—though we did become friends."[6]

Irving's ability to recognize, over the years, the dangers in the Jewish tradition of passivity and his ability to "become friends" with opponents were but two of the signs of his extraordinary

---

3 Irving Howe and Eliezer Greenberg, eds., *A Treasury of Yiddish Stories,* (New York, 1953), 38.

4 Irving Howe, *A Margin of Hope: An Intellectual Biography* (New York, 1982), 264.

5 Letter to the author, undated.

6 Letter to the author, 2 June 1983. See *A Margin of Hope*, 265.

disinterestedness. It was this quality which, combined with his acuteness of insight, his profound life-wisdom, his uncanny gift for *le mot juste,* his supple and lucid prose, and his unerring literary tact, gave him what Ruth Wisse called "perfect pitch" as a critic. When Matthew Arnold in 1865 called disinterestedness the *sine qua non* of the critic, he defined it as "a free play of the mind on all subjects which it touches...steadily refusing to lend itself to…ulterior, political, practical considerations about ideas."[7] Whether he wrote of literature or Jewish quandaries or politics (a realm in which he made many serious mistakes), Howe disdained the sectarian approach, which says "let us all stick to each other, and back each other up, since we are all in the same movement."

Probably no socialist thinker, with the possible exception of George Orwell, aroused—by his unvarnished, often unfashionable honesty—more hatred among other socialists than did Irving Howe. Who but he, among socialists, would have said that the reason why American Jewish workers never swerved from support of Roosevelt despite his administration's "shameful" record in helping to save or admit Jewish refugees from Hitler was that his domestic policies "seemed like a partial realization of their old socialist program"? What other Jewish radical could write that "Rebelling against the parochialism of traditional Jewish life, the Jewish radicals improvised a parochialism of their own—but with this difference; they called it 'universalism.'"?[8] What other Marxist could so perfectly encapsulate the absurdity of the current academic breed of Marxists as Howe did when he called them people who, having replaced the old-fashioned goal of taking over the government with the new one of taking over the English Department, had "gone to the universities to die in comfort"?[9] (He also pointed to the paradox whereby Marxist literary theorists now write in a prose of such "stupefying ... opacity"[10] that it

---

[7] Matthew Arnold, "The Function of Criticism at the Present Time," in *Essays in Criticism: First Series* (New York and London, 1865).

[8] Irving Howe, *World of Our Fathers* (New York, 1976), 392, 291.

[9] Irving Howe, The Treason of the Critics," *New Republic*, 12 June 1989, 31.

[10] Irving Howe, "The Value of the Canon," *New Republic*, 18 February 1991, 42.

is incomprehensible to the common reader; and he recommended that they "speak in English, a language that for some time served criticism well."[11] Even Howe's well-known dislike of Menachem Begin had an element of socialist self-criticism in it: "Begin: ex-socialists form the worst kind of reactionaries. They bring all the bad old habits to a bad new conviction."[12]

One wonders that Howe, so familiar from his youth with the "bad old habits" of socialists, should have been as surprised as he was when, as he put it, "some of [the New Left] spokesmen wanted not just to refute my opinions...but also to erase, to eliminate, to 'smash' people like me."[13] He never, to be sure, wavered in his conviction that socialism is a worthy (if also a lost) cause. This tenacity was disturbing to many of his admirers. I. B. Singer once complained to me: "A wonderful man, Irving Howe. He's done so much for Yiddish literature and for me. But he's not a youngster anymore, and still, still with this socialist *meshugas!*" Like Orwell before him, Howe would reiterate, as much in grief as in justification: "Good causes attract poor advocates." He was equally free of the constricting spirit of sect and party in literary matters. His very first teaching stint was at my own school, the University of Washington, to which he came, as he described himself decades later, "green and nervous," in the summer of 1952. The department was then divided between the disciples of Vernon Parrington, leftish social democrats (or even communists) and the New Critics, under the sway of the formalist methods developed by T. S. Eliot and the reactionary Southern Agrarian critics. Howe found himself drawn to the latter group rather than to his "natural" allies. "Your kindness," he later wrote to the most eminent of the New Critics in Seattle, Robert Heilman, was shared...by almost all the New Critics whom I met...Polemical disputes apart, there was a kind of largeness of spirit...which I've seldom found since then. "[14] I myself must have benefited from

---

11 "The Treason of the Critics," 31.

12 Letter to the author, 18 July 1977.

13 *A Margin of Hope*, 314.

14 Letter to Robert B. Heilman, 21 March 1991.

Howe's largeness of spirit towards opponents: he sometimes called me his "favorite reactionary." Once, shortly after his father had died late in 1977, I was in New York to visit my own father, hospitalized not far from Irving's apartment. "Come over," he said, "and let's talk about life and death—no politics."

What Howe used to call *edelkeit* (refinement, delicacy) could best be seen in this devotion to his own parents, whose moral image plays an important role in his writing. The finishing touch to his demolition of Kate Millett's inane book *Sexual Politics* is the sketch of his mother and father sharing years of trouble and affection during the Depression, working for slave wages in the garment center, helping one another, in shop, subways, and home, through dreadful years. "Was my mother a drudge in subordination to the 'master group'? No more a drudge than my father who used to come home with hands and feet blistered from his job as presser. Was she a 'sexual object'? I would never have thought to ask, but now, in the shadow of decades, I should like to think that at least sometimes she was. "[15] This affection was reciprocated by his parents, sometimes perhaps even to excess. I once had to collect Howe from his Seattle hotel room to deliver him to a lecture he was to give at the university, and we were delayed by a phone call. Irving listened for awhile, with rising impatience, and then said: "For God's sake, Pop, I'm 56 years old; you don't have to remind me to put on rubbers when it's raining."

One of Howe 's central ideas, to which I shall return, was that a religious faith apparently abandoned can exercise a far more powerful hold over a man than new, secular faiths adopted. Howe was not a religious man, yet I recall how once, when we were going (at his request) to Sabbath services at Seattle's Sephardic Bikur Cholim Congregation, he blurted out: "Tell me, Eddie, do you believe in God?" The question was entirely earnest, without a hint of irony or condescension; neither was it a prelude to debate or even discussion. But it was still, in his heart of hearts, the preeminent question. What answer he himself gave to it we cannot know. But it seems clear that for him as for the Yiddish writers he revered, the old faith, even the

---

[15] Irving Howe, *The Critical Point* (New York, 1973), 232.

partial or minimal Judaism that he inherited, was finally a far more imperious presence than such new creeds as socialism. He said that a good part of *World of Our Fathers* was no more than an extension of what he knew about his own father and the immigrant Jewish values and feelings he represented. Though Howe could see what was parochial in these values and feelings, "they also formed the firmest moral norms I would ever encounter. Again and again I would 'fail' my father...But his solidarity never wavered, and I came to feel that it was a solidarity more than familial, deriving from some unexpressed sense of what a Jew owed his son. Reading Mani Leib's sonnets and Moishe Leib [Halpern]'s poems, I learned to value that solidarity. Reading those sonnets and poems I learned where I had come from and how I was likely to end."[16]

This discovery of origins, this reconquest of Jewishness was begun relatively late in Howe's career. Before the Second World War he had been indifferent to Jewishness and, indeed, to the Jews. During the 1930s and 1940s Howe, like Lionel Trilling and Philip Rahv, was primarily interested in the fate of the Soviet Union and in the progress of socialism in America, not in the attacks the Jews were facing in Europe and Palestine. The Jewish intellectuals who did concern themselves with the Jews during those years—such writers as Hayim Greenberg, Marie Syrkin, Ben Halpern, Ludwig Lewisohn, Maurice Samuel[17]—would have laughed at anybody who predicted, let us say in 1942, that Irving Howe would one day become a Jewish literary hero writing books that would become standard bar-mitzvah presents. "In the years before the war," Howe confessed, "people like me tended to subordinate our sense of Jewishness to cosmopolitan culture and socialist politics. We did not think well or deeply on the matter of Jewishness—you might say we avoided thinking about it...Jewishness did not form part of a conscious commitment, it was not regarded as a major component of the culture I wanted to make my own, and I felt no particular responsibility for its survival or

[16] *A Margin of Hope*, 269.

[17] See, on this group, Carole Kessner, ed., *The 'Other' New York Jewish Intellectuals* (New York, 1994).

renewal."[18] Like his comrades in the Trotskyist movement, Howe argued strongly against American participation in the war against Hitler, taking the position that this was a war between two imperial and capitalist systems. He did serve four years in the U.S. army and later referred to his political position towards the war as a "deep error." Nevertheless, as Midge Decter (his one-time editor at *Harper's)* remarked in a hostile essay, "for a Jew, any Jew, to have proclaimed World War II merely a war between two 'imperialisms'... had to have been a significant and haunting act...Mr. Howe had taken himself beyond the cultural, and personal, identity given him by his birth into an immigrant Jewish family."[19]

According to William Phillips, longtime editor of *Partisan Review,* Howe "was haunted by the question of why our intellectual community...had paid so little attention to the Holocaust in the early 1940s...He wanted to know why we had failed to respond more strongly to the gravity of events...why we had written and talked so little about the Holocaust at the time it was taking place."[20] At the time it was taking place, of course, and even for a time after the war, Howe and his closest colleagues had no taste for and little interest in Judaism as a religion. They did not acknowledge themselves as part of an American Jewish community, since socialist dogma stipulated (erroneously, of course) that class loyalties and conflicts were decisive and superseded differences between Gentile and Jew. Nevertheless, starting in about 1947, Howe's attempt to grapple with the Holocaust led him to reconsider what it meant to be Jewish, even though he later admitted that if American socialism had not "reached an impasse in the postwar years," he might have continued to think of himself as "a cosmopolitan activist of Jewish origin, rather than a Jewish intellectual with cosmopolitan tastes."[21]

---

[18] *A Margin of Hope*, 251.

[19] Midge Decter, "Socialism and Its Irresponsibilities: The Case of Irving Howe," *Commentary*, 74 (December 1982): 27.

[20] William Phillips, "A Skeptic and a Believer," *Forward*, 14 May 1993.

[21] *A Margin of Hope*, 275-76.

A crucial turning point for him was Harold Rosenberg's rebuttal (in the January 1949 issue of *Commentary*) to Jean-Paul Sartre's *Reflexions sur la question juive,* which had appeared serially in *Partisan Review* and *Commentary* in 1946-47. Sartre had argued that Jews have no history, that the sole tie binding them is "the hostility and disdain of the societies which surround them."[22] This thesis, which originated with Spinoza, alleges that antisemitism itself creates Jewish consciousness, Jewish peoplehood, and Jewish persistence. The thesis, as writers ranging from Hannah Arendt to Robert Alter have pointed out, fails to explain why other peoples in the ancient Near East who suffered misfortunes similar to those of the Jews interpreted those misfortunes as proof that their national god had failed them and chose to surrender their religious loyalties in order to assimilate into surrounding cultures. The Jews, also conquered, banished, persecuted, chose to cling to their religion and national identity in exile. The real question, therefore, should have been not how antisemitism created Jewish consciousness but what inner compulsion led the Jews, unlike other unfortunate nations, to remain loyal to their god—to God—*despite* persecution.

Rosenberg answered by arguing that two thousand years of statelessness and powerlessness did not annul a people's history or its right to survive. Howe was impressed by the way in which Rosenberg demonstrated that the Jews "had lived in the narrow spaces of an autonomous history and a self-affirmed tradition"[23] and had survived because of an inner necessity derived from collective memory.

Although Howe saw that Rosenberg, like Sartre, ignored the significance of the emerging state of Israel—a powerful declaration of the Jewish people's will to live—he felt that Rosenberg, in his "insistence upon the integrity of the inner history of the Jews, despite the absence of governments, armies, and diplomacies," spoke for him and other "partial Jews," who believed that, without being a race or a nation or a religious community, Jews could nevertheless remain together as a people "in a net of memory and expectation." But, in

---

[22] Quoted by Howe in *Margin of Hope,* 254.

[23] *A Margin of Hope*, 255.

the very moment of identification with Rosenberg's affirmation of a Jewish identity rooted in history rather than religion, Howe introduced a devil's advocate into the midst of his most cherished beliefs. He conjectured that, had Sartre troubled to reply to Rosenberg, "he could have raised the question of whether the present historical condition of the Jews would long permit them to claim or keep ties with their 'ultimate beginnings.'" There might be a net of memory and expectation, but "what if the net grows increasingly full of holes?"[24]

Although Howe associated secular Jewishness, the creed he now adopted, with Polish Jewry between the world wars and the immigrant quarters in America, its history may be traced back to a much earlier time. Writing about nineteenth century European Jewry, Arendt, in her study of antisemitism, had described a new Jewish type defined not by nationality or religion but certain psychological attributes and reactions, the sum of which was supposed to constitute "Jewishness." She even foresaw the political direction that this perversion of Judaism would take. "Without faith in chosenness, which charged one specific people with the redemption of the world, Messianic hope evaporated into the dim cloud of general philanthropy and universalism which became so characteristic of specifically Jewish political enthusiasm."[25] (Arendt thus preceded Howe in pointing out that universalism is the specifically Jewish form of parochialism.)

Howe was too intelligent and honest to scant the problems bound to afflict Jews who did not believe in Judaism as a religion. Like Arendt, he saw the danger inherent in separating the concept of chosenness from the messianic hope. In *World of Our Fathers* he wrote that "A good portion of what was best in Jewish life, as also what was worst, derived from this secularized messianism as it passed on from generation to generation. The intense moral seriousness...was shadowed by a streak of madness, the purity of messianic yearning by an apocalyptic frenzy."[26] Even when he was lured into participating in

---

[24] *A Margin of Hope*, 256-57.

[25] Hannah Arendt, *The Origins of Totalitarianism*, 3 vols. (New York, 1951), III, 74.

[26] *World of Our Fathers,* 646.

one of Michael Lerner's grotesque jamborees designed to demonstrate that Torah follows an arrow-straight course from Sinai to the left wing of the Democratic Party, Howe would stand back and declare that there is no sanction in Jewish religion for liberal politics. "To claim there is a connection, he said in 1989, "can lead to parochial sentimentalism or ethnic vanity."[27] Neither did he conceal from himself the amorphous quality of this secular faith. "The very term' Jewishness,' "he acknowledged, "suggests, of course, a certain vagueness, pointing to the diffusion of a cultural heritage. When one speaks of Judaism or the Jewish religion, it is to invoke a coherent tradition of belief and custom; when one speaks of 'Jewishness,' it is to invoke a spectrum of styles and symbols, a range of cultural memories, no longer as ordered or weighty as once they were yet still able to affect experience. "[28]

In the late forties, Howe's feelings of "Jewishness" were strong but shapeless; in order to lend them coherence and provide for secular Jews a substitute for Torah, he hit upon the idea of establishing an "objective" body of sacred texts for the creed of secular Jewishness. These would be the stories, poems, essays of that most secular body of Jewish writing: Yiddish literature. Editing and translating this literature would become a major activity of Howe for the remainder of his life. "This wasn't, of course, a very forthright way of confronting my own troubled sense of Jewishness, but that was the way I took. Sometimes you have to make roundabout journeys without quite knowing where they will lead."[29] One might add that in order to make a return journey you must first leave.

For someone grappling with the implications of the Holocaust, Yiddish was a natural place to turn. It was the language of the majority of Nazism's victims. As a character in Cynthia Ozick's story "Envy; or, Yiddish in America" (1969) laments: "A little while ago there were twelve million people ... who lived inside this tongue, and now what is left? A language that never had a territory except

---

[27] Edward Rothstein, "Broken Vessel," *New Republic,* 6 March 1989, 19.

[28] Introduction to *Jewish-American Stories* (New York, 1977), 9-10.

[29] *A Margin of Hope*, 260.

Jewish mouths, and half the Jewish mouths on earth already stopped up with German worms."[30] Yiddish was also the language of many of Stalin's victims, particularly the Soviet Union's Jewish writers. If misgivings over his failure to attend to the fate of European Jewry led Howe to Yiddish literature, so too did his guilty awareness that an entire "generation of gifted Yiddish novelists and poets came to its end in the prison cells or labor camps"[31] of the state whose "experiment" in transforming human nature had been the primary magnet drawing Howe's attention away from the Jews in the thirties and forties.

Yiddish literature had begun, in the mid-nineteenth century, as an intensely secular enterprise, a result of the disintegration of the traditional world of East European Judaism. Its only religious aspect was what Howe liked to call the "religious intensity"[32] with which its practitioners turned to the idea of secular expression. Isaac Bashevis Singer recalls how, when he was a young man in Warsaw in the twenties, religious Jews "considered all the secular writers to be heretics, all unbelievers—they really were too, most of them. To become a *literat* was to them almost as bad as becoming a *meshumed,* one who forsakes the faith. My father used to say that secular writers like Peretz were leading the Jews to heresy. He said everything they wrote was against God. Even though Peretz wrote in a religious vein, my father called his writing 'sweetened poison,' but poison nevertheless. And from his point of view, he was right."[33] But in the aftermath of the Holocaust this largely secular literature took on a religious aspect. Traditionally, in the bilingual Jewish cultural household, Hebrew was the sacred tongue, Yiddish the *mame-loshen* or vernacular; but now Yiddish became for many the language of martyrdom while Hebrew was being used for, among other things,

---

[30] Cynthia Ozick, "Envy; or, Yiddish in America," *Commentary*, 48 (November 1969), 44.

[31] Irving Howe and Eliezer Greenberg, eds., *Ashes Out of Hope: Fiction by Soviet-Yiddish Writers* (New York, 1977), 1.

[32] Irving Howe and Eliezer Greenberg, eds., *Voices from the Yiddish: Essays, Memoirs, Diaries* (Ann Arbor, Michigan, 1972), 2.

[33] Joel Blocker and Richard Elman, "An Interview with Isaac Bashevis Singer," *Commentary*, 36 (November 1963), 368.

purchasing unkosher meat in Tel-Aviv. As Jacob Glatstein, whose poetry Howe championed above that of all other post-Holocaust Yiddish poets, wrote: "Poet, take the faintest Yiddish speech,/fill it with faith, make it holy again."[34]

In retrospect, we might view Zionism and Yiddishism as competitors for the loyalty of those who have believed that Jewish life can be perpetuated in secular form; the Zionists insisted this miracle could occur only in the Land of Israel, the Yiddishists believed it could happen in the Diaspora. For Howe, Zionism was not a serious option because he deplored nationalism and "wasn't one of those who danced in the streets when Ben-Gurion made his famous pronouncement that the Jews, like other peoples, now had a state of their own." What he himself called his ingrained "biases"—cosmopolitan socialism—kept him from such vulgar joy as might accrue from images of "a sunny paradise with stern pioneers on kibbutzim, rows of young trees, and the best hospitals in the world."[35]

In what sense, then, was Yiddish literature a seminal source for the creed of secular Jewishness? Howe undertook to tell its "brief and tragic history" in his lengthy introduction to *A Treasury of Yiddish Stories,* a crucial document because it is the first public expression of his "reconquest" of Jewishness. It is both celebration and mourning. The survival of Yiddish over the centuries "reflects the miracle of Jewish survival itself." Yet Yiddish literature itself began at an ending, long before the Holocaust. Yiddish literature deals with the *shtetl* when Jewish life there still had a culture and an inner world of its own but was under fierce attack from modernizing and external influences. "Yiddish reaches its climax of expressive power," he asserts, "as the world it portrays begins to come apart."[36]

Yiddish literature flourished in the interim between the dominance of religion and the ascendance of nationality; hence

---

[34] "In a Ghetto," *Selected Poems of Glatstein*, 110.

[35] *A Margin of Hope*, 276-77.

[36] *A Treasury of Yiddish Stories*, 21, 28.

Yiddish literature "became a central means of collective expression for the East European Jews, fulfilling some of the functions of both religion and the idea of nationality."[37] Unwittingly, perhaps, Howe here suggests the eventual triumph of Zionism—for which he had little affection in 1953—over Yiddishism; at least he intimates that once Yiddish had served the purpose of keeping Hebrew alive in a kind of warm storage over the centuries it would retreat and leave the two real adversaries—religion and nationalism—to contend against one another.

Howe praised Yiddish literature and culture for the very characteristics that made the opposing camp of secular Jews, the Zionists, reject it: "The virtue of powerlessness, the power of helplessness, the company of the dispossessed, the sanctity of the insulted and the injured—these, finally, are the great themes of Yiddish literature."[38] Howe did not ask whether pride in powerlessness was justified when there was no alternative to it. To a Zionist writer it seems the obvious question: "We Jews have been unique among the peoples of the earth," says Hillel Halkin, "for having lifted our hands against no one; yet is it not belaboring the obvious to point out that being so downtrodden ourselves, there was no one to lift them against?... It makes as much sense to take pride in such a record, or to attribute it to our superior moral instincts, as it does for a man starving for lack of money to buy food to boast of his self-control in keeping thin."[39] Writing at a time when the state of Israel had for five years been under what would prove a permanent state of siege by the Arab nations, Howe defiantly set the sacred texts of Yiddish literature in opposition to the imperatives of Zionism: "The prevalence of this [anti-heroic] theme may also help explain why Zionists have been tempted to look with impatience upon Yiddish literature. In the nature of their effort, the Zionists desired to retrieve—or improvise—an image of Jewish heroism; and in doing so they could not help finding large portions of Yiddish literature an

---

[37] *A Treasury of Yiddish Stories, 30.*

[38] *A Treasury of Yiddish Stories*, 38.

[39] Hillel Halkin, *Letters to an American-Jewish Friend: A Zionist's Polemic* (Philadelphia, 1977), 94.

impediment. The fact that Yiddish literature had to assume the burden of sustaining a national sense of identity did not therefore make it amenable to the needs of a national ideology. "[40]

Among the founding fathers of Yiddish literature, the crucial figure for Howe was I. L. Peretz, the Polish writer who believed in Jewish national-cultural revival in Poland, not political revival in Palestine. Peretz opposed religious orthodoxy: "Pious Jews are a suppressing majority. To the pious Jew everything is holy. The pettiest law recorded in Hebrew lore, the most insignificant and foolish custom—the entire Diasporal rope that winds from generation to generation around his neck and throttles and almost chokes him out of his breath—he regards as holy!" But Peretz was reluctant to undermine the foundations of traditional faith. "Yet one must confess—tragic as it may be and strange as it may sound—that this shortening of breath, this opiating of the Jewish life-pulse, has greatly helped the Jews to withstand and to endure the coal-black and blood-red times of the Inquisition, the massacres, and the like periods of woe that no other nation could survive...."[41]

Howe was like Peretz in seeking a secular version of Jewishness which would not only stiffen the Jews' collective wish to survive, despite the price to be paid for survival, but also the individual's will to live and adhere to an ethical code. He was attracted to George Eliot partly because, though deemed the first great godless writer of English fiction, "her 'godlessness' ... kept prompting her to search for equivalents to belief that would give moral weight to human existence."[42] One should not confuse Howe's frequent disparagement of organized religion or its virtual absence from *World of Our Fathers* with a contempt for religion itself. His complaint that "the temples grew in size and there was much busywork and eloquence, but God seldom figured as a dominant presence"[43] is not the snarl of an atheist. He chided socialists for

---

[40] *A Treasury of Yiddish Stories*, 39n.

[41] Quoted in Charles Madison, *Yiddish Literature: Its Scope and Major Writers* (New York, 1971), 107-08.

[42] Irving Howe, *Selected Writings: 1950-1990* (New York, 1990), 350.

[43] *A Margin of Hope*, 278.

obtusely disregarding the damage caused by weakening of religious belief: "No matter how alien we remain to the religious outlook, we must ask ourselves whether the malaise of this time isn't partly a consequence of that despairing emptiness which followed the breakup in the nineteenth century of traditional religious systems; whether the nihilism every sensitive person feels encompassing his life like a spiritual smog isn't itself a kind of inverted religious aspiration ... and whether the sense of disorientation that afflicts us isn't due to the difficulties of keeping alive a high civilization without a sustaining belief .... "[44]

Peretz was not a praying Jew; he rarely went to a synagogue; he never put on prayer shawl and *tefillin* at home. Maurice Samuel wrote of him that "Peretz paid no attention to the dietary laws, and he never made the benediction before eating a piece of fruit or drinking a glass of water—or of brandy. But what the benediction before food and the grace after it meant to a Chassid, he alone makes the non-Chassid understand ...."[45] Convinced that large portions of the Jewish community in Poland were turning away from religion to a secular European perspective, Peretz sought to establish, through literature, worldly equivalents for values that the religious tradition, in his view, no longer could sustain. Howe singled out, to exemplify both the promise and limits of Peretz 's secular Jewishness, the story "If Not Higher." In it an anti-Hasidic Litvak, skeptical of claims that the great rabbi of Nemirov disappears during the penitential season to intercede in heaven for the Jewish people, hides himself under the rebbe's bed to observe his rival. He discovers that at the time the rebbe's followers believe he ascends to heaven to conciliate God he is really, dressed as a peasant, felling a tree to supply a sick woman with firewood. While lighting the fire for her, he recites the penitential prayers. Witnessing this, the Litvak is "converted" to Hasidism. The rebbe really has been ascending to heaven, "if not higher." That is, he impresses the doubting Litvak as a saint after all, but a secular saint, whose religion is justified because it inspires him to selfless ethical behavior.

---

[44] *The Critical Point*, 16, 27.

[45] Maurice Samuel, *Prince of the Ghetto* (New York: Meridian, 1948), 178-79.

Howe interprets the story as "a parable of [Peretz's] own literary situation," making the Litvak a *persona* of Peretz himself, who can say nearly everything in favor of Hasidism—it is conducive to joy, to morality, to Jewish survival—everything except that it is true. "From Hasidism," Howe concludes, "Peretz tried to extract its life-strength, without finally crediting its source. The attempt was impossible...." Yet Peretz was able to transform Hasidic material into "fascinating parables of a dilemma that was not his alone."[46] It was the dilemma of Howe himself and of growing numbers of Jews no longer willing to credit or obey religious tradition. But if Peretz's attempt to substitute literature for religion was "impossible," how much more so Howe's attempt, given an audience of Jews without Jewish memories (and without Yiddish). At the very outset of his project to establish Yiddish literature as the spiritual source of secular Jewishness, Howe sounded a note of skepticism.

Peretz's ambivalent relation to Hasidic materials and Hasidic faith became for Howe the paradigmatic emblem of late nineteenth-century writers (gentile as well as Jewish) convinced of the utility of a faith in which they no longer believed. "He had abandoned strict faith, yet it must be remembered—this is perhaps the single overriding fact in the experience of Yiddish writers at the end of the nineteenth century—that faith abandoned could still be a far more imperious presence than new creeds adopted. Like...George Eliot and Thomas Hardy, he found himself enabled to draw upon traditional faiths and feelings precisely *through* the act of denying them intellectually; indeed, the greatest influence on the work of such writers is the rich entanglement of images, symbols, language, and ceremonies associated with a discarded belief."[47]

Yiddish literature flourished in an age of equipoise that could never come again. Had *haskalah,* Zionism, and socialism not encouraged secularism, Yiddish literature could not have developed or survived. But if secularism had obliterated traditional faith and rabbinical authority, Yiddish literature would have withered and died,

---

46 *A Treasury of Yiddish Stories*, 58.

47 Irving Howe and Eliezer Greenberg, eds., *Selected Stories: I. L. Peretz* (New York, 1974), 10.

or "evolved" prematurely into something like American Jewish writing in the Yiddish language. Instead, there was a "wonderful interregnum" in which "the opposing impulses of faith and skepticism stand poised, locked in opposition yet sharing a community of culture."[48]

The sacred texts of secular Jewishness to which Howe directed American Jewry in his volumes of translated stories, poems, and essays were redolent not of a self-confident golden age but of a precariously balanced one, with the forces of permanence and progression represented in creative tension: "You could denounce religion as superstition and worse, but the Yom Kippur service shook the heart and the voices of the Talmud lured the mind. You could decry the secular writers as apostates and worse, but no one with a scrap of Yiddish could resist Mendele's acrid satires or Sholom Aleichem's sadly ironic stories."[49]

But if the great Yiddish writers like Peretz already stood at one considerable remove from the faith which they celebrated without crediting, and Yiddish literature was itself a major break from Jewish tradition, could modern Jews derive strength and identity from that faith by reading Yiddish writers?[50] That Howe himself did we cannot doubt, despite his protestations that he would not let his work in Yiddish literature "become an unearned substitute for a defined Jewishness—especially at a moment when undefined Jewishness was readily becoming a substitute for traditional Judaism." He was strongly attracted to the idea of a Jewishness split away from yet dependent upon traditional Judaism, and the poems and stories helped him to renew his bond with his father as he embodied

---

[48] Irving Howe and Eliezer Greenberg, eds., *A Treasury of Yiddish Poetry,* (New York, 1969), 10.

[49] *Voices from the Yiddish*, 5.

[50] To some extent, Christian writers had already experimented with the idea of literature as a substitute for religion. In 1841, John Henry Newman wrote derisively that "a literary religion is…little to be depended upon; it looks well in fair weather, but its doctrines are opinions, and, when called to suffer for them, it slips them between its folios, or burns them at its hearth." Nevertheless, Matthew Arnold, almost forty years later in "The Study of Poetry," insisted that "The strongest part of our religion today is its unconscious poetry."

immigrant Jewishness. Howe claimed to have no thought of making his work a basis for some program that younger Jews might follow, especially those younger Jews "pinched into the narrowing sector of Jewish secularism."[51] Yet, given the permanently problematic condition of American Jewish life, the increasing unlikelihood of either a full return to religious faith or of a total abandonment of Jewish identification, who can doubt that Howe for a long time thought of his numerous volumes of Yiddish translations as offering a third way of being Jewish, neither religious nor nationalistic?

And why not? We have had two generations of American Jews educated in a Jewishness as far removed from their own immediate experience as Yiddish culture is. The Jewishness based on the European Jewish experience of the Holocaust and the Jewishness based on the Israeli Jewish experience of a constant burden of struggle against relentless enemies have been tried, and found wanting, if the epidemic proportion of intermarriage between Jews and unconverted gentiles and the suicidally low birth rate of Jews may be taken as valid indications of a people's loss of the will to live.[52] We have also, since the Six-Day War, witnessed the proliferation of Jewish Studies programs at the universities. The Jews who often fund them expect they will foster Jewish "identity." But it should come as no surprise that studying *about* Jews and Jewish history and culture does not produce Jews. As John Henry Newman famously said, we don't hire chemists when we require cooks, or mineralogists where masons and carpenters are needed.

So Howe might have been forgiven for thinking, even if he never quite said, that Yiddish literature was as good a basis for secular Jewishness as any other. Once upon a time American Jews did not require books to nourish the roots of secular Jewishness and connect them with their past. They had brought these from the old country, or they had parents who had brought them. Howe's most ambitious Jewish book, *World of Our Fathers,* celebrated the code of *menshlichkeit* (humanity) in the immigrant Jewish milieu as a rich and complicated

---

51 *A Margin of Hope*, 267-69.

52 See Jacob Neusner, "Jewish Secularism in Retreat, *Jewish Spectator* (Winter 1994-95): 25-29.

ethic, "a persuasion that human existence is a deeply serious matter for which all of us are finally accountable." He acknowledged that "We cannot be our fathers, we cannot live like our mothers, but we may look to their experience for images of rectitude and purities of devotion."[53] Nevertheless, he observed, very little of what had held the immigrant Jews together—customs, traditions, language—had been able to survive beyond a century; American society, by the lure of its receptiveness, induced Jews to surrender their collective self.

If Yiddish literature flourished, paradoxically, by depicting a traditional, religious society on the verge of disintegration, then American-Jewish literature found its voice in depicting the immigrant milieu, which is to say the society based upon secular Jewishness, on the verge of *its* disintegration. In his introduction to *Jewish-American Stories,* Howe argued that the distinctive note of second-generation Jewish writers in America was "the continued power of origins, the ineradicable stamp of New York or Chicago slums, even upon grandsons and granddaughters who may never have lived in or seen them...Is that not an essential aspect of the Jewish experience?—the way the past grips and forms us and will not allow us to escape even when we desperately want to."[54] But if Yiddish writers were at one large remove from Jewish tradition, then American Jewish writers who began with the secularized culture of Yiddish could have only the most feeble relationship with Jewish tradition in its fullness. Nevertheless, just as the Hasidic faith that Peretz cast aside had a more powerful hold over him than the secular faiths he adopted, so did the "broken and crippled" tradition of Yiddish and secular Jewishness still display enormous power over writers apparently ready, even eager, to shake it off.

This did not mean that every Jewish writer who made gestures in this direction was authentic. Howe saw the need, even when dealing with what might be called an imitation of an imitation, to enforce distinctions and uphold standards. Philip Roth, he thought, wrote out of "a thin personal culture," which meant either

---

[53] *World of Our Fathers*, 645.

[54] *Jewish-American Stories*, 6.

that he came "at the end of a tradition which can no longer nourish his imagination or that he has ... chosen to tear himself away from that tradition."[55] The spiritually anemic middle-class American Jews who were responsible for the travesty of Sholem Aleichem called *Fiddler on the Roof* were compounding their guilt for losing touch with their past by indulging in unearned nostalgia. Their popularization of Sholem Aleichem showed that Yiddish culture in this country was declining not from neglect, nor hostility, nor even ignorance, but from love and "tampering."[56]

Of all the American Jewish writers of the last few decades, Saul Bellow was for Howe not only the most gifted but the most serious, and most Jewish in his seriousness. He wrote in a style drawing heavily from Yiddish in intonation and rhythm, and showed a more confident and authoritative relation to Yiddish than most other American Jewish writers. "In him alone, or almost alone, the tradition of immigrant Jewishness, minus the *Schmaltz* and *schmutz* the decades have stuccoed onto it, survives with a stern dignity."[57] If, by the 1980s, there were no young writers in Yiddish, there were very few writing in English who were capable of much more than revisiting the old neighborhoods and the old Bolshevist politics.[58] In the very volume where he sought to make a case for the American-Jewish writers as a kind of regional sub-division of American literature, Howe declared that "My own view is that American Jewish fiction has probably moved past its high point. Insofar as this body of writing draws heavily from the immigrant experience, it must suffer a depletion of resources, a thinning-out of materials and

---

[55] *The Critical Point*, 147.

[56] "Tevye on Broadway," *Commentary*, 38 (November 1964): 75.

[57] *The Critical Point*, 135.

[58] See, on this subject, Cynthia Ozick: "Nothing is less original, by now, than, say, Parisian or New York novelists 'of Jewish extraction' who write as if they had never heard of a Jewish idea, especially if, as is likely, they never have....It becomes increasingly tedious to read about these hopelessly limited and parochial characters in so-called Jewish fiction whose Jewish connections appear solely in the form of neighborhood origin or played-out imitative sentence structure or superannuated exhausted Bolshevik leaning."—*Metaphor and Memory* (New York, 1989), 234.

memories ...."[59] That is to say, the younger practitioners of American-Jewish literature could not sustain themselves on the shards of secular Jewishness.

And what of Irving Howe himself? One of the sternest, most heroic aspects of his character was his insistence that Jewish authenticity "means not to claim more than one has a right to." He never claimed to be more than "a partial Jew." Showing his usual talent for attaching himself to lost causes, he had moved close to the Yiddish milieu just when it was nearing its end, and his own relationship with secular Jewishness was a reenactment of the relationship that had existed between the secular Jewishness of the Yiddish writers and traditional Judaism. Secular Jewishness had served him well (though not better than he served it), and "helped me get through my time." But whatever his initial hopes for the work in editing English translations of Yiddish literature might have been, he eventually "stopped pretending that this tradition could provide answers to the questions young people asked."[60]

In July 1977, shortly after the death of his long-time collaborator on the Yiddish volumes, Eliezer Greenberg, Howe offered this lament on secular Jewishnes: "When the writer Hillel Halkin sent from Israel a powerful book arguing that the Jews in the West now had only two long-range choices if they wished to remain Jews: Religion and Israel, faith and nationhood—I searched for arguments with which to answer him. But finally I gave it up, since it seemed clear that the perspective from which I lived as 'a partial Jew' had reached a historical dead end and there, at ease or not, I would have to remain."[61] Since his death in 1993, Howe has sometimes been invoked, especially by anti-Zionist Jews, as a prophet of secular Jewishness. But this is a mistake. He was its most brilliant expositor, and he endowed it with a special twilight beauty; but he ceased to believe in it long before he died.

---

[59] *Jewish-American Stories*, 16.

[60] *A Margin of Hope, 280-82.*

[61] *A Margin of Hope, 281.*

"From Zion: Academic and Personal"

Zev Garber
Los Angeles Valley College

In recognition of Saul Friedman's focused scholarship and sustained interest on issues of anti-Semitism and Zionism. He more than most appreciated the honest retelling of the Zionist idea and its proverbial effect on the destiny of the Jewish state and the far-flung Jewish Diaspora.

Zionism, A Success Story

20 Tammuz 5764 (July 2004) marked the 100th anniversary of the passing of Theodor (Binyamin Ze'ev) Herzl, father of political Zionism and founder of the World Zionist Organization. He was born in Budapest in 1860 and in 1878 his family moved to Vienna, whose enlightenment mores and values molded his career and worldview. In 1890, he served as the Paris correspondent for the *Neue Frei Presse* of Vienna, and though an assimilated Jew he was appalled by the growing anti-Semitism in the birthplace of "liberty, fraternity, and equality" and modern-day Jewish emancipation. His reporting on the Dreyfus Trial (1984) and the cry of the Parisian crowds, "Death to the Jews," convinced him that a national response was the only practical solution to local and international Jew hatred. And he devoted the last decade of his life to this mission.

By his words, we remember his legacy. His *conviction* ("The Jewish State is essential to the world; therefore it will be created," from *Der Judenstaat*, February 14, 1896) to *concern* ("Today as in every moment since I began to write, I am conscious that I always used my pen as a decent person. I never sold my pen, I never used it to mean ends, and not even for the purpose of winning friends. This will may be published. There will not be any man after my death who will contradict me," from his literary testament, February 12, 1897) to *vision* ("In Basle I founded the Jewish State. If I said this aloud today, I would be answered by universal laughter. Perhaps in five years, and certainly in fifty, everyone will agree," from his *Tagebocher*, September 1897) to *victory* ("If you will, it is no fairy tale," from *Altneuland*, 1902) to *triumph* ("I truly believe that even after we have obtained our land, Eretz Israel, Zionism will not cease to be an ideal. For Zionism, as I understand it, includes not only the aspiration to secure a legally recognized territory for our downtrodden people, but also an aspiration towards moral and spiritual integrity," from his message to youth, April 1904). In his day, Herzl was seen by the downtrodden masses as a charismatic leader and visionary, a second Moses, whose dream was fulfilled in the restored third Jewish commonwealth, the Zionist State of Israel.

The view of Zionism as a success story is often postulated by the role it played in bringing about the State of Israel as the fulfillment of Jewish self-determination. Notwithstanding this popularly accepted view, four observations are in order:

(1) Gershon Schocken's remarks that the fathers of Zionist ideology (Moses Hess, Leo Pinsker, Theodore Herzl, etc.) did not want "to establish a Jewish state, teach Hebrew, build a powerful army, or build a productive economy based on agriculture and industry."[1] They worked to abolish the Jewish problem, i.e., the inability of Jews in Diaspora to live safely as equals among equals. Their assumption was that a majority of world Jews, given the chance, would opt to live in an independent Jewish-controlled territory, established by public acclaim and recognized by international law. The goal "a secure refuge" for the majority not a protectorate for a minority of Jews who prefer to lose their identity by living the ways of Gentiles (ergo no *Jewish* problem). But the Zionist ideologues are in error. Despite the worst period of Diaspora history – the Shoah – and its aftermath, the existence of the State of Israel, and despite the full emancipation of Jews in the West, many of the Chosen People, like their forbears, voluntarily choose not to settle in the Promise Land. Why so?

(2) In the worst pre-Hitlerian days of East European suffering, the Jewish People survived due to a combination of factors, including acts of Gentile philo-Semitism and Jewish religious and moral resistance. Philo-Semitism ("love of Jews") is complex. It is found in religious, racial, nationalist expressions by a plethora of individuals and

---

[1] Gershom Schocken, "Revisiting Zionism," *The New York Review* (May 28, 1981): 41.

groups for a variety of reasons and gains. Yet not all actions by a supposed philo-Semite are intended to benefit Jews. Cases in point, "Edict of Tolerance" by Joseph II (February 2, 1782) and the benevolence of the Russian Czar Alexander II, who abolished the Cantonist system (1859) in his liberal policy of Russification of the Jews.

Also it can be argued that an action initially meant to harm Jews, in the long run had beneficial results for them. For example, the Ghettos of Europe were created to restrict Jews from social contacts with Christians, but the forced separation from Christian society enabled Jews to develop their own system of values and beliefs. However, the Dreyfus Affair (1894) in France, the birthplace of liberalism and Jewish emancipation, changed forever the agenda for Jewish survival. A few years later, Zionism declared its aim to create a Jewish homeland in which the Jewish People would be free to make decisions independent of the good will of its friends or the animosity of its enemies.

In terms of *Realpolitik*, this Zionist ideal has fallen short. It started with the illusion that Great Britain gave the Jewish People a ready-made Jewish State, it continued in a much more extreme way by the United Nations partition of Eretz Israel, and it is being pursued today by the parsing of Judea-Samaria and the call for the internationalization of Jerusalem, visible and undivided capital of Israel. Alas, Israel's political fortunes are not fashioned by the vision of Ben Gurion, nor the posturing of Golda Meir, nor the statesmanship of Menachem Begin, nor the expansionism of Yitzhak Shamir, nor the assassination of Yitzhak Rabin, nor the Pollyanna vision of peace of Shimon Peres, nor the confidence soundings of Benjamin Netanyahu. They are fashioned, paradoxically, in the final analysis on the whims of diplomacy with Israel's staunchest ally, the United States of America. How come?

(3) In the State of Israel, Israelis are faced with an identity problem: *kedushat ha'aretz* (security of the land) or *kedushat ha`am* (security of the people). Is Israel a sovereign state reaching its decisions in terms of different religious and social organizations and diverse power structure? Or are the Israelis a *bnei yisrael*, a family, bound to habits of solidarity and harmonious movement? If so, what to do with

the non-family-like debate without-an-end on "who is a Jew?", and now, "what is (legitimate) Judaism?"

(4) Teaching Zionism should be seen in terms of its central affirmations. The goal is to familiarize people with what the Zionist tradition regards as its essential genius and to provide an opportunity for an appreciation of the similarities and differences between ideologies and divisions within greater Zionism, which arguably are the tributaries that feed the stream of Jewish peoplehood today. Among the topics that we believe are beneficial in the quest and appreciation of Zionism are the following: (a) the theory of Zionism (nationalist messianism): political, cultural, religious, mystical, socialist, synthetic); and (b) the practice of Zionism: politics of statehood, social problems, the diversified and competitive role of religion-tradition and secularism; contemporary values, and the present state of Jewish belief (e.g., partition or retention of the land for peace, the morality of Jewish power, whose Jerusalem, etc.). The jury (read, Jewry) may be out on whether the State of Israel is the pinnacle or aberration of Zionism but it is certain that the Zionist idea challenged the notion that the Jewish People must remain a victim of world history. Succinctly put, the Zionist revolution, like an Ezekielian voice in the valley of bones, caused the people to rise from the deadly weight of the Shoah to statehood in Eretz Israel.

The role played by two founding pioneers of Modern Hebrew literature and language are illustrative of Zionism's early attempt to seed the exotic flower of cultural nationalism. Abraham Mapu (1808-1867) conceived the first modern Hebrew novel, *'ahavat ziyyon/ Love of Zion* (Vilna, 1853), which casts attention on the Holy Land by focusing pride in the national past.[2] Eliezer Ben-Yehudah's article, *she'elah lohatah*/ "A Burning Question" (published in P. Smolenskin's *ha-Shahar* in 1879), the first clear proposal of Eretz Israel as a spiritual center, takes issue with the elitism of *maskilim*, i.e., that Hebrew is only medium of the intelligentsia; Hebrew should be the language of all, and to accomplish this, there must be a "nation and a land." Ben-Yehudah's greatest literary accomplishment was his *milon* of the

[2] On Abraham Mapu and others who contributed to nineteenth and early twentieth century Hebrew fiction, see David Patterson, *A Phoenix in Fetters: Studies in Nineteenth and Early Twentieth Century Hebrew Fiction* (Savage, MA, 1988).

Hebrew language. Several volumes were completed by him, but the complete 17-volume work was finished in 1959 ---- thirty-seven years after he died.

Religious Zionism

> And the many peoples shall go and shall say:
> "Come, Let us go to the Mount of the Lord,
> To the House of the God of Jacob; That He
> May instruct us in His ways, and that we may
> Walk in His paths." For Torah shall come forth
> From Zion, the word of the Lord from
> Jerusalem.
>
> ---- Isaiah 2:3

In pre-State of Israel ideology, religious Zionism contributed an important *torah* (teaching): nationalism and religion are both necessary for the rebirth of a nation. Nonetheless, differences in methodology, personality, and philosophy existed that bear further exploration.[3]

Illustrations are in order. Rabbis Yehudah Hai Alkali (1798-1878) and Zvi Hirsch Kalischer (1795-1874) were religious activists bordering on the messianic who clashed with the authoritative rabbinical pietism, passivism and quietism of the day. Alkali spent his early years in Eretz Israel and then returned to his native Siberia in 1825, from where he advocated the preparation of the Land for later redemption. As early as 1834, he argued for Jewish settlement in Eretz Israel, which became an obsession for him following the Damascus Libel (1840). His book *Minhat Yehudah* (1845) posits the rabbinical dual messiahs, *Mashiah ben Yosef* and *Mashiah ben David*, in modern garb. The First Messiah is the process (philanthropic, military, political) that acquires and sustains the Land, the *atchalta di-geula* "the beginning of the redemption," which sets the stage for the ingathering of the exiles by the divinely appointed Second Messiah. For Alkali, the revival of spoken Hebrew as the language of instruction (teachers and students)

---

[3] On religious Judaism's contribution to *ha'umah ha-yisraelit*, see my review of Y. Zerubavel's *Recovered Roots: Collective Memory and the Making of Israeli National Tradition* in *Modern Judaism* vol. 18, no. 2 (1998): 197-200. My comments on G. Shimoni's *The Zionist Ideology* in *AJS Review* vol. 22, no. 2 (1997): 266-269) evaluates the major thinkers and venues of Zionist thought.

and of the streets (boys and girls) is the *conditio sine qua non* for the dawning and the eschatological fulfillment of the messianic age.[4]

Kalischer's book *Derishat Ziyyon* (1862) propounds the theory, by reference to scriptural and Talmudic sources, that the messianic era must be preceded by the establishment of Jewish colonies in Eretz Israel through the cooperation of willing governments, the benevolence of wealthy Jews (the Rothschild's, the Montefiores, the Baron de Hirschs, etc.) and "agricultural self-help." The latter inspired the Alliance Israélite Universelle to establish the Mikveh Israel agricultural training school near Jaffa and Petah Tikva, a Jewish agricultural colony.

Like a soul ablaze, the revolutionary religio-mystical philosophy of Rav Abraham Isaac Kook (1865-1935), first Chief Rabbi of Mandatory Palestine, is grounded in kabalistic particularity ("The People of Israel, the Torah, and the Land of Israel are One") but soars to heights of universality (the whole earth, and all therein, is His creation). In Kook's *Weltanschauung*, the love of God is fully demonstrated in the love for all God's creation; the impurity of the Exile, a cosmic distortion, is corrected by the return to Zion, a cosmic restoration; no longer to cast our sight on a heavenly Jerusalem but rather to look to our own (religious and secular alike) efforts here below to make the earthly Jerusalem a fit place to live in; an outpouring of divine "Light unto the Nations," perfecting the world *(tikkun 'olam)* through reconciliation, harmony and peace. Rav Kook's intellectual sincerity and piety was one giant step in bridging the chasm between secular Zionism and the religious tradition.

Less philosophy and theology and more history and politics characterize the rabbinic calling (Reform), community service, and Zionist orientation of San Francisco-born Judah L. Magnes (1877-1948). Orator and writer, socially and religiously committed, a pioneer of American Zionism, who is best known as a founder of the Hebrew University in Jerusalem (1925, chancellor; 1935, president) and for his humanistic, pacifistic plans of reconciliation between Arabs and Jews. However paradoxical and controversial were his position, and

---

[4] Alkali on Joel 3:1: "I will pour out my spirit upon all flesh and your sons and daughters shall prophesy."

sometimes misunderstood and misjudged, he remained his own dogged servant for his brand of Zionism in Judaism: his self-imposed distance from American Reform and departure from the American Zionist establishment; his unswerving pacifism, uncritical faith in cultural enlightenment and progress; and commitment to prophetic Judaism embarrassingly abated by events in World War II; and the opposition that greeted his founding of *Ihud*/ "Unity" (with Martin Buber in August 1942) that called for the establishment of a bi-national state in Eretz Israel. He taught as he lived --- "a dissenter in Zion."

Martin Buber (1878-1965)'s religio-cultural-mystical approach to Zionism, having its roots in Hasidism, which he discovered and interpreted for the West, is interlaced with his viewpoint on the nature of Man. His central question on the meaning of humanness is expressed in his recurring word *Wessen* (essence, being, nature), as understood in terms of two primary word-pairs: "I-You" and "I-It." The I-You relationship is total involvement of self and other in intimacy, sharing, empathy, caring, openness, and trust. The I-It relationship consists of self viewing the other in abstract terms, resulting in possession, exploitation, and distrust. The I-It pair permits the self to objectify the other, creating a state of manipulative dependency, and the I-You pair encourages an atmosphere of interdependence, permitting growth and respect. Only through genuine I-You encounters do people discover their humanity and, by mutually affirming and confirming one another, come face to face with the Eternal Thou. Thus, for Buber, Zionism is fundamentally social, consisting of interpersonal relations between "self and other," and the result is the nation's communal experience as expressed in righteousness, justice and moral action. The faith in Buber's strand of national religion gives rise to a new type of Zionist personality, in which the ideals of a nation and the interests of humanity coincide. For Buber, the deepest motive for Jewish presence in the homeland is in the religious-social arena, invoking and involving the cooperation of Israel and her neighbors on the basis of equality and brotherhood.

Against the crises in the Middle East (terror and nuclear), and fissures in Zionist ideal and practice, may the prophetic voice from Zion, written on the wall of the United Nations building in New York City, become the realized hope for all humanity:

> [A]nd they shall beat their swords into plowshares,
> And their spears into pruning-hooks;
> Nation shall not lift up sword against nation,
> Neither shall they learn war no more.
>
> --- Isaiah 2:4

Zion Skewed : Minimalist Abyss

On biblical Zion and related matters, I reconnect with thoughts expressed in my review of *David King of Israel Alive and Enduring?* (Hebrew), by O. Lipschitz, A. Mazar, A. Rofe, and Y. Zakovitch.[5]

This book of collected essays, the product of a conference convened at the Hebrew University of Jerusalem in 1996 to mark the tri-millennial anniversary of the founding of the "City of David," explores the life of Israel's most famous king and ponders if indeed, "David, King of Israel, is alive and existing" (b. Roš. Haš. 25a). Not completely path breaking nor of equal parts --- about two-thirds of the content are written by Lipschitz and Zakovitch --- this volume, nevertheless, has much to recommend it. Each chapter deals with a well-defined topic, reviews past research in the field, offers a workable bibliography, and when possible coordinates and evaluates biblical historiography and rabbinic tradition to Jewish non-rabbinic tradition and modern scholarship. Two chapters are noteworthy

An overview on the biblical David by O. Lipschitz introduces the book, showing the extreme position taken by biblical minimalists (P. R. Davies, N. P. Lemche, T. L. Thompson and others), who claim more mythology than history by Israel's chosen king (and his son, Solomon) as well as by the biblical account. They propose that "(t)he figure of King David is about as historical as King Arthur;[6] "Biblical Israel never existed in fact, but is a literary construct of the editors of the Hebrew Bible in the Hellenistic period";[7] and, "The ancient

---

5 Garber, review of *David King of Israel Alive and Enduring?* (Hebrew), by O. Lipschitz, A. Mazar, A. Rofe, and Y. Zakovitch, in *Journal of Biblical Literature* vol. 119, no. 1 (2000): 189-190.

6 P. R. Davies, *Biblical Archaeology Review* vol. 20, no. 4 (1994): 55.

7 N. P. Thompson, *Scandinavian Journal of the Old Testament*, vol. 9 (1995): 63.

Israelites were invented by the Old Testament writers… no Israelite empire ever existed in the tenth century BCE."[8] Here the minimalists deal with empirical rationality ("There is not a single sherd from the tenth century,"[9] with a deconstruction of biblical narratives along these lines. However, Lipschitz careful epigraphic and historical read of the Aramaic inscription from Tel Dan places the "House of David" within the chronology of Levantine Iron Age stratigraphy.

The other essay on King David by A. Mazar reviews the archaeological evidence from Megiddo, Hazor, and Gezer (see 1 Kgs 9:15) and other places and concludes that the United Monarchy of David and Solomon is feasibly dated to the tenth century BCE. This view, first made popular by Yigael Yadin, diametrically opposes the position of I. Finkelstein and D. Ussishkin, who argue that the gate at Megiddo is not Solomonic but rather dates forward to the ninth century BCE. In place of neo-fundamentalism and radical reconstructionism, Mazar's methodology suggests, wisely in our opinion, a dialectic approach to the Bible, one which recognizes in light of archaeological data that the history of *mamlekhet dawid _ûšelomoh* (1005-925 BCE) as reflected in the biblical texts contains a mixture of early, reliable historical elements and late, untrustworthy, historiosophical components. Though data from the earth do not unequivocally establish a mighty Israelite empire in the days of David and Solomon (so Scriptures) they do suggest grandeur public works constructed by a powerful central authority in the tenth century, a "dark period" in biblical historiography.

In the realm of biblical social media, *Bible and Interpretation* is an oft visited website dedicated to "delivering the latest news, features, editorials, commentary, archaeological interpretation and excavations relevant to the study of the Bible for the public and biblical scholars." In August 2012, an opinion piece by a major Minimalist Bible scholar, Emeritus Professor Phillip Davies (University of Sheffield) was featured. The coordinator of the website asked me to comment on Davies, "Secular Values and Biblical Scholarship." I welcomed the

---

[8] T. L. Lemche, *Scandinavian Journal of the Old Testament*, vol. 8 (1994): 168.

[9] T. L. Lemche, *Biblical Archaeology Review* vol. 23, no. 4 (1997): 35.

opportunity to engage in dialogue with a fellow senior scholar but was distraught by the author's insistence in the Zionist myth of biblical proportion in the making of biblical Israel and the founding of the State of Israel.

> I (Davies) observe, for example, a State of Israel—for whose existence I can accept some secular reasons—that is using the Bible, archaeology, and a biblical discourse in which 'Israel' is the object of divine favor, to repeatedly disregard international law, human rights conventions, and United Nations resolutions (except the one that gave it birth), and is colonizing land that it does not have a right to (the total of Israeli West Bank settlers is now 350,000). This regime has bulldozed homes, villages and olive groves, inflicted collective punishment and detained persons contrary to the Geneva Convention. Such behavior concerns me professionally. I have been, for example, invited to attend conferences in Jerusalem, a city illegally 'unified' by a regime now seeking to minimize non-Jewish habitation by dubious means, including archaeological excavation, land development and extensive Jewish settlement ('population transfer' has been going on in Israel ever since 1948, in fact). Historical research, especially archaeological survey and excavation, are being illegally conducted (Gerizim, for example), and historical artifacts with which I have to deal in my work are appropriated from what is legally non-Jewish territory. (Quite regardless of international law, I cannot, as a secular scholar, see in what sense the West Bank could be said to 'belong' to the Jewish 'people').

Davies's quarrel is not with Judaism but with certain forms of Zionism which are the nexus of the State of Israel's policies against Palestinian minorities (rights, territory expansion). He cites Jewish peace advocacy groups, the US Presbyterian Church, and UN resolutions as examples of his non-bias position. Davies and like minded academics see disparities towards Palestinian rights and privileges spoken, written, and executed by the government of the State of Israel. Succinctly put, Jewish nationalism disqualifies due process of law for non-Jews, and, in particular, Palestinian Arabs. Thus Zionism is inherently flawed.

Sidney Hook proclaimed in his autobiography; "The one indispensable role of colleges and universities is teaching." More than once Davies has argued the sanctity of secular higher education and the triumphalism of Humanism, and this pleases many or some or whatever. What is not acceptable is the unwarranted broadside opinion-cum-factual attack against the State of Israel and "occupied" Jerusalem (apartheid state, expansionist, usurper of land), warped definition of Judaism (religion only), redefinition of terms ("anti-Semitism" *is* hatred of Jews, only *not* Arab Semites), and on. Cheap shots I do not expect from a respectable scholar. At the 2011 SBL Annual Meeting in San Francisco I was called to my face "bigoted" when I asked a worker at a Jewish peace table why are you working on the Shabbat disseminating anti-Israeli propaganda? I sought a peaceful exchange; I received instead verbal curses and veiled threats. I did not deserve the accusations and innuendos on that Sabbath morn. Sadly, its credo permeates the ant-Zionist section of Davies essay.

Minimalist spokesperson Niels Lemche (University of Copenhagen) offered me a refresher course in Zionism and European diplomacy

> That Zev Garber does not like the anti-Zionist bias of Philip Davies is hardly difficult to understand. It is clear that modern Israel and its followers—mainly in North America—have tried to censor biblical scholarship to conform with Israel's chosen foundation story. Maybe you should also read the other side. They have a quite different foundation story. Recent works by Nur Masalha (The Bible and Zionism, 2007, The Palestine Nakba, 2012), Ilan Pappe (The Ethnic Cleansing of Palestine, 2006) and more are recommendable, and then you will know more about what has happened. The reaction of a well-known and respected Israeli scholar to Shlomo Sand, The Invention of the Jewish People (2009, Hebrew original 2008) is typical: The worst book ever written, sloppy scholarship, and I have no intention of reading it. A typical reaction from those who do not want to know more, especially when it becomes an embarrassment. However, in light of your experiences at the SBL 2011 meeting, it must be sad to Israeli Jews to see how Israel has simply lost Europe because it has become clear over here that we have been cheated.[10]

---

[10] N. Lemche, 08/05/2012

Niels Peter Lemche's misrepresents my critical comment on Philip Davies "anti-Zionist bias." What I questioned is why a very clear anti-Zionist political agenda is inserted in an essay dealing with the merits of non-bias secular scholarship. Strongly stated, I see flaws in Davies opinionated facts on Jews, Judaism, and the Land of Israel. Respectfully disagree but do not make light of my sincerity or suggest a reading list from post-Zionist historians on the true intent of the Founding Fathers of the State of Israel. Book suggestions on Lemche's reading list are marginal (Sand) or changed position (Pappe). I see my role in the classroom more as a knowledge-facilitator and less of a knowledge-dispenser and certainly *not* a Zionist autocrat as the Copenhagen Minimalist sneeringly suggests. Lastly, the SBL statement. My reference to the Jewish Peace table fiasco is because from the Peace advocacy I expected tolerance and respect of differences. I received neither, and from Prof. Lemche I received a cautionary warning that Europe (scholarship) will never again be the victim of Zionist duplicity. Amazing grace.

Anatomy of a Boycott

On April 22, 2005, delegates and administration of Great Britain's main university teachers' union, the Association of University Teachers (AUT), voted to boycott two Israeli universities, Haifa University (for infringing the academic freedom of a post-Zionist academic) and Bar-Ilan University (for association with a West Bank college), and to blacklist their faculty. Also, resolutions to inquire whether to extend the boycott to Hebrew University (for appropriating Palestinian land to build student dormitories and engaging in research to benefit an occupying state power) and a comprehensive blacklist of most Israeli academics were approved. The response was a widespread dismay by a conglomerate of voices within and without the United Kingdom. At stake were the issues of due process of debate and resolution, the hallowed principle of academic freedom, and the acrimonious charge of anti-Semitism. In its condemnation of the AUT resolution, for example, the American Association of University Professors (AAUP) stated: "AAUP (is) committed to preserving and advancing the free exchange of ideas among academics irrespective of government policies and however unpalatable those policies may be viewed. We reject proposals that curtail the freedom of teachers and researchers to engage in work with academic colleagues, and we reaffirm the paramount importance of the freest possible international movement of scholars and ideas."[11]

Implicit in the AUT accusation is that the State of Israel is an apartheid state that practices racism; Israeli universities are a think tank in the advocacy of Zionist colonialism; Israeli democracy is tainted by anti-Palestinianism and ethnic cleansing, and so forth. However, the anti-boycott advocates see the situation differently. They wonder why there is no similar declaration against universities in China, Africa, and Arab countries where state sponsored infringement of civil rights are common. They point out that Israeli academics are overwhelmingly anti-racist, in favor of Jewish-Arab coexistence, and critical of government encroachment policy. They are puzzled that Zionist loyalty is inherently evil. And both sides, by word and deed, suggest to me that variant political viewpoints on the current Israeli-Palestinian impasse are at the center of the disputation.

Politics – right, left, and shades in between – has no legitimacy in Academia. To boycott in the marketplace of ideas is wrong and to boycott the boycotters is equally distasteful. Freedom to pursue, teach, and share relevant knowledge and to discuss it freely without interference from academic institutions and associations are the hallmark of academic freedom and the stuff of responsible education. Indeed, the joint declaration by Sari Nusseibeh, president of Al Quds University in East Jerusalem, and Menachem Magidor, president of Hebrew University, before an international gathering of scholars meeting in London debating human rights, are instructive: "Our disaffection with, and condemnation of, acts of academic boycotts is predicated on the principles of academic freedom, human rights and equality between nations and among individuals" (NY Times, May 20, 2005).

On May 26, 2005, Reuters reported, AUT repealed its boycott of Israeli institutions "after a heated debate that stirred up accusations of anti-Semitism in academia."

---

[11] http//www.aaup.org; see statement on "Academic Boycott," posted on 5/3/05.

Pilgrim's Progress: Vatican, Zion and I

I am a Jew. I was born in the Bronx, New York during *die milhomeh yahren*, and I was raised by religious parents (European-born and Yiddish-speaking). They exposed me early to the traditionalist way of life, exemplified by yeshiva learning and Orthodox observance. Day in and day out, I dangled between the concepts of *de-orayta* (regulations of the Torah) and *de-rabanim* (decisions of the Sages) and of being an American. I lived the way of Torah prescribed by the "four cubits of Halakhah" and the American dream formed by the "four civil rights"; together, they shielded me from the ideology of Jew hatred.

But this was all to change. In the seventh and eighth grades at Yeshiva Rabbi Israel Salanter in the Bronx, I was taught by refugee rabbis from the ghettos of Eastern Europe. More than once, they related painful accounts of European anti-Semitism and countered its catastrophic climax by teaching strict adherence to the Judaism of the Dual Torah, and they taught halakhic ethical behavior in the spirit of *musar* (moral deliberation).[12] Thus, in my Bar Mitzvah year, I discovered the terrible price – and honor –of being a Jew.

My high school years planted in me a young student's view of the war against the Jews (1933-1945). I was equally interested in learning the who and what, and in understanding the how and why. My formidable introduction to anti-Semitism and the path to the Final Solution and the *Shoah*, however, was at Hunter College in the Bronx.[13] There I read about the terrible fate of a noble faith, conceived in the Abrahamic covenant; forged at Sinai in thunder, lightning and fire Exod 19:16, 18) ; and consumed in the smoke of Hitler's inferno. This sad story took a shocking twist when I read Malcolm Hay's *Europe and the Jews* (1961) and James Parkes's *The Conflict of the Church and Synagogue* (1961). In them, I discovered the role of Christian anti-Judaism (New

---

12 The Musar movement was founded by Rabbi Israel Lipkin Salanter (1810-1883) to counter the increasing secular influences on Lithuanian Jewry.

13 The Security Council of the United Nations held its first formal meetings on American soil in Hunter's (now Lehman College) Gym Building (March 25-August 15, 1946), at which time the United Nations Economic and Social Council established a preliminary Commission on Human Rights headed by Eleanor Roosevelt.

Testament passages, writings of Church Fathers, Roman Catholic Saints, Protestant Reformers) and anti-Semitism in contributing to and sustaining the oldest hatred. I was determined to learn more about the role played by religious doctrine and prejudice in abetting the mass murder of innocents in the cradle of Christendom.

This may explain why the Second Testament and Church History were among my areas of concentration at the Graduate School of Religion at the University of Southern California. I had a driven desire to know the interrelationship – if any -- between classical Church history and doctrine and the Shoah. I was driven by the Torah's teaching, "Justice, and only justice, you shall pursue" (Deut. 16:20), and the Prophets' admonition that without the constant vigil of justice and righteousness, religion is a sham, abhorrent to God. In my studies, I discovered that the Church is a professing and confessing "Body of Christ." Nonetheless, on the road to Christian-Jewish reconciliation, the path is bumpy. Case in point, whether Christian leaders and the Vatican in particular did enough to sound the alarm and to save Jews during World War II is an endless debate among scholars, clerics, and lay people as recent scholastic and non-scholarly articles and media indicate. But few deny that the tie of Catholic-Jewish history turned for the better when Pope John XXIII, who deleted the phrase "perfidious Jews" from the Good Friday service, directed the Second Vatican Council to deal with replacement theology of the wandering Jew cursed by God. Despite conservative supersessionist teaching, opposition from Arab Christians, and fear of anti-Christian backlash in the Muslim world, Vatican II issued the document *Nostra Aetate* ("In Our Times"), the first-ever Catholic document repudiating the collective Jewish guilt for the death of Jesus.

The Second Vatican Council's document on the Jews inspired numerous dioceses and archdioceses in Europe, Latin America, and the United States to implement *Nostra Aetate* (1965) and to rid the anti-Jewish bias of *contra Judaeos* found at the crossroads of Christian teaching and preaching. Noteworthy, is the philo-Semitic leadership of Pope John Paul II, who has done more in his 22-year papacy than centuries of predecessors to rid the Church of "the hatred, acts of persecution and displays of anti-Semitism directed against the Jews by

Christians at any time and in any place."[14] He set the pastoral tone that condemned hatred of the Jew as Jew as a sin against God, referred to the Jews as Christianity's "elder brother" with whom God's covenant is irrevocable, and established diplomatic relations with the State of Israel in 1994. Also, The Vatican document *We Remember* (1998) and "Confession of Sins Against the People of Israel" (2000)[15] are major milestones in the Church's efforts to reconcile with the Jewish People.

Needless to say, Pope John Paul II's pilgrimage to Eretz Israel was fraught with diplomacy, politics, religious and national claims and counterclaims. Still, the pontiff visited the birthplace of Jesus, walked where Jesus walked, prayed where Jesus prayed, preached where Jesus preached, demonstrated his faith where Jesus died – in short, he came as a pilgrim to the places where the Church owes its origins. However, for me as a non-Christian, the telling moment of the pontiff's pilgrimage of truth and love was his talk at Yad Vashem, a powerful mixture of prayer and confessional, publicly said and personally transmitted. His visible *t'shuvah* (penitence) – "we wish to remember (the Shoah) to ensure that never again will evil prevail, as it did for the millions of innocent victims of Nazism"[16] -- mixed with the heart-felt *t'shuvah* (response) of *'Ani Ma'amin* and *'El Malei Rahamim* memorial prayer for the murdered Children of Israel during the Shoah in the lands of Christendom: "*R'vavot, r'vavot, r'vavot* – "Tens of thousands, tens of thousands, tens of thousands." And the Holy Father cried.

For one moment, unprecedented and irrevocable, on a sacred hill in Jerusalem, called the City of God, I sensed a post-Shoah symbiosis of the Teaching and the Word:

---

[14] From Pope John Paul II's speech at Yad VaShem, March 23, 2000.

[15] Paragraph IV of Pope John Paul II's landmark confession for Catholic sins past and present said on the Day of Pardon Mass in St. Peter's Basilica, March 12, 2000.

[16] Pope John Paul II's profound expression of identification with Jewish suffering at Christian hands was reiterated in his note that he left at the Western Wall (March 26): "God of our fathers, you chose Abraham and his descendants to bring your Name to the Nations. We are deeply saddened by the behavior of those who in their course of history have caused these children of yours to \suffer, and asking for your forgiveness, we wish to commit ourselves to genuine brotherhood with the people of the Covenant." The note was transferred to Yad VaShem for permanent display.

> The Lord our God made a covenant with us … Not with our ancestors did the Lord make this covenant, but with us, who are all of us here alive today (and) the Lord spoke with (us) face to face at the mountain, out of the fire.[17]
> Uniting Zion and Shoah

On April 12, 1951, the Knesset declared *Nisan* 27 as *Yom ha-Shoah u-Mered ha-Getaot* ("Shoah and Ghetto Revolt Remembrance Day"). The declaration recalls antecedents to the Nazi brutality done to Ashkenazi Jewry in European lands; chooses biblical prooftexts that narrate exile, plight, mercy, justice, return, redemption, and responsibility; maintains that in the month of *Nisan*, many communities were destroyed by the Crusaders; and offers a fable suggesting a useful truth:

> A man and his son were walking along the path. The son tired and asked his father: "Father, where is the state?" The father replied: "Son, this should be your sign, if you see a cemetery close by, the state is near."

In our day, the catastrophic destruction of the Jewish People is the Shoah ("cemetery"), which is forever linked to the rise of Israel ("state"). Indeed, Israel Independence Day is celebrated on *Iyar* 5, showing a connection between *Yom ha-Shoah* and *Yom ha-Atzmaut.*

On April 12, 1951, the Knesset read first the declaration on *Yom ha-Atzmaut* followed by the declaration on *Yom ha-Shoah.* The order of the readings is important; it suggests that only a non-relentless commitment to life and hope (Zionist dream and *tikvah*) can withstand the pain and grief of remembering the Shoah. The reverse is unimaginable and unthinkable.

At the Wannsee Conference in January 1942, the blueprint for the "Final Solution" was unveiled in fifty eight minutes by the authority of the Nazi state. In less than twenty minutes on April 12, 1951/6 *Nisan* 5711, by the authority of the Jewish state, an eternal manifesto

---

[17] Deut 5:2-4. Words of the Torah (Teaching) describing the assembly of Israel at Horeb, when Moses, our Teacher, proclaimed the "Ten Words" (Deut 5: 6-21); slightly different than the Decalogue mentioned in Exod 20:2-17.

was sent forth from Zion committing a post-Shoah age to life, hope and action.

Returning to Zion and the Beyond

Celebrating Zionism commemorates a truly Hebrew Enlightenment: the return of a people to the desolate land of its forebears; the re-establishment of its political sovereignty; and reviving to the fullest extent the old-new language and literature of Hebrew.

Flashed before my eyes is a note from my last class lecture (Spring semester 1991), "to name is to destroy, to suggest is to create." Several days later my father, Morris (Moshe) Benjamin (Binyamin) Garber *niftar* (died) in Jerusalem (7 June 1991).

In my class on modern Hebrew literature in translation, we were discussing selected short stories from the pen of S.Y. Agnon, winner of the Nobel Prize for Literature in 1966. His stories reflect disintegration of traditional forms of life, the loss of faith, and the subsequent loss of identity. In this particular session, I was lecturing on Agnon's "The Fable of the Goat" (1925) and "Agunot" (1908). The latter was his first major tale, from which he adopted the name in which he lived and wrote.

In "Agunot" disembodied souls are condemned to be anchored (*aguna*) to that which they desire but cannot obtain. In the end, all five protagonists are exiled from Jerusalem. This is a story of paradise lost, in which the *Shomer Yisrael*, who is inseparably linked with the destiny of Israel, cannot or will not prevent their abolishment. The former, i.e., God's seeming indifference to Man's self-alienation, leads to an uncertainly about a moral rule in the universe; and the latter, i.e., human action is responsible for human destiny, suspends God's providential role in history.

The literary motifs of Agnon's stories became my reality. I sensed at the news of my father's death and burial (which my sister, my physically challenged mother, and myself were not able to attend) that realism is transient and that permanency is surrealistic. My structured life, well defined by everyday routines, such as scholarship and teaching, became jagged by an electronic voice from Zion. It left me with an Agnonian pursuit of wholeness -- symbolized by my father's now permanent absence from home. The yearning for such wholeness will forever remain unfulfilled.

"The Fable of the Goat" is about a well-rehearsed Jewish theme, exile and redemption, with a novel Agnonian twist. Israel was exiled from the Land because of its sins but the hope for redemption never ceases. When will redemption come? Perhaps when we take hold of it as the youthful protagonist in the story grabbed hold of the tail of the goat and followed it through a hidden passageway to the Promise Land. In truth, however, redemption is more complicated. Animals may find their way to Eden by chance; people, however, will find their way only by confronting God and their own souls.

Oftentimes, however, we lack a meaningful correlation between our hopes and our actions, thereby, impairing our destiny and fate. "Agunot" is a tale of five individuals, who are incapable of communicating honestly their feelings one to another. They have been stripped of their earthly potential and strength.

What is the Jewish response to death? The laws of mourning require the mourner to behave as if he or she is dead. No normal activity (positive religious requirements, work, study, food preparation, excessive personal hygiene and grooming, conjugal relations, etc., is permitted during the period of *Shivah*, the seven days following death. The mourner is touched by the anti-life and his/her activities reflect this sense of incompleteness. The mourner returns to religious requirements and social amenities by degrees. Paradoxically, in the mourning observances, the mourner and the mourned are united; that is to say, by observing the absence of life, the mourner is sensitized to the value and quality of life.

In Judaism danger is called mixture, the enemy is called chaos. My father's *yiddishkeit* caused him to live separately from others but not against others. His whole life – from childhood in the Hasidic dominated *Shtetl* Zwehille, Central Volhynia in the Ukraine, to retirement in Jerusalem and all the Bronx neighborhoods in between – was committed to separate light from darkness, Shabbat and Holidays from regular days, the sacred from the profane, the pure from the impure, the return from the exile. At his death, I learned to unchain life from death and to understand that to mingle categories is to destroy uniqueness.

"Separation" is Judaism's teaching of order. In Hebrew, *Kadosh* ("Holy") means to detach from the whole; thus, Holy Land (from all lands); Holy Tongue (from all languages); Holy People (from all nations); and Holy Person (from laity). Similarly, the Holy Shabbat, a taste of eternity, is divided from the days of the week, temporal time. Thus, the rules and regulations of mourning are suspended on the Shabbat. The Torah's admonition became my advocacy: "Set before you (is) life and death, the blessing and the curse, therefore choose life" (Deut 30:19).

The liturgical symbol for "life" in the period of mourning is the Kaddish, recited for eleven months in the case of a parent's death. The prayer talks not of death but of the task of building God's kingdom on earth, of restoring the world. Its doxology is an affirmation of the unity of the generations in their dedication to sanctify His Name in life. As my father said the Kaddish for his parents, and I say it for him, and one day my children will say it for me, the message is poignantly clear: for the Jew the finality of death is overcome in the eternity of Israel and guided by the principle "to love the Lord your God, to hearken to His voice, and to cleave unto Him, for that is your life and the length of your days" (Deut 30:20). My first obligatory Kaddish was recited on the Land which the Lord swore unto the patriarchs, to give them; a land in which my father chose to live and die.

Reciting the Kaddish during the year of mourning became a matrix around which memories of my father were spun: the family name Garber in honor of the bachelor who saved my father's great grandfather from a 25-year conscription in the army during the reign of Czar Nicholas I (1825-1851); the flight from Russia at the tender age of 9½ ; selling from a crude pushcart on Bathgate Ave. in the Bronx after a full day of school at Townsend and Harris High School; graduation from St. John's University in Brooklyn, and then a Shomer Shabbat drugstore for four decades in the Bronx; devotion and love to family; the visit to Israel in the summer of 1951 and the decision to make Aliya seven years later; and the multiple brushes with death: rheumatic fever as a child, untold holdups, and several strokes.

Through it all, my father was there when we needed him and he rarely criticized when we departed from his principles. True to form, he minimized problems and never spoke of medical ailments until after they passed, lest the children worry or be inconvenienced. Alas, he was buried without his family present, leaving me to question, Daddy dear, is this the pattern you and He have planned?

My introduction to the Kaddish brought to mind a rabbinic lesson. In an ancient collection of rabbinic homilies, *Likkutei Rachman*, as interpreted by S.Y. Agnon, we learn a reason for the recitation of the Kaddish: "We recite the Kaddish after the death of a human being because the Almighty is praised thereby … When a king of flesh and blood looses one of his soldiers, his army is diminished – but since he has thousands of soldiers, his sense of loss is very light. Not so with the Holy One, Blessed be He: even though a single individual dies, the Kaddish is recited and the Name of the Holy One is praised."[18]

An individual in the eyes of God is unique. There never was, is, or will be another like him or her. We are told that it is not God's desire that anyone shall die (Ezek 18:32). And when a human being dies there is none to be set in his or her place.

When individuals recite the Kaddish, they offer God consolidation for His loss. *Yitgadal, v-Yitkadash, Shemeh Rabba'*: may the power of the Name be magnified, and may no lessening of power (brought upon by death of a person, who is made in the image of God) come to Him who is blessed and sanctified. It is a somber and awesome thought, this ancient thinking: saying the Kaddish is not only an act of repairing the cohesion of the family (group), which has been profoundly shaken by death, but simultaneously, it is a task of restoring cosmic order. In death as in life, Man is seeking God and God is seeking Man.

For my sister and me, the rhythm of the *Shivah* was out of sync for the first two days. On the day of our father's burial, we were in flight to Israel. *Keriah*, the rendering of the garment on the left side of the mourner's garment opposite the heart was done after the Sabbath. By day three, things returned to "normal." I commenced my morning, afternoon, and evening services at the synagogue. My sister, mother, and I sat in mourning attire and posture. Every day, all day in the *Shivah* period, streams of neighbors and friends of my parents visited, chatted, and comforted. Food and other basic needs were provided. I genuinely

---

[18] On this Agnon analogy, see M. Lamm, *The Jewish Way in Death and Mourning* [rev. ed.] (Middle Village, NY, 2000): 149-150.

felt that all activities of *Shivah* week were interpenetrated with traditional values, mores, and folkways. For this, I was grateful.

Nonetheless, by being suspended between death and life, inadvertently, my being became the issue of a *halakhi*c dispute. One day, I was "kidnapped" by the Sephardim to complete their prayer quorum for the *Shaharit* (morning) service. In the evening, I was asked by a Galicianer where I was earlier in the day. I explained the situation. He then turned to a Moroccan, one of the "chappers," who joined the Ashkenazim for the *'Arvit* (evening) service.

The Galicianer said, "You know, the son of Moshe Binjamin, z"l, is an *'Avel* (mourner); he is obligated to pray in his father's place at the synagogue."

The Moroccan replied, "But the son fulfilled a greater *mitzvah* (obligatory good deed). He completed our *minyan* (prayer quorum), thereby, enabling proper recitation of public prayers, including the Kaddish said by him and by others."

The Galicianer was puzzled and appeared intellectually defeated. He pondered, mumbled something in Yiddish, and then excitedly declared, "How do you know that we did not need him to complete our morning *minyan*? Aha!"

"Aha," meaning, granted both prayer quorums are equal before the Almighty, however, the constant duty of the *'Avel* during *Shivah* is to pray where his father prayed; to pray in another place is not a constant but periodical duty. Where there is a constant duty and one not constant, the constant duty has the precedence.

On the seventh day, at the conclusion of the *Shaharit*, the week of *Shivah* officially ended. At the end as in the beginning, I was greeted with the words, "May the *Makom* (divine presence) comfort you among the mourners of Zion and Jerusalem." It was the last time that I was to hear these soothing and touching words. The cool breeze of a sunny Jerusalem day welcomed me back to the living.

"The Dreyfus Affair and Its Echoes"

Monty Noam Penkower
Professor Emeritus of Jewish History at the Machon Lander Graduate Center of Jewish Studies, Jerusalem

On 5 January 1895, Alfred Dreyfus stood in a cobblestone courtyard of the *Ecole Militaire* in Paris. At the north end of the Champ-de-Mars loomed the Eiffel Tower, then six years old and the monument of modernity. The only Jew on the French Army general staff, Dreyfus had been convicted two weeks earlier of selling military secrets to the Germans, and he now faced public degradation for this act of high treason. Shouting "an innocent is dishonored! Long live France – long live the Army!" the 35-year-old prisoner stood erect as a senior officer proceeded to strip off his braid and buttons and to break Dreyfus's saber in two. "His face is grey, flattened and base, showing no sign of remorse . . . a wreck from the ghetto," wrote the journalist and future fascist Léon Daudet.[1] Dreyfus was marched around the courtyard, still exclaiming loudly in an atonal voice that he was innocent. A huge crowd, waiting outside the gates that cold, clear morning, began to whistle and chant "Death to Dreyfus! Death to the Jews!" Soon thereafter, in accord with the unanimous sentence of the court martial, Dreyfus was dispatched to a life of imprisonment on the infamous penal colony of Devil's Island, a parched, desolate spot in the Atlantic off the coast of French Guiana. From this incident developed the Dreyfus Affair, a lengthy controversy that presented the Third Republic with its greatest political and moral crisis.[2]

---

[1] Daudet quoted in Adam Gopnik, "Trial of the Century: Revisiting the Dreyfus Affair," *New Yorker*, 28 September 2009.

[2] Of the many books written about the Dreyfus Affair, I have found the following most helpful: Louis Begley. *Why the Dreyfus Affair Matters* (New Haven, 2009); Jean-Denis Bredin, *The Affair: The Case of Alfred Dreyfus*, Jeffrey Mehlman trans. (New York, 1986); Michael Burns, *Dreyfus, A Family Affair, 1789-1945* (New York, 1991); David L. Lewis, *Prisoners of Honor: The Dreyfus Affair* (New York, 1973); Michael R. Marrus, *The Politics of Assimilation: The Jewish Community in France at the Time of the Dreyfus Affair* (Oxford, 1980); Louis Snyder, ed. *The Dreyfus Case: A Documentary History* (New Brunswick, 1975); George R. Whyte, *The Dreyfus Affair: A Chronological History* (New York, 2008).

The tale of Alfred Dreyfus begins with the city of Mulhouse, located on the southern plain of Alsace, north of Switzerland and only fifteen kilometers west of the Rhine River and the German border. This thriving textile center was also a bastion of Protestantism in the midst of an overwhelmingly Catholic Alsace. For that reason Jews found refuge in the Calvinist stronghold. By the middle of the nineteenth century, when the 600-year-old republic had ceased to exist and Mulhouse became part of French Alsace, the Jewish population approached 2,000, or nearly seven percent of the city's residents. By contrast, the Jewish population of Paris stood at less than one-half of one percent at the time.

Jacob Dreyfuss, like many Alsatian Jews in the first half of the century, traveled during the week from his village (Rixheim) to Mulhouse, peddling old clothes, secondhand objects, engravings, and trinkets before returning home to spend the Sabbath with his family. A moneylender to supplement his peddling and retail trade, like many Jews of the region, Jacob was subject to threats during any rural crisis in Alsace, most recently in 1832. With only one child, Raphael, and having amassed a respectable amount of savings, Jacob, along with thousands of Jews who had lived for a millennium throughout the Alsatian countryside, left his rural world. He, like them, would never return. Shortly after settling with his wife and Raphael in Mulhouse, Jacob died.

A few years later, Raphael married Jeannette Libmann, a seamstress. Together, they launched a cotton mill. Jeannette bore nine children, seven of whom survived (four sons and three daughters). By the end of the century, three sons managed their father's well-to-do business. The youngest, Alfred, did not pursue his father's trade. After the Franco-Prussian War of 1870, which witnessed the unification of Germany, Alfred moved with his oldest sister to her husband's home in Carpentras and then in Paris. There, in 1878, he entered the Etude Polytechnique and the officer corps of the French Army, committed to the republican values of the French Revolution.

By then, Jews in France numbered no more than 86,000 out of a total population of nearly 40 million. That religious community was administered through the government-sponsored *Consistoire Central*, whose "Prayer for France" read: "Almighty protector of Israel and humanity, if of all religions ours is the most dear to You, because it is Your own handiwork, France is of all countries the one which You seem to prefer, because it is the most worthy of You."[3] Much was modeled on Christian practice, including flowers on coffins, collection-plates, and the use of organs in the synagogue service, with rabbis dressed almost like Catholic priests. There were perhaps 500 Orthodox Jews in all of France.

Jewish lay leaders echoed Rabbi Joseph Hermann of Rheims in thinking that France was designated by God to direct the destinies of humanity, to spread the great ideas which had formerly been "the exclusive patrimony of Israel." It was necessary for all French Jews, advised the historian Leon Halevy, that "the name of Jew become accessory, and the name of Frenchman principal." James Darmesteter, director of the prestigious *Ecole des Hautes Etudes*, asserted that France and the Jews would bring about the messianic age, which would take the form of "the terrestrial triumph of justice in humanity." [4]

Alfred Dreyfus was another adamant, assimilated French-Jewish patriot. His father's choice of French citizenship in 1871, when the Germans obtained possession of Alsace, had signified an initial step in this direction. Obtaining a commission in the French Army had been Alfred's boyhood ambition. To be the first Jew selected for staff duties in 1892, promoted to the rank of captain and attached to the War Ministry, was a matter of tremendous pride for the ambitious, self-confident individual. This bourgeois family man, always marked by a cold and correct demeanor, eventually settled with his wife, Lucie née Hadamard, and their two children, Pierre and Jeanne, in a grand apartment on the Avenue du Trocadéro.

Popular writings in French should have given Dreyfus considerable pause, however. In the 1840s, the socialist Alphonse Tousennel had fulminated that the "usurious" Jewish financiers

---

[3] Quoted in Paul Johnson, *A History of the Jews* (New York, 1988), 381.

[4] Quoted in Johnson, *A History of the Jews,* 381.

(Rothschild being the most prominent) controlled the country as "kings of the epoch." In 1853, the conservative diplomat Count Joseph Arthur de Gobineau published his *Essay on the Inequality of Human Races.* This classic of European racist thought, which had a great impact on German antisemites like Richard Wagner in its justification of Nordic supremacy, distinguished between Aryan virtue and Semitic (and Latin) degeneration. Concurrently, Ernst Renan, in his analysis of Semitic languages and especially in his book *Life of Jesus* (1863), asserted that the Semitic race, compared with the Indo-European, "represents an inferior level of human nature."

Edouard-Adolphe Drumont joined the views of Toussenel and Renan to produce a far more influential treatise of more than one thousand pages, *La France Juive* (1886). In contradistinction to the Frenchman, argued this journalist, the Jew lacks a creative impulse, and he is correspondingly ugly: a hooked nose, contorted fingers, an unpleasant body odor. Moreover, the Jews are by nature spies, traitors, criminals, and carriers of disease. Through cunning, the so-called "Jewish race" has all but subjugated the benign, yet careless, Aryans of France. For Drumont, the clutches of the predatory Jew, who, he claimed, controlled at least half of France's natural wealth, ought to be broken. A specially created government office could confiscate Jewish wealth by decree, avoiding violent revolution and unemployment.

La France Juive went through more than one hundred editions, and was said to be the most widely read book in France. It enabled its author to establish the Anti-Semitic League, primarily supported by students and lower echelons of the Catholic clergy. In 1892, Drumont founded a daily newspaper, *La Libre Parole*, which reflected his unbridled animosity toward Jews, a paternalistic concern for the poor, and a repugnance of what he termed "Jewish capital."

Beyond this pseudo-scientific hatred of Jews, a second layer of French antisemitism was clerical. Backed by the papacy, religious orders like the Assumptionists organized mass pilgrimages to Rome and new miracle centers, such as Lourdes. The Assumptionists also established a very successful publishing house, La Bonne Press, and subsequently a mass-circulation daily, *La Croix.* That newspaper had been founded in 1883 to fight what was considered to be a satanic conspiracy of Protestants, Freemasons, and Jews, which the

Assumptionists believed had caused the collapse of the Catholic banking organization Union Generale one year earlier.

Their conspiratorial theory made Catholics a natural ally of the right-wing in domestic politics. Ever since the French Revolution of 1789, Conservatives and Republicans fiercely battled for the country's soul. Between March and May 1871, a faction of anarchists and left-wing elements in Paris known as the Communards fought troops loyal to the new Third Republic, whose leaders had just signed a peace treaty with Germany following the Franco-Prussian war. The ensuing death toll of thousands on both sides left a legacy of hatred between the right and the left that poisoned French politics thereafter.

With the rightist royalists unable to put forth a credible leader, the Republicans dominated French politics during the next forty years. Putting their main effort into reducing the power of the Catholic Church, they issued a number of decrees in the 1880s, separating the state from the church, secularizing public schools, and requiring their teachers to be members of the laity. The Republicans also sanctioned trade unions and gave the working class basic security.

Loathing the Third Republic, the Conservatives plotted its overthrow. A scheme to have a nationalist general, Georges Boulanger, seize the government in dictatorial fashion collapsed at the last moment in the late 1880s when Boulanger lost his nerve. In 1892-1893 the Conservatives exploited the "Panama Scandal" against the government. That scandal resulted from the bankruptcy of a company chartered to dig the Panama Canal, in which a number of prominent Republican politicians were implicated for accepting bribes to vote for authorizing the company's stock lottery in order to raise additional capital. Since some Jewish financiers were involved in this labyrinth of financial manipulation, Drumont's steady charges in *La Libre Parole* fell on receptive ears.[5]

---

[5] For the historical context, see Hannah Arendt, *The Origins of Totalitarianism* (New York, 1958 ed.; Jay R. Berkovitz); *The Shaping of Identity in Nineteenth-Century France* (Detroit, 1989); Phyllis Cohen Albert, *The Modernization of French Jewry: Consistory and Community in the Nineteenth Century* (Hanover, 1977); Eugen Weber, *France, Fin-de-Siècle* (Cambridge, 1986); Stephen Wilson, *Ideology and Experience: Antisemitism in France at the Time of the Dreyfus Affair* (Rutherford, New Jersey, 1982).

Amidst this orchestrated campaign of vilification, ordinary Frenchmen suddenly faced what Drumont and company termed "*la question Juive.*" In one generation, France had taken in 120,000 Jews, many escaping pogroms in Russia following the assassination of Czar Alexander II in 1881. More than doubling the size of French Jewry, these poor, Ashkenazic Jews appeared to conform to the caricatures which regularly surfaced in *La Libre Parole* and *La Croix*. That these Jews had the slightest German connections made them additionally suspect in a country seeking revenge against the Hun and simultaneously paranoid about further German assault.[6]

All these varied circumstances fused to serve as the backdrop for the immediate events which resulted in Alfred Dreyfus's condemnation to life imprisonment. On 24 September 1894, a cleaning woman who spied for the French army's counter-intelligence service had found a suspicious onionskin paper torn into six pieces in the wastebasket of Major Max von Schwartzkoppen, a military attaché at the German embassy in Paris. On the letter, subsequently called the *bordereau* (memorandum), appeared a list of French military papers which the writer intended to hand over in return for cash. The nature of the list indicated that a French officer, presumably one who was a member of the French general staff, was supplying the Germans with important military information. Two days later, the *bordereau* reached Major Hubert Henry of French military intelligence. Colonel Jean-Conrad Sandherr, chief of the Statistical Section of the General Staff who directed the office responsible for uncovering the *bordereau*, was unable to identity the handwriting authoritatively; nor could the handwriting experts whom he consulted.

Yet Henry, an antisemite, persuaded Sandherr, a German-hating antisemite from Alsace whose Protestant father had converted to Catholicism, that Captain Alfred Dreyfus was the most likely culprit. The handwriting bore little resemblance to Dreyfus's script, and all the internal evidence of the *bordereau* pointed to Marie Charles Ferdinand Walsen-Esterhazy, then an Army major and commander of the 74th Infantry. Esterhazy, the ne'er-do-well son of an illegitimate daughter

---

[6] Vicki Caron, *Between France and Germany: The Jews of Alsace-Lorraine, 1871-1918* (Stanford, 1988).

of an illegitimate claimant to the Hungarian royal line, was a man staggered by gambling debts. Nonetheless, Sandherr had Dreyfus arrested on October 13 and formally charged by a military court with treason. Several declared "experts" on handwriting offered testimony, none more aggressive than the antisemitic Catholic royalist Maj. Armand Mercier du Paty de Clam. An amateur graphologist and firm believer in the occult, du Paty proceeded to interrogate Dreyfus night and day in Cherche-Midi Prison, trying to obtain a confession of guilt by locking the hapless man in a mirror-lined room, using sleep deprivation, and waking him suddenly in the middle of the night with a bright light directed at his face. In the meantime, Henry informed the panel of officers that he had "other" information implicating Dreyfus, but could not reveal it without jeopardizing France's military position.

At first, given such slim "evidence," the court martial hesitated to pass judgment. The trial was held *in camera*. Contrary to all legal procedure, the ministry of war had placed a file of secret documents (part of which were forgeries arranged by Henry) before the tribunal. The actual trouble began when Drumont's newspaper broke the story that a Jewish officer had been secretly arrested for treason. By November 9th, *La Libre Parole* proclaimed that all of Jewry was behind the traitor, "the Judas Dreyfus;" *La Croix* joined in the witch hunt, as did the royalist press. This violent campaign particularly fingered the German-speaking Jewish population, which served as scapegoats for the loss of Alsace and other territory to Germany as a result of the Franco-Prussian War.

The Dreyfus family, led by his indefatigable brother Mathieu, consistently supported Alfred's plea of innocence. Yet, as Michael Marrus has documented, the leaders of the Jewish community tried to play things down. Eventually, the vindictive clamor of the headlines and editorials against the "international Jewish conspiracy" helped convince the Minister of War, General Auguste Mercier, to intervene in order to guarantee that the court officers convict Dreyfus. The Jewish officer was found guilty on December 22, and, after the humiliating public ceremony at the *Ecole Militaire*, sent in shackles to the pestilent French island off the coast of South America. He was the sole prisoner there.

Dreyfus denied his guilt from the outset, at one point crying out in his jail cell, "My only crime is to have been born a Jew!" Imposed to a regime of silence and chained to his bed at night, Dreyfus saved his sanity by reading. As Louis Begley observes, he read Tolstoy, Nietzsche, the French classics, and made intelligent notes on them. He especially focused on all the great tragedies of Shakespeare — teaching himself to read them in the original, and found in those stories a language suitable to his own condition. He copied out Othello's lines on honor, and sent them to his wife.

Theodor Herzl found himself in the crowd watching the degradation of Dreyfus. According to an article which Herzl wrote in 1899, the founder of modern political Zionism subsequently insisted: "What made me a Zionist was the Dreyfus trial." Herzl had covered the trial for his Viennese newspaper, but his reports then do not confirm the later personal assertion. Herzl did not say at the time of the proceedings that he accepted the fact of Dreyfus's innocence. Nor is the trial mentioned in his diary, which surely would have been the case had it produced his conversion to Zionism in May 1895. Rather, as Jacques Kornberg has convincingly shown, what preoccupied Herzl in 1894-1895 was Austrian antisemitism.[7]

Herzl's relatively optimistic judgment on French antisemitism prior to the Dreyfus trial is explained by the fact, pointed out by Robert Byrnes, that the anti-Jewish movement there, unlike in Austria, never translated its popular support into political gains. Indeed, when Captain Armand Mayer was killed in a dual in 1892, fought in response to a campaign launched by *La Libre Parole* to impugn the loyalty of Jews in the French Army, his military funeral through the streets of Paris attracted thousands of sympathetic onlookers. Mayer's sacrifice "will not have been useless," announced Chief Rabbi Zadoc Kahn at the funeral service, "if it serves to dissipate the fatal misunderstandings, and lets shine forth, through the veil of mourning which covers it today, the flag of France, this glorious and immortal symbol of justice, of concord, of fraternity."[8] Drumont's defense of political

[7] Jacques Kornberg, *Theodor Herzl: From Assimilation to Zionism* (Bloomington, 1993), chaps 4 and 8.

[8] Robert Byrnes, *Antisemitism in Modern France* (New Brunswick, 1950), 335-339; Kahn quoted in Marrus, *The Politics of Assimilation*, 199.

assassinations forced him to flee to Belgium in June 1894, after the president of France was killed by an anarchist.

One week after Dreyfus's conviction, Herzl praised France: "The energies of the Republic are by no means exhausted....[France] is the land of experiments...the great vessel where political innovations simmer for the whole civilized world." [9] Like other Jews, Herzl was shaken by the trial, which strengthened French antisemitism. Through 1895, however, he did not endow the case with special significance. Seven judges, after all, had voted unanimously for conviction; no one knew of Henry's forgeries, nor that the incriminating secret file had been kept from Dreyfus's lawyer. Under these circumstances, the entire French press welcomed the court's decision, and Dreyfus became a forgotten man.

But not by Bernard Lazare. Born Baruch Hagani, a young Symbolist poet from Nimes, Lazare had been attracted by anarchism and socialist movements once he shifted to Paris. In a collection of articles which formed his book *Antisemitism, its History and Causes* (1894), Lazare maintained that hatred of Jews could be useful in bringing about the advent of socialism by teaching hatred of capitalism in all its forms. Assimilation into "the mass of the nation," he postulated, would bring an end to Jew-hatred. The book contained violent expressions, often quoted later by professional antisemites, against some sectors of the Jewish community. The Dreyfus trial challenged Lazare's views to their roots, however, and completely altered his attitude on the so-called "Jewish problem." He wrote two articles at the end of 1894 about the antisemitic aspects of the case, yet expressed no interest in defending a bourgeois army officer in trouble.

Eventually, pressed by Alfred's brother-in-law, Joseph Valabregue, the pugnacious Lazare began to investigate the case. Although providing critical information about what he termed the "judicial error," Mathieu and others of the upper-class Dreyfus family followed the *Consistoire's* line of not wishing to criticize the Army in the press. Awaiting Mathieu's green light to proceed with publication of a

---

[9] Herzl quoted in Kornberg, *Theodor Herzl*, 181.

manuscript that was ready by the summer of 1895, Lazare turned to the writing of articles which taunted Drumont (a duel followed in which neither man was injured), as well as the "atavistic pusillanimity" of France's Jews. Eventually, seeing no results from the cautious stance adopted by the *Consistoire* and his Catholic lawyer, Edgar Demange, Mathieu provided the necessary funds to the militant journalist, who published a pamphlet in Brussels (to avoid legal action in France) in November 1896, entitled *A Judicial Error: The Truth about the Dreyfus Affair.* It vigorously raised the antisemitic issue for the first time publicly from the Jewish perspective: "Because he was a Jew he was arrested, because he was a Jew he was convicted, because he was a Jew the voices of justice and of truth could not be heard in his favor." For Lazare, Dreyfus was the archetypal Jewish martyr:

> He incarnates in himself, not only the centuries-old sufferings of the people of martyrs, but their present agonies through him...all of those whom desperation drives to seek some haven in the far corners of the inhabited world where they will at last find that justice which the best of them have claimed for all humanity.

Lazare sent the pamphlet to members of the French Senate and to public figures, thereby breaking the general silence which had prevailed for the last two years. [10]

Independently, Lt. Col. Georges Picquart, who succeeded Sandherr in July 1895 after the latter took command of the 20th Infantry Regiment at Montauban, had sensed something suspicious about the Dreyfus trial. In March 1896, he had obtained a second document, later called the *petit bleu.* This special-delivery letter, written on blue paper and resembling a postal card, was addressed by military attaché Schwartzkoppen to Major Esterhazy (clearly a German agent). Picquart then compared Esterhazy's handwriting with that of the original *bordereau* and, although an arch conservative and an avowed antisemite himself, concluded that Esterhazy was the traitor. Further, the *bordereau* was written on the same onionskin paper that Esterhazy

---

[10] Lazare quoted in Johnson, *A History of the Jews*, 386. The best full study is by Nelly Wilson, *Bernard Lazare: Antisemitism and the Problem of Jewish Identity in Late Nineteenth Century France* (Cambridge, 1978).

had used to correspond with his stock broker and mistresses. Henry responded by forging additional documents to prove that the court martial had not erred, then notified his superiors that Picquart was about to make embarrassing investigations into the original conviction. When Picquart submitted his evidence to the deputy director of the General Staff, he was told to say nothing. He found himself soon transferred to a frontier post in Tunisia. Fearful that he might die with this evidence undisclosed, on the eve of his departure for remote Africa, Picquart transmitted the story to his lawyer, Louis Leblois. At the same time, he forbade the attorney to inform anyone else.

Fortunately, Leblois did not keep his pledge. He brought the crucial new information to the attention of Auguste Scheurer-Kestner, the liberal vice-president of the Senate. This respected Alsatian patriot immediately realized that the Army's determination to protect its "honor" rather than admit error, a point which Henry had made, in fact, to Picquart, undermined equality before the law. Announcing in the Senate that Dreyfus was innocent and openly accusing Esterhazy, Scheurer-Kestner and his colleagues quickly began to campaign for a retrial. The right-wing premier, Jules Meline, refused to accept his statement, however, and tried to hide the facts.

At about the same time, Mathieu Dreyfus managed to obtain a facsimile of the *bordereau*. He submitted it to a number of bank officials, who identified the handwriting as Esterhazy's. While releasing the information to the press, Mathieu denounced Esterhazy in a letter to the minister of war on 15 November 1897. An uproar broke out in Paris and throughout France. Esterhazy demanded a court martial.

The evidence against him was considerable. Aside from the incriminating handwriting, it was clear that Esterhazy's forays in gambling halls and boudoirs left him regularly short of cash. The diaries of this Hungarian-born aristocrat, moreover, revealed his personal detestation for France. Yet the court, in another secret hearing, acquitted him on 9 January 1898, and arrested Picquart, who was punished with sixty days' imprisonment.

By now, the case had attracted widespread attention and split France into two opposing camps. The issues were regarded as far exceeding the personal matter of the guilt or innocence of Alfred

Dreyfus. The anti-Dreyfusards (those against reopening the case) viewed the controversy as an attempt by France's enemies to discredit the Army. It had become an issue of national security against international socialism and Jewry, pitting France against Germany. Many Roman Catholics, including monarchists, joined this camp in the hope of revenge for the actions directed against their church during the century since the French Revolution; Conservatives, for their part, attempted to remove a government which threatened their economic and political interests. On the other side, Dreyfusards (those seeking Dreyfus's exoneration), considering themselves heirs of the Revolution, saw the matter as the principle of individual freedom subordinated to that of national security. From their perspective, civilian authority had to stand firmly against a military authority which acted independently of the state.

Lazare, who in 1898 would publish a second book on Dreyfus's innocence, played a significant role in this development. The native Jewish establishment, personified by Chief Rabbi Kahn, whom Lazare had unsuccessfully urged to work for a revision of the case, chose a stance of abject political quietism. If Dreyfus were innocent, these leaders reasoned, let the Republicans undertake the attack on his behalf rather than have attacks by Jews foment antisemitism. In their view, as Kahn put it in the preface to a book in 1886 on Jewish life, with their homeland signifying "deliverance for all those who suffer oppression," "Jews above all feel a love for France without limit....They are proud...to work for her prosperity and to defend her flag."[11] Lazare persisted nonetheless, winning over the eminent Jewish lawyer-politician Joseph Reinach and several young Jewish intellectuals, among them Marcel Proust. A "petition of intellectuals" began, with prominent writers, most notably Anatole France, signing on in Dreyfus's defense.

What became known as the Dreyfus Affair truly commenced on 13 January 1898, four days after Esterhazy's acquittal, with Emile

---

[11] Burns, *Dreyfus*, 86. For related expressions by French Jewish leaders, see Marrus, *The Politics of Assimilation*, Chap. 5.

Zola's open letter to the president of the Third Republic, Felix Faure, published on the front page of *L'Aurore*. Zola, the country's most popular author, had undertaken his own crusade after receiving information from Schuerer-Kestner and reading Mathieu's public letter denouncing Esterhazy. As a result, Zola wrote a lengthy, eloquent broadside accusing various French generals and statesmen by name of Dreyfus's unjust condemnation, and brought it to *L'Aurore*. Georges Clemenceau, one of that liberal newspaper's leading columnists and a rising Radical politician, suggested the key words of the final paragraphs. The final manifesto, offered as nothing less than "a radical measure to hasten the explosion of truth and justice," appeared under the bold headline *"J'Accuse!"*

"L'Affaire", as it came to be called, erupted at that moment. Some 300,000 copies of *"J'Accuse!"* were sold in Paris within a day. Nationalists pressed the government to bring Zola to justice; antisemitic riots, with the patent complicity of the police, broke out across France. In Algiers, the assaults lasted four days and involved the sack of the entire Jewish quarter. Pope Leo XIII remained silent while allowing the official Jesuit review to inflame Catholic opinion against the Jews. Officers of the General Staff, which had been instrumental in organizing the mob, threatened to resign if Dreyfus were acquitted. Zola was charged, as he had intended, with libel. His public trial began on February 7, with Clemenceau's eloquent address on his behalf to the jury raising the primary issue at stake: "See to it that the supremacy of the law is undisputed, and through the law rid our hearts of this respect for reasons of state that is absurd in a democracy."[12] On February 23 Zola was found guilty, and sentenced to a year's imprisonment and a fine of 3,000 francs. He was also removed from the *Légion d'honneur*.

On the advice of friends, Zola fled to England for a few months. The intellectuals' petition drew 3,000 signatures. In February, the Dreyfusards formed the League of the Rights of Man; their

---

[12] Clemenceau quoted in Gopnik, "Trial of the Century."

opponents, spearheaded by the writer Charles Maurras and his newspaper *L'Action Française*, replied at the year's end with the League of the French Fatherland to "defend the honor of the army and France." Clemenceau fought a duel with Drumont (neither was hurt); there were at least 32 other duels over the controversy, one Jew being killed. The spring 1898 elections resulted in a clear victory for the anti-Dreyfusards.

Yet, during the ensuing months, it was discovered that one of the decisive pieces of evidence against Dreyfus had been forged by Henry, and that he had fabricated a number of other documents between 1894 and 1898 in order to conceal the original forgery. When these revelations surfaced in August, Henry confessed and was immediately put in prison, where he committed suicide the next day. The chief of the General Staff and the minister of war resigned. Du Paty, whom Zola described as the "diabolical" mastermind of the Dreyfus Affair, was retired and put on half-pay for punishment. In panic, Esterhazy absconded to Belgium and, ultimately, London. The royalists refused to admit defeat, however. Officers, aristocrats, and hundreds of Catholic clergymen subscribed to a "Henry Memorial Fund," endorsing *L'Action Francaise* in believing that Henry was a hero and even a martyr. Nevertheless, Henry's confession ensured that the appeal of the Dreyfus family for a retrial would now be irresistible.

By the summer of 1899, a distinct class of intellectuals (the word "intelligentsia" was now coined), including a growing number of secular Jews, emerged as a major power in European society. The anti-Dreyfusards boasted authors including Paul Valéry, Jules Verne, and Maurice Barrès, as well as twenty-six out of forty members of the *Academie Francaise*. Degas, Renoir, Cezanne, and Rodin allied with this camp, opposed by fellow artists Pissarro, Monet, Signac, and Cassatt. The latter Dreyfusards were joined by the Socialists. The hammering away on Dreyfus's behalf by this important but numerically limited cadre finally began to swing the tide.

Following several political crises, a new cabinet, led by the moderate Pierre Waldeck-Rousseau, took office in June 1899, resolving to put an end to *"l'affaire."* Dreyfus was brought back from Devil's Island, still in chains, passing through a large soldiers' guard which stood with backs turned as he entered a courtroom in Rennes on August 7. Until then totally unaware that his conviction had created a furor in France, Alfred had been left to waste away, his voice turned to a rasp, in a vermin-infested cell. The courtroom now saw a dazed thirty-nine year-old man, stooped, gaunt, practically bald. "All that had survived against crushing odds," in David Lewis's felicitous phrase, "was an indomitable will for vindication." Yet, despite the overwhelming evidence, after only an hour's deliberation on 9 September 1899, the new court martial, by a vote of five to two, found Dreyfus guilty. The judges in this secret hearing were prepared, at the same time, to reduce his sentence to ten years (five of which he had already served) because of what they termed "extenuating circumstances." "The traitor convicted," crowed the headline in *La Libre Parole* after the verdict: "Down with the Jews!"

"A thrill of horror and shame ran through the whole civilized world," editorialized the London *Times* twenty-four hours later. Demonstrations against the verdict were held across Europe and the United States. In France, Jew-haters and reactionaries saw the court judgment as a justification of their position. The pro-Dreyfus forces were divided. Some like the poet Charles Péguy, looking at the issue in political terms, wanted Dreyfus to continue the struggle. Yet Alfred, concerned for his steadfast wife and their children, and having his siblings' support in light (as he later wrote) of his "seriously undermined health," chose to secure his own release. Following the premier's advice, Dreyfus withdrew his appeal and was finally granted a "pardon" by the new, liberal president of the Third Republic, Emile Loubet. The government's hopes for the upcoming Paris Exposition of 1900, with France's prestige involved, may have played a significant role in this decision. Dreyfus accepted the act of clemency, but reserved the right to do all in his power to establish his innocence.

In 1904, a retrial was granted by the leftist government. In July, 1906, a civilian High Court of Appeal declared the Rennes judgment "wrongful" and "erroneous," and reversed all previous convictions. The Senate passed a bill reinstating Dreyfus; on July 21, he was formally reinstated and decorated as a Chevalier of the *Légion d'honneur* only steps from the site of his degradation in January 1895. "Long live the Republic! Long live truth!" this unyielding, self-controlled patriot responded to the small crowd present. After a further year of service in the French Army, whose honor he had always sought to restore and in which he attained the rank of major, Dreyfus retired to the reserves. Picquart was promoted to the rank of brigadier general. On 4 June 1908, the government transferred the ashes of Zola, who had died four years earlier of accidental asphyxiation in his Paris home and was buried in Paris's Montmartre Cemetery, to the Pantheon. There he shares a crypt with Victor Hugo and Alexandre Dumas.

What were the consequences in France of the Dreyfus Affair? In December 1905, the union of anticlerical socialists and a leftist bloc in the Chamber of Deputies pushed through legislation which formally separated church and state, thus liquidating the Concordat of 1801 agreed upon by Napoleon and the Vatican. The gap widened between the extremists of both sides—right-wing nationalists and left-wing anti-militarists, haunting French life until 1914 and even later. France was weakened as a European and world state: its reputation as the most enlightened country on the continent became greatly tarnished, while the Army's strength would be vitiated in the face of an emboldened pacifist movement during the crises that led to World War I.

What of the Affair's impact on French Jewry? In 1899, the die-hard anti-Dreyfusards organized the movement *Action Française* to defend their ideas and to serve as a rallying point for overthrowing the Third Republic. (With these Conservative forces staking so much on Dreyfus's guilt, it is understandable that his full rehabilitation occurred only in 1906.) The extreme nationalist *Action Française*, led by Maurras, Barrès, and Léon Daudet, would provide the intellectual foundation for French fascism in the 1930s and for some in the collaborationist Vichy regime after the German victory against the Republic in June 1940. On the other hand, the radical Marxist wing in France, which identified Jews with the capitalists and viewed the Dreyfus Affair as an internal concern of the middle-class, retreated before the socialist-humanitarian wing led by Jean-Leon Jaurès. Léon Blum, who first entered the political arena via the Affair and his strong admiration of

Jaurès, also serving as an assistant to Zola's lawyer, would become the first Jew and Socialist to be chosen premier of the Republic in 1936. [13]

The French-Jewish establishment believed that its faith in the Republic and emancipation had been vindicated by the outcome of *"l'affaire."* The Consistoire's main publication announced that "the Dreyfus Affair has concluded for the Israelites and its conclusion would make us love even more, were that possible, our dear country." The *Univers Israelite* went even further: "The Affair...had particularly fortunate results for our coreligionists, for in giving birth to the Dreyfus Affair, anti-Semitism has died." [14]

Like Reinach, Dreyfus himself thought Zionism an "anachronism" in modern society, in which Frenchmen were obligated to protect the liberal promise of the Revolution of 1789 and to strive to create a secular state. Together with Mathieu, Alfred believed to the end that triumphant French justice, not a Judaism whose rituals he did not practice, had saved him.

Other Jews were hardly sanguine. As reflected by the aesthete Swann's disillusionment in the last books of *A la recherché du temps perdu*, the Dreyfus Affair destroyed Proust's belief in a natural merger of the educated bourgeoisie, mostly Jewish, and the aristocratic wellborn. Lazare, whom Péguy later memorialized as "the prophet of both Israel and the world" in the controversy,[15] converted to a militant socialist Zionism as the answer to antisemitism. He died from cancer in 1903 at the age of thirty-eight, practically forgotten. Herzl had first met Lazare in July 1896, and Lazare's pamphlet of that year probably persuaded the founder of political Zionism of Dreyfus's innocence. For Herzl, the virtues which he previously had believed Jews were to gain through assimilation—independence, physical courage, idealism, as well as an end to worldwide hatred of Jews—would be realized, instead, by the establishment of a secular Jewish state.

---

[13] For the historical context, see Paula Hyman, *From Dreyfus to Vichy: The Remaking of French Jewry, 1906-1939* (New York, 1979).

[14] Both publications quoted in Paula Hyman, *The Jews of Modern France* (Berkeley, 1998), 113.

[15] For Lazare's influence on Péguy, see Sidney D. Braun, "Péguy and Bernard Lazare: A Common Mystique," *Symposium*, 4:1 (1950), 131-140.

Antisemitism and anti-Dreyfusard did not always go together. Some anti-Dreyfusards were not fanatical antisemites; conversely, certain Dreyfusards harbored anti-Jewish prejudices. Further, some anti-Dreyfusards did not really believe Dreyfus to be a traitor. Yet they considered the defense of the French Army or "the nation" more important than the fate of one man. Similarly, for some Dreyfusards, the importance of defending universal values far outweighed the importance of the personal destiny of Alfred Dreyfus. In this war of ideas, two systems confronted each other: truth versus authority, justice versus order, reason versus instinct, and universalism versus exclusive nationalism.

These opposing systems of value resurfaced in all of France's political crises to come, including the Vichy years of 1940-1944. Yet the policies of the Vichy government after France's surrender in June 1940, can only be understood within the context of the German occupation and World War II. Vichy was neither a military dictatorship nor a clerical government, but rather a regime possessed of its own ideological ambitions and of a vision, sparked by the consequences of World War I, that situated France as a member of Nazified Europe.

The recollection of the Dreyfus Affair during the Vichy regime was dim, observes Henry Rousso. A regime which asserted during the country's occupation by Hitler's forces that the Jews had been responsible for the war against the Third Reich in 1939-1940 and that this was a war which "French people" had not wanted would not harp on a controversy where a Jew had been accused of spying for Germany, and which had divided the French people as sharply almost a half-century earlier. In addition, anyone in France attempting, together with the Nazis, to promote antisemitism anchored in French tradition would hardly refer explicitly to a case which, first and foremost, had resulted in a major defeat for the anti-Jewish movement.[16]

---

[16] Henry Rousso, *The Vichy Syndrome, History and Memory in France Since 1944* (Cambridge, 1991).

The *Statut des Juifs* in October 1940, and the immediate antisemitic legislation of Vichy, launched on its own initiative (the only instance in occupied Western Europe) under the direction of some fanatical disciples of Maurras, were all marked by the heritage of the Dreyfus Affair. Yet these laws against Jews were also an extreme expression of the xenophobic tendencies and measures that had emerged towards the end of the 1930s, when France accepted well over 300,000 refugees (perhaps 55,000 Jews) from Central Europe. The most brutal manifestations of this xenophobia were Vichy's establishment of a dense network of very primitive concentration camps in the southern zone; its special efforts to suppress Jewish Communists within the Resistance movement; and the far harsher treatment meted out to foreign-born Jews.

Early on the morning of 16 July 1942, 13,152 Jews from occupied Paris and its suburbs were arrested by French police—on the basis of lists that the gendarmerie themselves had drawn up—before being sent to Nazi death camps in Poland. Childless couples and single people were interned in a camp in the working-class suburb of Drancy. The others were taken to the Vélodrome d'Hiver, a bicycle stadium. Thrown together for five days in inhuman conditions, they were taken from there to the camps of Pithiviers and Beaune-la-Rolande. The Vichy administration had issued a clear directive that the children "must not leave in the same convoys as the parents."[17] So, after heartrending separations, they departed—the parents on one side, the children on the other—for Auschwitz-Birkenau, where the deportees of Drancy had preceded them by a few days. Only 811 of

---

[17] Vichy order quoted in Francois Hollande, "The Crime Committed in France, by France," 22 July 2012. www.consulfrance-miami.org/spip.php?article3235. After this brutal roundup, several leading French churchmen did speak out indignantly against the Vichy regime. Among them was Archbishop Jean-Geraud Saliege of Toulouse, who declared on August 30, 1942, that "the Jews are our brothers, like so many others, and no Christian can forget this fact." The defiant attitude of those churchmen after 1942, Roger Cohen points out, contributed to the fact that that three-quarters of France's Jewish population survived, many of them protected by French Catholics. On the other hand, some churchmen, including Alfred Cardinal Baudrillart, the rector of the Catholic Insitute in Paris, were outspoken supporters of the Vichy government and the Nazis. Cardinal Baudrillart called Hitler's mission a noble and inspiring one. Roger Cohen, "French Church Issues Apology To Jews on War," *New York Times*, 1 October 1997.

these Jews survived the war. In the next two years, more than 67,000 French and foreign Jews were deported from these transit camps to the death centers; 2,500 returned.

Active collusion by Vichy in the Holocaust from mid-1942 onwards stemmed less from a determination to participate in the Third Reich's mass murder of the Jews than from an overall strategy to assert Vichy sovereignty in the face of the occupier, and to achieve some reciprocal benefit in exchange for cooperation with the Nazis. In the end, Marrus and Paxton show in their joint study of the subject, this "colossal miscalculation" sanctioned the turning over to Germany of foreign and French Jews from *both* the northern and southern zones. Close to 75,000 Jews (one-third French citizens) lost their lives as a consequence. [18] These included Alfred Dreyfus's favorite grandchild, Madeleine Levy, a "Combat" Resistance fighter who was responsible for hiding Jewish children in the French countryside. Deported from Drancy in November 1943 to Auschwitz, she died of typhus two months later at the age of twenty-five.

Fortunately, Dreyfus did not live to witness this singular tragedy. He was recalled to active service during World War I and, as a lieutenant-colonel, commanded an ammunition column. After the war, the now colonel retired permanently into obscurity; the publication of Schwartzkoppen's papers in 1930 reaffirmed his innocence. On 12 July 1935, Dreyfus died quietly in his Paris home after a long illness, surrounded by Lucie and their two children. Burial followed two days later, on the Republic's Bastille Day, in the Montparnasse Cemetery on the left bank of the Seine, final resting place for many of the country's illustrious citizens. By his own wish, the funeral was strictly private, relatives only in attendance.

In the prosperity and general confidence of the 1920s, antisemitism in France subsided. Drumont's *La Libre Parole* folded in 1924 for lack of funds; Pope Pius XI condemned *L'Action Française* two years later. The crises of the late 1930s stripped away this veneer, however. When Blum became premier as head of a Popular Front leftist government, he was denounced in the Chamber of Deputies by

---

18 Michael Marrus and Robert O. Paxton, *Vichy France and the Jews* (New York, 1981). Also see Nicholas Fraser, "Toujours Vichy: A Reckoning With Disgrace." *Harper's*, October 2006, 86–94.

Xavier Vallat, a right-wing Deputy and sympathizer of *L'Action Française* (and later Commissioner for Jewish Affairs in the Vichy government), who said: "Your coming to power is undoubtedly a historic event. For the first time this ancient Gallo-Roman country will be governed by a Jew....to govern a peasant nation such as France, it is better to have someone whose origins, however modest, are deep in our soil...than to have a subtle Talmudist." Blum immediately responded: "I for one know neither Jews, as you say, nor Protestants, nor Catholics. I know only Frenchmen."[19]

For the first time, political antisemitism had been openly shown in France. Street demonstrations in Paris and the provinces broke out against the new government. Before long, a popular, ominous slogan in conservative circles surfaced: "Better Hitler than Blum." Blum resigned in June 1937, a few months before noted author Louis-Ferdinand Céline published *Bagatelles Pour Un Massacre*, a scurrilous emotive litany critical of Jews and their influence on French society, and which called for a pogrom. That same year, "The Life of Emil Zola," starring Paul Muni (originally Meshulem Meier Weisenfreund of Lemberg), won the Oscar for Best Motion Picture. Blum landed in the Buchenwald concentration camp in early 1943 after Hitler's armed forces took control of the Vichy-run zone in the south of France.

In May 1945, U.S. Army forces liberated Blum, who became a hero of France and of the international socialist movement. When Maurras was condemned that same year to life imprisonment for collaboration, he cried, "It's the revenge of Dreyfus!" (His sentence was commuted in 1952 to forced residence in a private clinic; he died a few months later.) By the mid-1950s, the secular Jew Pierre Mendes-France would achieve power as the most dynamic and admired premier of the Fourth Republic. And in early 1994, Jean-Marie Le Pen's extremist right-wing Front National notwithstanding, a public opinion poll reported that 81 percent of French citizens questioned in a poll responded that they would have no problem in voting for a Jewish candidate for the presidency. Three years later, the country's Roman

---

[19] The Vallat-Blum exchange is quoted in Pierre Birnbaum, *Anti-Semitism in France, A Political History from Léon Blum to the Present* (Oxford, 1992), 243. Also see Paul J. Kingston, *Anti-Semitism in France During the 1930s: Organizations, Personalities and Propaganda* (Hull, 1983).

Catholic Church issued an apology for its silence over French collaboration during the Holocaust, declaring that "we beg for the pardon of God." [20]

The Dreyfus Affair still periodically roiled French politics, however. In 1984, two years after a terrorist bomb planted outside the Copernic synagogue in Paris killed four people – only one of them Jewish, Minister of Culture Jack Lang of President Francois Mitterrand's socialist government commissioned a statue of Dreyfus, to be placed in the courtyard where the officer had been degraded a century earlier. Since the minister of defense refused to allow it to be displayed there, the army wishing no embarrassing reminders of its role in the tumultuous affair, the rough-hewn bronze statue by the Polish-born Jewish political cartoonist Louis Mitelberg (TIM) was kept out of the public eye for three years upon its completion in 1986. After being put in a little-publicized corner of the Tuileries Gardens, the same year that Dreyfus's tomb was desecrated, the twelve-foot high sculpture was eventually moved in October 1994 to the Left Bank's Place Pierre Lafue at the corner of Boulevard Raspail and Notre-Dame-des-Champs in conjunction with the 100th anniversary of Dreyfus's first conviction. (At the same moment, the army formally acknowledged Dreyfus's innocence.) A copy of this "*Hommage au capitaine Dreyfus*," bearing his words to Lucie from Devil's Island "*Si tu veux que je vive, fais-moi rendre mon honneur*" and showing Dreyfus holding a broken sword, stands in front of the Museum of Jewish Art and History on Rue du Temple.[21]

In 1993, the Dreyfus Society was inaugurated in Bonn under the name of the *Dreyfus Gesellschaft für Menschenrechte und activ Toleranz*. Its defined objectives were to participate in appropriate projects during the Dreyfus Centenary and to establish a platform dedicated to cultural projects combating antisemitism and racism. Publications and the fields of performing arts are especially encouraged. Since its inception

---

20 Cohen, "French Church Issues Apology To Jews on War."

21 Thomas A. Bass, "Still Wandering," *Tablet Magazine*, 11 October 2011.

the Society has also cooperated with numerous international organizations such as *Inter Nationes Bonn*, *The Moses Mendelsohn Zentrum Potsdam; Evangelische Akademie Arnoldshain*; The National Association of Jewish Students in Germany; *the Deutsche Oper Berlin, Oper der Stadt Bonn, Theater Basel*, and the New York City Opera. These projects have been further recognized by the Goethe Institute New York, National TV and Radio Channels in Germany, France, the United Kingdom, Sweden, Finland, Hungary, Canada, Slovenia, and Switzerland. They have also led to numerous presentations, lectures, and debates held by the Guggenheim Museum in New York, Memoire 2000 in Paris, Barnes & Noble New York, the Jewish Book Week in London, and the *Institut Français* in London.

In 1994, a major work by French military historian and army reserve officer Jean Doise provided support for Esterhazy's admission, made before his death in 1923, that he had written the bordereau under orders from Sandherr. *Un secret bien gardé: Histoire militaire de l'affaire Dreyfus* argued that, as an agent planting disinformation for French counter-intelligence, Esterhazy was peddling "secrets" about the technologically obsolete 120 mm Baquet howitzer, which the French army was about to replace. Selling old secrets and framing Dreyfus to make this information look important was a ruse designed to keep the Germans from discovering France's real military secret, the development of the new quick-firing 75 mm field gun. The French 75 was ahead of its time technically. The Germans and Americans did not produce a field gun that matched its performance until twenty years later, on the eve of World War I. In fact, in 1918, the U.S. Army simply adopted the French 75 as its own and began building the gun under license in the United States. In Thomas Bass's apt summation, Dreyfus was sacrificed for reasons of state—or, to borrow from current usage, for national security.[22]

On 13 January 1998, France paid solemn tribute to Zola on the centennial of the publication of *J'Accuse!* Standing before the vaulted stone crypt in the Pantheon, Prime Minister Lionel Jospin acknowledged that the country continued to struggle with the consequences of its role during the Holocaust years. "Truth is on the

---

[22] Bass. "Still Wandering."

march, and nothing can stop it," Zola had declared in *J'Accuse!* "History proved him right," Jospin concluded. A reproduction of the novelist's ringing manifesto, emblazoned across the front page of *L'Aurore* and reproduced in many other daily newspapers, hung on the classical pillars of the National Assembly, with blue, red and white lighting in the colors of the French flag. *La Croix* apologized for its antisemitic editorials during the Dreyfus Affair. While Communist and Socialist leaders stood alongside Jospin, President Jacques Chirac, a Gaullist conservative, sent letters to the descendants of Zola and Dreyfus noting that the Dreyfus Affair was "a black spot unworthy of our country and our history, a colossal judicial error and shamefully compromising for the state." During a speech in 1995, speaking then as mayor of Paris during the rededication of TIM's statue of Dreyfus, Chirac had acknowledged for the first time that France itself, and not just the Vichy regime, had been responsible for crimes against the Jews in World War II. "Half a century after Vichy," he now wrote to Dreyfus's granddaughter, Simone Perl, "we know that dark forces, intolerance and injustice can insinuate themselves into the very summit of the state."[23]

Yet while French Jewry possessed by then a far greater sense of collective self-assertion than in the past, its ranks swelled by 300,000 Sephardi immigrants from North Africa in the 1950s and 1960s and its spirits boosted after Israel's stunning victory in the Six-Day War of 1967, that community's future is not certain. The Fifth Republic's culture, beginning with the rise to power of the left in the 1980s, increasingly questioned the setting of one's community apart from national society; open support for Israel, particularly after its war in Lebanon against the Palestine Liberation Organization in 1982, became difficult for French Jews to sustain. The emergence of a large Arab minority (currently estimated to be about 10 percent of France's population of 67 million), joined to the bitterness in the suburbs of Paris and other cities of a neglected underclass from West Africa and elsewhere, sparked antisemitic attacks from 2001 onwards. The Palestinian Second Intifada heightened tensions. President Chirac denied this upsurge, even accusing American Jewish organizations in

---

[23] Craig R. Whitney, "A Repentant France Honors Zola." *New York Times*, 13 January 1998.

2002 of waging an anti-France campaign under orders from Jerusalem. That same year, along with assaults against Jewish school children, vandals spray-painted Dreyfus's statue with the yellow star that Jews had been forced to wear under Nazi rule.

Also in 2002, the Johns Hopkins University Archives, in Baltimore, acquired illustrated material which documents the reaction of the French public to the Dreyfus Affair during the 1890s. The material, catalogued as the Alfred Dreyfus Collection, MS. 422, consists of material obtained from the collection of Jean Marie Goulemot, a collector of French intellectual history and a member of the *Institut Universitaire de France*. The Collection includes a set of hand-colored lithographs, titled the *Musée des Horreurs* (Freak Show), which depict prominent supporters of Dreyfus, statesmen, journalists and Jewish leaders as animals. They were originally published as a series of fify-one political posters starting in the fall 1899, at the opening of the Paris Exposition, and after Dreyfus' re-trial at Rennes. Among those depicted in caricature are Zola, Dreyfus, Picquart, Clemenceau, Henri Brisson (prime minister), Louis Lépine (prefect of the Paris police), Fernand Labori (defense attorney for Dreyfus) and Ludovis Travieux (minister of justice and prominent Dreyfusard). The lithographs had been created by an artist operating under the pseudonym V. Lenepveu, and were eventually confiscated by the police, who also stopped their production.[24]

Attacks since 2004 against the Jews of France, when the police recorded close to 1,000 such incidents of hatred, continue to revive memories of "*l'affaire.*" When a gang of youths tortured to death the twenty-three year-old Jew Ilan Hilmi in February 2006, first seeking a large ransom for the Moroccan-born telephone salesman because "Jews were rich," Prime Minister Dominique de Villepin met with Jewish leaders. De Villepin cited the Dreyfus Affair as "the indestructible link uniting the Jews in France and the destiny of the Republic." By exonerating Dreyfus, he explained, French truth and

---

24 For additional background, see Noram L. Kleebatt, ed., *The Dreyfus Affair: Art, Truth and Justice* (Berkeley, 1987).

justice had triumphed.[25] Assaults on Jews and Jewish institutions continued nonetheless. Catcalls of *"sale Juif"* and graffiti such as *"à bas le Juif"* and swastikas became commonplace.

Not surprisingly, this escalation in turn has resulted in a marked increase in the number of French Jews moving to Israel. When Israeli Prime Minister Ariel Sharon remarked in the summer 2004 that French *aliya* "is a must and they have to move immediately," the CRIF Jewish-umbrella organization was embarrassed; Chirac even suggested that Sharon, equated by the political left with Hitler, was not welcome in France. Sharon responded by lauding the French government for its vigilance against antisemitism, but Orthodox Jews (some thirty percent of the community and strongly pro-Zionist) responded to his provocative call. From about 1,000 a year before the Palestinian Arab *intifada* had erupted in September 2000, the number of French-Jewish immigrants to Israel tripled by 2006. Another 20,000 or so have made the final decision to move to their new homes there, and more are expected to arrive in the coming years. Their presence is already felt in Ashdod, Netanya, Ra'anana, and Ramat Bet Shemesh, as well as in Jerusalem's German Colony, Herzliya Pitah, and
Caesarea. [26]

The vast majority of France's 480,000 Jews, by far the largest Jewish center in Europe and third largest worldwide after Israel and the United States, is not prepared to join this wave. At the same time, in addition to the presence of a vocal Arab population, its members have to contend with an increasingly decentralized French political culture that challenges directly the old model of Jewish identification and legitimacy as a community. Further, Shmuel Trigano has noted, "the possibility of a unique communal framework which will include the majority of French Jews seems increasingly remote."[27] Ultra-Orthodoxy, the direction in which religious renewal has gone, is largely cut off from the wider Jewish community; non-observant Jews have failed to establish institutions of cultural transmission; pro-Israel

---

25 Stanley Meisler, "History's new verdict on the Dreyfus case," *Los Angeles Times*, 9 July 2006.

26 Larry Derfner, "Vive Israel." *Jerusalem Post Magazine*, 13 October 2006.

27 Shmuel Trigano, "Is There a Future for French Jewry?," *Azure* 20 (Spring 2005): 45-61.

activities lack communal and institutional support. An estimated forty percent of French Jewry is religiously unaffiliated. The next generation of French Jewish leadership, asserts this professor of the sociology of religion and politics at Paris University in Nanterre, "is nowhere to be found."

On 12 July 2006, exactly one hundred years after Alfred Dreyfus's official exoneration, France's president held a state ceremony together with descendants of Dreyfus and Zola. Standing in the cobblestone courtyard of the *Ecole Militaire*, Jacques Chirac called Dreyfus "an exemplary officer" and a "patriot who passionately loved France," a man "suddenly caught in the snowball effect of a judicial error." The two words "judicial crime" never passed his lips, to the disappointment of Alfred's great-grandson, Michael Dreyfus. [28]
Later that day, the first stone was laid for a *Musée Dreyfus* on Zola's property in Medan, thirty kilometers west of Paris, in an initiative under the patronage of Elie Wiesel. Scheduled to open in September 2009, the museum was to be devoted to *"l'affaire"* and to its "timeless and universal" significance—the fight against antisemitism and all other forms of racism—so that remembrance prevails over ignorance and vigilance over oblivion. On 3 October 2011, it was announced that the Zola House would be closed for four years of construction, aimed to restore the property and develop a Dreyfus museum.

A few months earlier, the Touro College Jacob D. Fuchsberg Law Center of Central Islip, New York, sponsored a conference in Paris to examine the Dreyfus Affair and its legacy. For three days, sessions at the *Ecole Militaire,* the *Palais de Justice*, the Museum of Jewish Art and History, the *Palais de Luxembourg*, and two academic centers explored the issues from the viewpoint of justice, of media, and of politics. In the presence of some descendants of Dreyfus and of Zola, eminent professors, Jewish community leaders, journalists, and jurists delivered their remarks under the theme of "persecution through prosecution". While no government officials took an active part, the conference was held under the patronage of President Nicolas Sarkozy.

The climate of Jew-hatred escalated dramatically with the fatal

[28] http://www.ambafrance-uk.org/Speech-by-M-Jacques-Chirac.

shooting by twenty-three year old Mohamed Merah on 19 March 2012, of a rabbi, his two small children, and another child at the Ozar HaTorah school in the Roseraie district of Toulouse. The murderer, a Frenchman of Algerian descent who had also killed three unarmed French soldiers earlier, filmed the attack and wounded several other pupils before making his escape. Sarkozy, then campaigning for reelection, declared a day of national mourning when he visited the scene and described the shooting as a national tragedy. Chief Rabbi Gilles Bernheim declared himself "horrified" by the attack. Before being fatally shot by police three days later while seeking to escape his apartment, self-styled al Qaeda jihadist Merah declared that he had been motivated by the fate of the Palestinian Arabs, the French military presence in Afghanistan, and France's ban on the *burqa*. French Friends of Israel blamed "anti-Zionist propaganda" for encouraging "the murderous lunacy of fanatics." Mohammed Moussaoui of the French Council for the Muslim Faith said he was "horrified by this indescribable criminal act" and he wanted to express the solidarity of France's Muslim community. At the same time, thirty young people, mostly girls, demonstrating to honor Merah's memory in the district where most of Toulouse's Muslims live, compared their pain to that of the victims' families.[29]

For the French Jewish community, appalled by the murders in Toulouse, one of the key issues in the second and final round of the country's presidential elections two months later was how each candidate might combat the new antisemitism that has developed under the mask of anti-Zionism. Following a bruising campaign, dominated by ten percent unemployment in France and a challenge to the German-led policy of economic austerity in the euro zone, Sarkozy's loss to socialist Francois Hollande signaled the possibility that far-Left parties who are anti-Israel would enter the new government. (Further, a poll for *Le Figaro* of 10,000 voters indicated that ninety-three percent of the two million French Muslim participants backed Hollande.) In addition, the important issue of

[29] *BBC News*, 22 March 2012; *Los Angeles Times World*, 21 March 2012.

secularity will lead to difficulties in the legal adjustments to Jewish religious practices such as *shechita* (kosher butchering). In the view of Richard Prasquier, past president of the CRIF (Council of French Jewish Institutions) and an open supporter of Sarkozy's candidacy, the Jewish community which is, regardless of its political leanings, very close to Israel, cannot avoid confronting these new challenges.[30]

The Toulouse massacre "triggered an explosion" in antisemitic attacks across France. In a report released on 4 June 2012, by the *Service de Protection de la Communauté Juive* (SPCJ), more than ninety such incidents occurred in the ten days after that shooting, and a total of 148 in March and April—forty-three of these classified by the French Interior Ministry as "violent." In the report's last recorded incident, a Jewish man and his friend were assaulted by people who self-identified as Palestinians and promised to "exterminate" the Jews. On June 2, three Jewish teenagers, the two boys wearing *kippot* on the Sabbath, were assaulted in the city of Villeurbanne, near Lyon. The group of young male attackers first hurled racial slurs, left, and then returned with hammers and iron bars. The Jewish teens were then beaten, leaving one with an open wound on his skull and the girl with a neck injury. French Interior Minister Manuel Valls decried this "deliberate attack against the Republic", while CRIF President Marcel Amsellem denounced the "climate of animosity and stigmatization of the State of Israel leading to hatred and unacceptable acts." "Jewish citizens are a recurring target," observed Johan Sportouch, the secretary-general of the Union of Jewish Students.[31]

On 22 July 2012, seventy years after the Vel d'Hiv roundup, President Hollande laid a wreath and paid his respects in front of a commemorative plaque that was erected on the site of the demolished Winter Velodrome. In an official booklet released before the anniversary, Hollande declared, "This crime was committed in France by France," before adding that it was "also a crime against France, a betrayal of its values." A recent poll by France's Jewish Student

---

[30] Richard Prasquier, "Jews to Face New Challenges in Post-Elections France," *Haaretz*,26 April 2012.

[31] Joseph Stritch and Marc Benchtetrit. "French Police: 3 Jewish Teens Attacked in City Near Lyon." *Jerusalem Post*, 5 June 2012. Also see Robert I. Weiner and Richard E. Sharpless. *An Uncertain Future: Voices of a French Jewish Community, 1940-2012* (Toronto, 2012).

Association revealed that forty-two percent of the country's citizens did not know what the "Vel d'Hiv" round-up was. The figure was even higher among French youth, with sixty percent of eighteen to twenty-four year-olds saying they were not aware of that round-up or of the active part taken in it by French gendarmerie. At the same time, beyond the annual wreath-laying ceremonies, "the City of Love" is committed to making sure that its youth is taught about France's dark past. At least once during their school years, all students pay a visit to a freight car, once used to deport Jews, and the nearby granite memorial in Drancy or to a mini-museum in the area. An annual writing contest organized by the Ministry of Education and Historical Foundations, seeking to raise awareness about the main events of World War II, offers as a first prize a visit to the camps. In September, a Memorial to the Shoah was inaugurated on the site of the Drancy transit camp.[32]

Perhaps the last revelation on the Dreyfus Affair occurred half a year later, when the French Ministry of Defense for the first time made public the entire contents of the long-sealed file that the French army had used against Dreyfus. (The posting online of that file is the work of Pierre Gervais, Pauline Peretz and Pierre Stutin, historians who recently wrote *Le Dossier Secret de l'Affaire Dreyfus*.) Encompassing about 1,000 pieces of evidence, many of them forgeries, this dossier included a series of intimate letters between Schwartzkoppen, to whom Esterhazy had sold French military "secrets", and Lieutenant Colonel Alessandro Panizzardi, an Italian military attaché who was sexually involved with his German counterpart in Paris at the time. Although neither man had anything to do with Dreyfus, their correspondence revealed an irrefutable liaison between them, and thus lent an air of veracity to other documents which Dreyfus's persecutors forged in order to lend retroactive credibility to his conviction as a spy. Some of these fake documents even made reference to the foreigners' affair directly, in which "Alexandrine" informs his lover "Maximilienne" that if "Dreyfus is brought in for questioning," they must both claim that

---

[32] Andrea Davoust, "City at Heart of Jewish Deportations Confronts Past." *France 24*, 22 July 2012. For Hollande's public address to mark 70 years after the Vel D'Hiv roundup, see Hollande, "The Crime Committed in France, by France."

they "never had any dealings with that Jew....Clearly, no one can ever know what happened with him."[33]

The spies' letters, real and fake, conveniently allowed the top officers to justify placing the whole dossier under seal, on the grounds that "dishonoring" Germany's and Italy's military attaches by uncovering their illicit entanglement could spell disaster for France's diplomatic relations with both countries. At a time when male homosexuality still constituted "an affront to decency" under French law, it seemed all too logical that the high command should suppress its proof of the foreign soldiers' sexual crimes. In keeping the Dreyfus dossier shrouded in secrecy, the French military also fueled right-wing paranoia about a "Jewish conspiracy."

According to Gervais, Peretz and Stutin, *fin-de-siecle* antisemites and homophobes of the Belle Epoque both envisioned "hidden vices" with which members of those putatively deviant and immoral "races", along with their advocates, were secretly corrupting the nation. It is in what Caroline Weber characterizes as the "phantasmagoric convergence" of Jewishness, homosexuality, *dreyfusisme*, and covert criminality that the French army's secret dossier evokes the masterpiece by Marcel Proust, who was himself half-Jewish, gay, and a Dreyfusard. In *Sodome et Gomorrhe* (1921-22), volume four of the seven-volume *A la recherche du temps perdu*, Proust emphasizes that societal persecution and prejudices have transformed homosexuality and Jewishness into unspeakable transgressions, the two groups ostracized "save on the days of general misfortune when the majority rally round the victim as the Jews rallied round Dreyfus." Further, Proust writes, this criminalization has in turn forced the members of these so-called races underground, like so many spies, forcing them into a tacit conspiracy not to destroy the community at large, but to "make a secret of their lives" until the day of "the scandal when these lion-tamers are devoured."[34]

At the end of May 2013, an exhibition entitled "Phantom House" by Ahlam Shibli, an Israeli Bedouin woman, opened at the

---

[33] Quoted in Carolyn Weber, "Dreyfus, Proust, and the Crimes of the Belle Epoque," *Bloomberg View*, 13 May 2013.

[34] Proust cited in Weber, "Dreyfus, Proust."

city's *Jeu de Paume*. This renowned museum of contemporary art, which is subsidized by the French Ministry of Culture and Communications, featured sixty-eight photographs of Palestinian Arab suicide bombers. The museum's website describes suicide bombers as "those who lost their lives fighting against the occupation," and the exhibition as being about "the efforts of Palestinian society to preserve their presence." According to CRIF, the people commemorated in the photos are "mostly from the [Fatah-affiliated] al-Aqsa Martyrs' Brigades, the Izz ad-Din al-Qassam Brigades [of Hamas], and the Popular Front for the Liberation of Palestine." All three are designated by the European Union as terrorist groups. One of the photos is of Osama Buchkar, a PFLP operative who killed three people and wounded fifty-nine in a terrorist attack he carried out at an open market in Netanya on 19 May 2002. The caption to his picture says that Buchkar "committed a martyr mission in Netanya." The exhibit's introduction in the museum catalogue describes captured Palestinian terrorists convicted in Israel as "Failed Suicide Martyrs"— who have yet to fulfill their unfinished mission of suicide. Israeli Arab volunteers in the Israel Defense Forces are shown as confused or mentally coerced victims and collaborators serving Zionism against the Palestinian cause.

In a letter to France's Culture and Communications Minister, Aurélie Filipetti, CRIF President Roger Cukierman asserted that it was "particularly lamentable and unacceptable that such a display should justify terrorism from the heart of Paris." In response to numerous protests, the Jeu de Paume released a statement "strongly denying accusations that it either condones or is complicit in terrorism." Shibli added: "I am not a militant… My work is to show, not to denounce or judge."[35] Yet this artist, going so far as to juxtapose Palestinian Arab resistance to Israeli rule with French resistance to Nazi occupation, is decidedly judgmental.

As of August 2013, the future for French Jewry remains unsettled. In light of the fifty-eight percent rise in attacks against Jews in France during the previous year, with one in four attacks involving

---

35 "Paris Museum Features Photos of Palestinian 'Martyrs.'" *Jewish Telegraphic Agency*, 7 June 2013.
Also see Richard Landes, "Terrorist Chic in France, From the Jeu de Paume Exhibit to Al Durah to Mohamed Merah," *Tablet* Magazine, 30 July 2013.

a weapon, it is not surprising that French Jews are quietly moving to London, New York, and Israel. [36] The ferment of that Jewry's plight has manifested itself in terrorist attacks, arson, assaults, the planting of a fake bomb near the Hillel Center in Lyon in March, and the stabbing of a rabbi and his son outside their synagogue in Paris one month later.

In addition, writing in *Tablet* magazine, Jillian Scheinfeld outlined an actual, popular trend of antisemitic hate speech on Twitter. The previous October, when the hashtag #UnBonJuif reached the top three on Twitter's trending topics list in France, the Union of French Jewish Students complained directly to the San Francisco-based social networking giant asking for the names of Twitter users promoting the antisemitic hashtag. "We are taking this extremely seriously," Guillaume Ayne, director of SOS Racisme, told *France24*: "There is a deep-rooted anti-Semitism in France, and there is a very small step between racist words and racist acts."[37] When Twitter failed to respond, the students took their case to a French court—and won. But, as Adam Chandler observes, even if a court order may ultimately impel Twitter to police its users more thoroughly, there is still a whole world offline and in the dark.[38] As of May 2013, Twitter has not yet cooperated.

A related phenomenon is the success of Dieudonné M'bala M'bala. This French-Cameroonian comedian, actor, and political provocateur has attracted thousands to his shows brimming with antisemitic "jokes," and has been awarded the prize of "political incorrectness" by the aged Holocaust denier Robert Faurisson. The prize was presented to him on stage by a sound technician, dressed in stripped pajamas which resembled those worn by Jews in the Nazi death camps. In responding to his critics, Dieudonné fashions himself

---

[36] Anna Sheinman, "Exodus to the UK as French Jews Escape Antisemitism." *Jewish Chronicle Online*, 29 February 2013.
[37] Julian Scheinfeld, "#FrenchJewHating," *Tablet* Magazine, 13 March 2013; Ayne quoted in Tony Todd, "Twitter May Face Legal Action Over Anti-Semitic Tweets," *France24*, 17 October 2012.

[38] Adam Chandler, "The Very Real Jewish Exodus from France." *Tablet* Magazine, 14 March 2013.

as a defender of freedom of speech, and a victim of the powerful Zionist plot against it.

At present, President Hollande has so far failed to give answers to a nation plagued by debt, taxes, and all-time high unemployment. This deleterious climate damages the image of France as a safe haven for its minorities, with Jews possibly serving as the ideal scapegoat. In addition, Clémence Bouloque notes that the prevailing perception among many French today is that members of the Left, past champions of the country's republican values, are unwilling to deal strongly with anti-Zionist or antisemitic rhetoric out of ostensible sympathy with the plight of the Palestinian Arabs or, worse, that they are merely using the Palestinian situation as an excuse to mask their own Judeophobia. On the other side of the political coin, one cannot forget President Charles De Gaulle's statement at a press conference in November 1967, where he not only questioned Israel's legitimacy as a nation-state, but also denounced Jews in general as an "elite, self-assured, and domineering people," equipped with "vast resources in terms of money, influence, and propaganda." The anti-American, pro-Arab, and objectively anti-Israel policies initiated by de Gaulle in the 1960s have remained to this day an essential tenet of French foreign affairs and French political culture, whether under conservative or socialist governments.

In the course of his speech at the *Ecole Militaire* in 2006, then President Chirac had asserted that "the combat against the dark forces of intolerance and hate is never definitely won." Confronted by these same but more sinister adversaries today, the 480,000 Jews of France, comprising less than one per cent of the population, also face a culture which steadily questions their existence as a community. To the historian, this quickly recalls the moment when, during debates over the civic enfranchisement of French Jews, the liberal nobleman Stanislas de Clermont-Tonnerre rose in the National Assembly on 23 December 1789, to declare: "To the Jews as individuals, everything; to the Jews as a people, nothing." In France, as elsewhere in Europe, Jews are increasingly subject to pressures that they separate themselves from their fellow-Jews in Israel, realize that many ethnic Europeans and especially radical Islamists wish them ill, and accept Europe's proscription of some of the most basic practices of their faith. Together with European Jewry as a whole, the prospects for their survival as Jews depend on their will and their ability to live as a collectivity while affirming a sense of peoplehood. The resolution of this dilemma of Jewish identity will be given in the new century unfolding.

August 2013[39]

---

[39] Professor Monty Noam Penkower is Professor Emeritus of Jewish History at the Machon Lander Graduate Center of Jewish Studies, Jerusalem. He is the author of numerous books, including most recently the two volume *Palestine in Turmoil: The Struggle for Sovereignty, 1933-1939* (Newport, RI: Touro College Press, 2014).

"A Meditation on Memory and Mortality"

Rochelle L. Millen
Wittenberg University

> Memory is the basis of individual personality,
> Just as tradition is the basis of the collective
> Personality of a people. We live in memory
> And by memory, and our spiritual life is at bottom
> Simply the effort of our memory to persist, to
> Transform itself into hope, the effort of past to
> Transform itself into our future.[1]

Introduction

When Stanley Kraemer's 1961 movie, *Judgment at Nuremberg,* came out, I and my three siblings, having seen it, decided that our father surely should not view the film. Father had arrived in the United States in 1937, having married our mother in Poland[2] in 1936. She had been in the United States since 1930, and after becoming a naturalized citizen, took the boat back to Poland, on her own and married Father, thus gaining entry for him into the United States.

Many years later—I was already married with three small children— Mother shared that Father's sisters had made a scene at their small wedding in Sambor, near Lvov. They had yelled out in Yiddish "Avraham, Avraham, do not go to America; do not leave us!"[3] Although the youngest in his family, Father had helped support his sisters since both of my grandparents had already died. And the few times I tried to speak with him about his family in Europe, the tension

---

[1] Miguel de Unamuno, *Tragic Sense of Life*, trans. J.E. Crawford Flitch (New York, 1954): 8-9. The present essay is reprinted with permission from the University of Washington Press from the volume edited by Sarah Pinnock, *After Death: Facing Mortality in the Holocaust and Ourselves.*

[2] Their town, Sambor, in Eastern Galicia, is now in the Ukraine.

[3] According to the story, they actually used the affectionate diminutive in Yiddish, "Avrumchele."

was palpable. Here he was in America, the *goldena medinah (*the golden land), with a wife, four children, and a small store. The sisters, whose behavior had considerably diminished the joy of a long-planned wedding, had perished, together with all Father's relatives. Either they had been murdered by Ukrainians during the pogrom in 1941 subsequent to the German occupation of the city; during the mass action in the Sambor ghetto[4] which took place April 10-14, 1943; or at the time of the ghetto's final liquidation on June 9, 1943.[5] From Mother's family, her oldest brother, from whose home she had been escorted to the wedding canopy on August 2, 1936, was murdered together with his wife and two young sons.

But Mother's parents and three siblings were alive in the States, while Father was left an orphan. He had survived by following his heart and defying his sisters' wishes, leaving them in the vulnerable political and social environment of 1937 Poland. Not only had they and their families been murdered, but his brothers as well. As my late sister and I sometimes discussed, Father was a survivor. He had not endured the concentration or labor camps, he had not been tortured or beaten, but he was a survivor nonetheless. He could not endure any depiction or description of Nazi atrocities. They aroused loss, grief, and guilt. *Judgment at Nuremberg* remained a movie he did not see.

In 1961, when the movie appeared, I was 18 years old, the second oldest of four siblings all born in the United States. My parents owned a small store on Long Island that sold linens, and custom upholstery, and draperies My two brothers, sister and I attended an excellent public school and went to Hebrew school several afternoons a week and on Sunday. There was almost never conversation about "what happened to the family in Europe." We children picked up bits and pieces of information and rarely had the awareness to question our parents or Mother's siblings who resided in Brooklyn. We knew Uncle Aaron, Aunt Leiba[6] and their two sons had been murdered by the

---

[4] The closed ghetto in Sambor was established on December 1, 1942. Jews had already been concentrated in the Blich area of the town since March, 1942.

[5] See *The Book of Sambor—Stari-Sambor: A Memorial*, Alexander Manor, ed. (Tel Aviv, 1980). Most of the text is in Hebrew. These dates are on p. XLI

[6] Often called "Leibcha" by my parents, an endearing and affectionate form of her name.

Germans, as had all Mother's aunts, uncles, and cousins and Father's entire family. We knew that a special monument to the murdered Jews of Sambor had been erected in the Old Montefiore Cemetery in Queens; that friends of our parents would sometimes gather in our living room and talk about those no longer alive. But we were American; our parents were so proud of the education they had provided us. Not only were we in a good school, but Mother and Father took satisfaction in making available ample nourishment. It was only later in life that I understood my father's great pleasure in the wooden crate of oranges and that of apples kept cool in our garage. Mother had once told me, wistfully, that one year in Sambor her Chanukah gift was an orange! It appeared as a miracle in the Polish winter: the deep, lush color of the skin, the juicy pulp; the sweet taste. I listened, taking in the emotional cues perhaps unknowingly expressed. But I do not recall asking about Chanukah in other years in Sambor. So much went unasked and now remains unanswered, except for that which historical research and speculation uncover.

My parents—their stories and the family members central to those stories-- are nearly all gone. For reasons of family dynamics and professional interests, the position of family historian, keeper of the legacy, sleuth and collector of tales has become mine. It is a privilege that drives me and often I am overcome with a palpable and deep, deep sense of loss. The first time I walked through the Valley of Destroyed Communities at Yad Vashem—it was still under construction that day in the summer of 1991—I found the name "Sambor" etched on the Jerusalem stone, surrounded by the names of hundreds of other villages, towns, and cities now almost entirely *Judenrein.* The architecture of the valley is like a silent orchestra, playing the music of grief and loss and emptiness and tribute without a sound being heard; rather, the experience resonates in deeply tangible fashion. The silent notes tremble and are somber, sad, low, and full of pain. But they belong where they are—those notes, those names on huge pinkish-beige boulders. Walking among the stones, I felt the murdered had finally come home[7] to rest –in the land of Israel, on the hills of

---

[7] On the concept of "home" in the post-Holocaust era, see John K. Roth, *Ethics During and After the Holocaust: In the Shadow of Birkenau* (New York, 2007): 30-34.

Jerusalem. I felt small, miniscule, tiny against the backdrop of towering rocks, symbols of unimaginable loss. I was a diminutive, minute embodiment of the Jews who once flourished in those villages, towns, and cities. Their memory had become my legacy.

I have said to my students when we read excerpts from post-Holocaust theology that living in the post-Holocaust era requires of us responsibilities different from those of earlier times. Hatred of those unlike us has always existed; violence and aggression have deep roots in human history. But the widespread abhorrence of Jews, Roma and others on allegedly racial grounds fomented an ideology that justified organized slaughter across the European continent. The many victims in World War I—civilians and soldiers both[8]—were not targeted in the same way as those murdered by the Nazis and their allies. Their deaths were the results of war, not the outcome of modern technology allied with a broad systematic and intentional use of racial ideology. Nationalism played an essential role in each conflict, but not in the same ways. [9]

This chapter explores the relationship between my personal connections to the Holocaust, my family history, and its influence both on my sense of self and my professional identity as professor of religion and Jewish studies. In the latter capacity, I teach courses relating both directly and indirectly to the Shoah, among them "Reflections on the Holocaust: History, Literature, Theology" and "Germans and Jews: Culture, Identity, and Difference." What are my aims as a teacher in the classroom? What do I hope to accomplish, to implant in my students as I guide them through the complex vortex of Holocaust-related materials? In what way(s) might my objectives be affected by the diminishing number of Holocaust survivors? The chapter then draws associations from these core aspects of my identity and briefly comments upon memory, history, and the sense of mortality.

---

[8] The literature on World War I is huge. One recent source focusing on civilians is Tammy M. Proctor's, *Civilians in a World at War* (New York, 2010).

[9] Two classic studies of nationalism are Hans Kohn, *Living in a World Revolution: My Encounters with History* (New York, 1964) and Isaiah Berlin, *Against the Current: Essays in the History of Ideas* (Princeton, 2001).

The Last Survivors and Holocaust Education

Emanuel Levinas tells us: "When man [*sic*] truly approaches the other, he is uprooted from history." [10] Yet my task as teacher of the Holocaust is to immerse the student in its history, literature, and discussions of post-Holocaust theology. Is it feasible, while so absorbed, simultaneously to "uproot" him/her from that deep involvement? Will such action, as Levinas claims and hopes, indeed lead the person truly to approach and see the face of the other? I do not know. I am not aware of controlled studies or statistical analyses to corroborate—or disconfirm—this claim. But I do know that Levinas's affirmation is also my own. I see my task not only to disabuse students of historical naïveté and ignorance, to increase insight into the perspectives through which complex histories develop, to help structure and enrich their emotional imaginations, but also—and indeed primarily—to challenge them morally and ethically. The study of history is a process that gives meaning to the past.[11] Connecting to the past implies engaging our imagination and empathy in ways that lead us to respect the past and to comprehend that all actions have consequences; once certain choices are made, they cannot be undone. History enlarges our understanding of moral and ethical actions and leads to a deep sense of moral obligation. The steady attenuating of Holocaust survivors has led to a sense of urgency among educators: Can we convey their legacy when they are no longer with us? Can we effectively transmit the moral conundrum of that genocide in their absence?

Early in the semester, I talk with my students about who they are, their identities, their sense of self. "You are adults," I say, "molded by your first, primary, and most powerful teachers: your parents. You already have a strongly developed moral compass." Can I, I ask rhetorically, complicate that compass in the ways that study of genocide impels us to do? Can I create a cognizance in that – would/should the circumstances be such—help you incline against evil

---

[10] Emanuel Levinas, "Useless Suffering" in *Entre Nous: Thinking-of-the-Other* (New York, 1998): 52.

[11] See Gerda Lerner, *Why History Matters: Life and Thought* (New York, 1997): esp. 113-118.

and toward the good? "Here I am, in a liberal arts institution, sharing these aspects of Holocaust study with you after most of your personality has been formed and doing so with a specific ethical purpose: to increase your awareness and make you more able to choose the good. I am never sure, I say, that I can be effective. And probably I will never know." The absence of an actual survivor to bear witness to the moral ambiguity and horror increasingly complicates my task. For my students, 1933-1945 is long ago and far away.

Several years ago, Lisa L., a survivor from Cincinnati spoke to the class in which there were 25 students. She had traveled on the ship *St. Louis* as a nine year old, together with her mother and brother. In Havana at the port, she could see her father, who had been admitted to Cuba several months earlier. She waved and he waved back. It was May, 1939, and Cuba had decided not to admit more than the 2500 Jews already allowed entry. She was not re-united with her father. With over 900 others, she returned to Germany on the ship doomed to carry Jews toward death. Her family was fortunate; they survived.

Lisa's narrative conveyed not only events, but also and most significantly a distinctive emotional timbre: that of a nine year old separated once again from a beloved father; and of a then 72 year old woman reflecting on the history and memory of that heartbreak, anguish, fear, and dislocation. Then there is Murray E., who stood before a group of perhaps a hundred or more students relating how, in the Cracow ghetto while playing with other boys, he was suddenly taken to a truck with other young fellows. Their job was to remove tombstones from the central Cracow Jewish cemetery and use them to build a road. "My mother," he said in a soft tone, looking down, "I never got to say goodbye, "said this man of then 68 years, "to my mother." The hush in the large room was palpable. Memory made immediate in the retelling created unusual attentiveness. The only voice to be heard—in its pathos, poignancy, pain, and lament of the child within—was his. No one stirred.

I see my task as teaching in a manner that uses, yet transcends historical analysis. Horror can be an object of history, but at the same time, it must be very personal, suffused with individual memory and inner feeling. As Lisa L., Murray E. and other survivors reach their eighties, we must ask: why and in what ways does the death of the last survivor alter how we keep the immediacy of the Holocaust vigorous, animated, and vital? Will the archives[12] of taped interviews not suffice? On one level, the archives will be all we have; but on another, the screen is not the person.

In their journals, nearly every student wrote about the survivors whom they heard speak. The students asked many questions and then reflected, in written form, on both the presentation and the questions. Young people –especially Americans—often have a limited sense of history. Living in this huge country, only 247 years old with few wars having taken place on its soil, the centuries-old conflicts in Europe, the Balkans, the Middle East and Asia are incredibly distant and seem out-of-touch with the cornfields of Kansas and the cultural life of Chicago, New York or California. The presence of a person who represents a slice of the history brings the perspective of scale to the horrors and complexities of Holocaust history. For how do we experience the pursuit of and the death of another? Especially in instances of large-scale killing, the sense of death can be functional, abstract, disconnected. It is difficult to feel when encountering a number, a statistic. A summary of such murders causes us to protect ourselves without allowing the identification, empathy and fright a personal perspective engenders. Greater abstraction leads to less comprehension. Over the years, survivors—whether in public schools, universities, or communal gatherings on Yom Hashoah - –have shared their stories, thereby conveying the personal and human aspects of Nazi history. A member of our synagogue, a man now 100 years old, was in six camps and was 60 pounds when liberated. Another, now gone, was saved in one of Wallenberg's houses. Another member of the community, together with members of his family, was hidden in a small Dutch village close to the German border. As a small girl, a woman stayed for two years in a Catholic monastery in Paris. She still recalls the cape she wore and some of the Catholic liturgy she learned. A former Chief Rabbi of Israel finally put into book form the many

[12] The most extensive archives of taped interviews are to be found in the Fortunoff Archives at Yale University and the Spielberg Archives in California.

talks he has given about outliving death.[13] A woman in Toronto, incredibly, found her two sisters in a Swiss Red Cross hospital after the war. These survivors and their narratives bring life to a history whose objective was death.

In but a few years, the survivors will be gone. At every community Yom Hashoah commemoration in Columbus, OH where I live and in the communities of Dayton and Springfield, OH, near Wittenberg University, where I taught for twenty-five years, the number of survivors diminishes. Teaching of the Holocaust continues even as the events become more distant and the remaining survivors fewer. Yet the need to preserve their stories seems to me even more pressing than in the past. As the survivors face mortality, they know they will be buried in a marked grave after a proper funeral. They know their lives will not be abstractions, but rather personal narratives embedded in family and community. And most realize that their past, their personal history and experiences, duly acknowledged, are necessary for our future. How else to instruct the next generation? As their vivid or somber or fearful tales fade, as their powerful memories are transformed into history, we educators have an obligation to seek out other means of maintaining the immediacy and impact of their experiences. Two years ago in Jerusalem, I interviewed a woman, a dentist and noted sculptor born in Sambor, my parents' town, in 1937. During the final liquidation of the ghetto in 1943, her mother had pushed her—then six years old—through a small window onto the roof of a neighboring house; then the mother also managed to squeeze through. Until the liberation, they remained hidden in the home of a former neighbor. At the beginning of Dora N.'s narrative, she related how first her father had been taken, and later her grandmother, the beloved *Bubbe* who had lived across the street. The memory of her grandmother being led away was so powerful, immediate, and alive that in the telling, this sophisticated woman of over 70 wept and sobbed. The decades conflated, the wounds reopened.[14] Can this be replicated for contemporary and future students? In what ways can the impact of

---

[13] Israel Meir Lau, *Out of the Depths: The Story of a Child of Buchenwald Who Returned Home at Last* (New York, 2011).

[14] See Lawrence L. Langer, *Holocaust Testimonies: The Ruins of Memory* (New Haven, 1991).

personal testimony continue to help our students as they consider the many nuanced faces of evil and work toward a commitment to individual responsibility, ethical obligation and the possibility of—to reiterate Levinas' terms—being "uprooted from history" so as to act on moral principles? I understand Levinas describing moral and ethical action as embedded in the concrete circumstances of history, leading to human obligation most powerfully when decisions to act hover above the circumstances themselves; that is, they are "uprooted." The motivations and decisions and ethical impulses arise deep within the person, not in the history itself. History is the stage upon which human responsibility to each other plays out. Once the personal dimension erodes, educators are faced with issues both pedagogic and moral; one wishes to be an effective teacher so as to present the moral and ethical challenges implicit in the history, literature, and theology.

As survivors leave us, we must rely on other means of conveying that which we wish to impart. The archived testimonies, although once removed from the immediacy of a personal encounter, can be effective. Speakers from the second-generation —or even third-generation—can be significant. Those who know family histories can share their knowledge and feelings. Memoirs written by those of the second- generation are multifaceted tools in maintaining the memories in personal fashion.[15] And of course, there is film. But none can replace those who came from Minsk or Prague or Paris or Warsaw or Sambor; who managed to avoid a mass grave; who lived to be a witness to genocide. We must be grateful for the tales and traces they have left us of a history replete with bestiality, brutality, and savage perversion of morality. From that period of evil, we must educate toward the good. It is our obligation.[16]

---

[15] Several such memoirs come immediately to mind: Helen Epstein's *Where She Came From: A Daughter's Search for her Mother's History* (New York, 1998); Carl Friedman, *Nightfather*, trans Arnold and Erika Pomerans (New York, 1994); and George Clare's *Last Waltz in Vienna: The Destruction of a Family, 1842-1942*(London, 2007). Each of these helped students identify with the historical context and created conversation and discussion about moral obligation.

[16] As John Roth states, "Why learn about the Holocaust? One of the best reasons is because doing so is a crucial reminder of the importance of putting children first, " and "No work that I know does more than study of the Holocaust to make me remember to take nothing good for granted." *Ethics During and After the Holocaust, 36.*

Yet, given the increasing paucity of survivors, my concern is substantial. Will the absence of eyewitnesses lead fewer students to study the Holocaust, to feel its vast but personal impact, to struggle with its nuances and ambiguities? Will university Holocaust courses become more abstract, engaging students less at the levels of moral and ethical conflict? Will young people thus be left with a less powerful sense of obligation, empathy, and activism? I do not know. I can only hope that creativity and technology will help fill the void left by the increasingly smaller number of survivors, and do so in such a way as to retain the power—even if second-hand—of the survivors' presence. These are questions and issues we must confront.

Conclusion

Every Friday night, I light the Shabbat candles on a five-branched sterling candelabrum. It has a classic, simple design that is much to my taste, not being overly ornate and baroque in style. But its aesthetics is not what impels me to care for the candelabra with especial attentiveness. Rather, its history and the story attached to this elegant object connect me to my family's history and the era of the murder of so many in Nazi-occupied Europe.

When my mother traveled to Sambor in 1936, her parents and three siblings were in the United States. She was brought to the marriage canopy by her oldest brother, Aaron, and sister-in-law, Leiba, then the parents of two small boys. Leiba came from a middle-class family, while my mother's family was of more modest means and my father's quite poor. The sterling candelabrum was a wedding gift to my parents from Aaron and Leiba. It was related that Leiba also said to my mother, "Toiba, I have more silver flatware than we need. Please take some with you to America." Mother demurred; the silver forks, spoons, and knives remained in Sambor, in my aunt and uncle's home. Only the candelabra crossed the Atlantic, and throughout my growing up it welcomed the Sabbath with its polished surfaces and warm glow of candles. My late sister and I would speculate: where is Aunt Leiba and Uncle Aaron's flatware these many years later? Melted down for the "war effort?" Taken as tokens to a wife in Bremen or Munich or Halle? In the home of a Polish family in Sambor, being passed from generation to generation? Yet seventy-seven years after my parents received this beautiful wedding gift, the candelabra, with its Sabbath candles, continues to illuminate our home with its soft light. Aunt Leiba and Uncle Aaron are with us still. Objects too can connect us to the past. The piles of children's shoes or heaps of eyeglasses in Auschwitz and elsewhere speak loudly. They tell more general stories than the individual tales of survivors, but stories nonetheless. They stimulate our imaginations, create memories, and lead the heart to weep.

I am a child of parents who left Poland before the conflagration. Many—and in Father's case all—family members perished. It is only as an adult that I have come to understand subtleties of conversations and interactions that took place in my home when a youngster. Perhaps my parents' history unconsciously impelled me to teach religion and intellectual history; to study at Yad Vashem and the USHMM; to organize an international conference on teaching the Holocaust in 1993; and to offer a course titled "Reflections on the Holocaust: History, Literature, Theology."

As a child of survivors, a parent, grandparent, and teacher, I find the issue of memory haunting. Memory is the crux of personal identity, psychological wholeness, cognitive awareness. Memory has formed me in ways both broad and small. As a Jew, I participate in the collective memory of a people as old as the *Tanakh,* the Hebrew Bible. All the festivals are about remembering historical experiences as a people and as an individual member of a nation; the Passover Seder, the command to remember the Sabbath in the two versions of the Ten Commandments,[17] to remember Amalek,[18] and the thirty-six ethical admonitions to treat well and take care of the vulnerable—the widow, orphan, the poor, the hungry because, as must be remembered, "You were slaves in the land of Egypt."[19] Collective memory is thus integral both to the Jewish community and the Jewish individual. It spurs religious ceremony and symbolism through ritual actions on various

---

[17][17] Exodus 20:8 and Deuteronomy 5:15.

[18] Deuteronomy 25:17-19.

[19] See Nehama Leibowitz, *Studies in Shemot (Exodus), Vol. 1*, trans. by Aryeh Newman (Jerusalem, 1976): 372-379.

festivals as well as ethical acts in everyday living.[20] Historical memory is the focal point of Jewish tradition.

When I consider the question of Holocaust memory,[21] I tend to put it in the framework of how Judaism construes memory in human existence. The 1951 controversy in Israel regarding the establishment of Holocaust Remembrance and Martyr's Day (*Yom Hashoah*) as a national day of commemoration is testimony[22] to the strength of memory as a *sine qua non* of Jewish history and culture. Yet the vehicles and vessels of Holocaust memory are dying. The profusion of poems, music, paintings, stories, and memoirs—and the archived testimonies—are our archeological building blocks, our portal into the Holocaust experiences. Those of us who are second and third generation have the responsibility to explore and share our legacy, to educate and sensitize the next generation. I do not think my children know enough about my parents' background—the trauma, the dislocation, the rebuilding in the face of unimaginable loss, the ability to look forward while mourning the past. While I am working to change that[23], I wonder in what ways my eventual demise will leave a gap for them. I am unsure how the immediacy of family histories can be retained even with the best of efforts. Yet, I hope to enable those of the next generation—both family and students—to continue the work in which I have been so deeply involved: educating toward goodness. The inevitability of death—that of the survivors, and eventually of the second and third generation, cannot mean the erosion

---

[20] The classic analysis of the relation of Jewish memory to modern Jewish historiography is found in Yosef Hayim

Yerushalmi's *Zakhor: Jewish History and Jewish Memory* (New York, 1989) which is based on a published lecture in 1982 from University of Washington Press. The entire issue of *The Jewish Quarterly Review*, Vol. 97, No. 4 (Fall 2007) is devoted to an analysis of Yerushalmi's study.

[21] "Remembering the Holocaust confers obligations in the present and for the future." John K. Roth, *Ethics During and After the Holocaust,* 33. An interesting analysis of collective Polish memory about the Holocaust is found in Jolanta Ambrosewicz-Jacobs, "The Holocaust and Coming to Terms with the Past in Post-Communist Poland," Ina Levine Annual Lecture, April 12, 2012, USHMM, esp. 5-9.

[22] See Chapter 10 of Irving Greenberg, *The Jewish Way* (New York, 1988): 314-373.

[23] I am writing a history of our family. It will include all the photographs and correspondence to which I have access.

of ways to make vital, meaningful, and intellectually and emotionally complex an understanding of the forces of human nature that twisted into what became the knot of Holocaust genocide.

In *The Contract of Mutual Indifference: Political Philosophy after the Holocaust,*[24] Norman Geras speculates as to what would be necessary for a society to transform its neutral contract of mutual indifference into a social ethic of caring for the other. He asks:

> Could one feasibly entertain the vision of a global human community in which an obligation to come to the assistance of others in danger or distress was widely felt as among the most powerful of imperatives, moving people to action…making of shame, and the foretaste of it, an effective, mobilizing norm of social life?[25]

Geras sees this vision as part of "an enduring battle…an open process…" [26] It is a battle in which I have been—and continue to be—a part. Only with a staunch and committed cadre of soldiers is victory a possibility.

> Myth and memory condition action. There are myths that are life sustaining and deserve to be reinterpreted for our age. There are some that lead astray and must be redefined. Others are dangerous and must be exposed.[27]

---

[24] Published by Verso in 1998.

[25] Norman Geras, *The Contract of Mutual Indifference: Political Philosophy after the Holocaust* (New York, 1998): 57.

[26] Geras, 115.

[27] Yosef Hayim Yerushalmi, 99-100.